Organizing Spirit

T&T CLARK STUDIES IN ANABAPTIST THEOLOGY AND ETHICS

Series Editors

Paul Martens and Laura Schmidt Roberts

Organizing Spirit

Pneumatology, Institutions, and Global Imagination

Jamie Pitts

t&tclark

LONDON • NEW YORK • OXFORD • NEW DELHI • SYDNEY

T&T CLARK

Bloomsbury Publishing Plc, 50 Bedford Square, London, WC1B 3DP, UK
Bloomsbury Publishing Inc, 1385 Broadway, New York, NY 10018, USA
Bloomsbury Publishing Ireland, 29 Earlsfort Terrace, Dublin 2, D02 AY28, Ireland

BLOOMSBURY, T&T CLARK and the T&T Clark logo are
trademarks of Bloomsbury Publishing Plc

First published in Great Britain 2025

Copyright © Jamie Pitts, 2025

Jamie Pitts has asserted his right under the Copyright,
Designs and Patents Act, 1988, to be identified as Author of this work.

For legal purposes the Acknowledgments on pp. xiii–xvi constitute an
extension of this copyright page.

Cover design: Gita Kowlessur

All rights reserved. No part of this publication may be: i) reproduced or transmitted in any form, electronic or mechanical, including photocopying, recording or by means of any information storage or retrieval system without prior permission in writing from the publishers; or ii) used or reproduced in any way for the training, development or operation of artificial intelligence (AI) technologies, including generative AI technologies. The rights holders expressly reserve this publication from the text and data mining exception as per Article 4(3) of the Digital Single Market Directive (EU) 2019/790.

Bloomsbury Publishing Plc does not have any control over, or responsibility for, any third-party websites referred to or in this book. All internet addresses given in this book were correct at the time of going to press. The author and publisher regret any inconvenience caused if addresses have changed or sites have ceased to exist, but can accept no responsibility for any such changes.

A catalogue record for this book is available from the British Library.

A catalog record for this book is available from the Library of Congress.

ISBN: HB: 978-0-5677-1259-2
PB: 978-0-5677-1258-5
ePDF: 978-0-5677-1261-5
eBook: 978-0-5677-1260-8

Typeset by Integra Software Services Pvt. Ltd.
Printed and bound in Great Britain

For product safety related questions contact productsafety@bloomsbury.com.

To find out more about our authors and books visit www.bloomsbury.com
and sign up for our newsletters.

For Brittany

free spirit

CONTENTS

Preface ix
Acknowledgments xiii

1 Picturing Spirit 1
   Spirit and Organizations in Contemporary Theology 4
   Contemporary Theology's Pneumatological-Sociological
      Picture 11
   Organizing Relations: Theological and Sociological
      Perspectives 20
   Picturing Spirit 31

2 Hovering Spirit 39
   The Organizational Politics of Anabaptist Environmental
      Ethics 41
   Hovering Spirit 46
   Creation, Election, and Hovering Spirit 52
   The Elkhart River Watershed 56
   The Spirit Hovers over the Watershed 67

3 Sanctifying Spirit 71
   The Sanctifying Spirit, Gender, and Sexuality 74
   The Sanctifying Spirit and Institutional Reform: The Case of
      North American Mennonite Women 84
   From Pessimism to Progress? 100
   Conclusion 108

4 Doubling Spirit 111

Vincent Harding: Life and Work 115
Freedom Institutions and Pneumatological Doubling 122
Doubling Spirit, Movement Institutions, and the Church 129
Identity, Theology, and Politics 136
Conclusion 146

5 Organizing Spirit 153

Picturing Organizing Spirit 153
Neoliberalism, Global Imagination, and Pneumatological Political Theology 161
Democratic Institutions and the Organizing Spirit 173

References 179
Index 197

PREFACE

In the summer of 2013, the Institute of Mennonite Studies hosted a gathering of church leaders at Anabaptist Mennonite Biblical Seminary (AMBS). The group was tasked with discerning major conversations that the church would need to have over the next decade. Although I was unable to attend the conference, I was intrigued to see that one of the named conversations concerned the relationship between the Holy Spirit and institutions. The question, it seemed, was how to understand the work of stable church organizations in light of the Spirit's fluid, often disruptive movement. Weren't social movements, and the small communities that nurtured them, a better expression of life in the Spirit than institutions? Fresh off a doctoral dissertation in which I related Mennonite theology to Pierre Bourdieu's relational sociology, I thought I could easily respond to this question by showing the limitations of dualistic sociologies that pitted movements and institutions against each other. I saw the question posed by the church leaders as a reflection of older sociological models that juxtaposed charisma and bureaucracy (Weber) or community and institutional society (Tönnies). A Bourdieusian intervention, I wagered, would reveal the relational complexity at the heart of different modes of social organization, thereby opening a way to imagine the Spirit as working across a variety of organizational forms.

When a handful of AMBS faculty began to meet regularly during the 2015/16 academic year to collaborate on a project related to the Holy Spirit, I brought an outline for an article that would articulate my response. Rebecca Slough, then AMBS academic dean, looked at the outline and immediately said, "[T]his looks like a book, not an article." I was skeptical, confident in my ability to fire off an article that would address the issue. Almost a decade and several articles later, it seems Rebecca was right!

The book's argument does build on my initial intuition. Throughout the book I employ conceptual tools from Bourdieu's sociology (particularly the concept of a social "field") to suggest that a relational understanding of organizations militates against any strong dualism between movements or communities and institutions. But I position this sociological argument within a larger pneumatological argument about the character and work of the Holy Spirit. The first chapter accordingly begins to sketch a picture of the Spirit as divine initiator, present influence, and ultimate goal of creation's relational web. Chapter 2 further explores the relationship between Spirit and creation, and identifies the latter's dynamic structural complexity as a sign of Spirit organizing. Human participation in the ongoing process of structuring creation—e.g., through the organization and reorganization of social structures—might therefore be seen as a form of participation in the Spirit. In Chapter 3, I examine literature on the Spirit, gender, and sexuality to suggest that the Spirit's work of sanctification might take not only the form of personal transformation but also the reformation of ecclesial institutions. Chapter 4 engages resources from African American history and theology to depict the Spirit as calling forth the "doubling" of movements for justice through institutions. The book concludes in Chapter 5 with a discussion of possibilities for theologians to help imagine global institutions that would correspond to the global dimensions of the Spirit's work—and thereby respond to noxious global political economic and cultural forces.

The book can therefore be read not only as a social theoretical intervention with implications for how theologians think about organizational structures, but also and above all as an invitation to think differently about the Spirit and the organizational shape of participation in the Spirit. I accordingly focus my argument on the nexus of pneumatological and sociological imaginations, describing the book's critical target and its alternative proposal in terms of a "pneumatological-sociological picture." This phrase indicates that how we theologians imagine the Spirit working impinges upon what organizational activities and forms we regard as legitimate means of pneumatological participation. The goal of the book is to widen the range of such activities and forms that we regard as legitimate by widening our imagination of the Spirit.

I regard this widening as important and valid on theological grounds as well as on pragmatic grounds related to specific challenges facing the church and world today. Among these challenges is the global climate catastrophe that is unfolding under the auspices of an anti-democratic global political economic and cultural order, frequently referred to as "neoliberalism." Facing up to this order, I contend, requires an alliance of global democratic institutions acting in defense of planetary life. Yet Christian theologians have in recent decades almost entirely neglected the institutional and often the global dimensions of this defense, preferring to emphasize local politics and "community." This emphasis is frequently advanced in the name of the Spirit, who is described as working primarily to form local communities and movements. Although I do not wish to diminish the importance of local organizations, which of course include Christian congregations, I do seek to challenge my fellow theologians to think more—and to think more theologically—about the place of national, regional, and global institutions in Christian ministry and witness. Along these lines, the book can be read as an appeal for constructive political theologies of denominations, global church bodies, ecumenical institutions, Christian aid organizations, and so forth—not to mention of "extra-ecclesial" institutions with which Christians interact in various ways. This book takes a first step of situating institutional organization, leadership, and reformation as possible means of participation in the Spirit.

The task of construing institutions as legitimate arenas of Christian participation should not be confused with the idolatrous identification of specific institutions with God. In addition to the theological injunction against idolatry, recent attention to racism, sexism, and other abuses perpetrated by and within institutions strictly prohibits the labeling of this or that institution simply as a work of the Spirit. I repeat this point over and over in the pages that follow—this book is *not* an argument for taking some institutions as specially organized by the Spirit in a way that would provide moral or political cover for their conduct. The Spirit organizes—hovers, sanctifies, doubles—by inspiring and encouraging organizational activities aimed at life and creaturely solidarity, healing, and justice. Nowhere in the book do I describe any particular organization as organized by the Spirit, and in general I describe organizations as *potential* means of pneumatological participation. Whether or not some institution is deemed to genuinely participate to some limited degree in the work of the Spirit—and it will always be only to some limited degree—is a matter of discernment. Discernment compares an institution's structures and activities with theological criteria that aim to specify how the Spirit works. All institutions (like all individuals, communities, and movements) will fall short of these criteria. Discernment is, moreover, an ongoing process that rightly makes space for disagreement about both the institution's conduct and the criteria employed to assess it. Part of the objective of this book is to offer a variety of criteria for discerning when and how an institution is or is not participating in the work of the organizing Spirit. But, of course, theologians will take issue with some or all of the criteria I put forward. Although I feel strongly about the integrity of the criteria offered here, I am most concerned that we begin talking about them—and talking about institutions as potential means of pneumatological participation.

ACKNOWLEDGMENTS

I am grateful to Rebecca Slough, Mary Schertz, Barb Nelson Gingerich, Malinda Berry, and Daniel Schipani for conversations about the Holy Spirit during the 2015/16 Scribes for the Reign of God collaborative faculty research project at AMBS. The project included opportunities to engage the AMBS faculty, students, and constituency, the latter during the 2016 Pastors Week event at the seminary. Mary, Barb, and Rebecca also organized and led a conference held at AMBS in June 2017 titled (Un)Holy Mix: The Holy Spirit in Movements and Institutions. At that conference I was able to workshop some of my initial thoughts on the topic with a group facilitated by Rachel Miller Jacobs that also included Nekeisha Alayna Alexis, Suella Lehman Gerber, Benjamin Isaak-Krauss, Richard Kauffman, John Lapp, Jonathan Nahar, and Willard Roth. Although this book looks quite a bit different from the proposal I shared then, I hope my interlocutors in those early discussions will at least judge that I tried to heed their counsel at various points.

In 2016, Pastor José Luis Gutiérrez of Comunidad Cristiana Adulam (Goshen, Indiana) invited me to give two talks on "the Holy Spirit in the Bible" at a regional gathering of Assemblies of God pastors in Mexico City. Some of this material is included in Chapters 1 and 2. That year I also participated in the first of two official dialogue sessions between Mennonite Church USA and the Church of God (Cleveland, Tennessee), where I presented a paper on historical Anabaptist-Mennonite theologies of the Spirit. Feedback from Nancy Bedford, Gayle Gerber Koontz, Alan Kreider, Crip Stephenson, and other conference participants—as well as later editors and peer reviewers as I revised the paper for publication—improved the paper, which proved formative for the pneumatological outlook I develop in this book.[1]

---

[1] References to these and other publications occur in the chapters where I refer to and/or make use of portions of them.

I returned to Mexico City for two months during a sabbatical leave from AMBS in 2018. Thanks to my host, Carlos Martínez García of the Conferencia de Iglesias Evangélicas Anabautistas Menonitas de México, I was able to enjoy mostly undistracted research time while staying at the Comunidad Teológica de México—within walking distance of the beautiful San Ángel neighborhood and the famous murals of the UNAM campus. When distractions came, they were always welcome invitations from Fernando Sandoval Guzmán to explore the city. My conversations with Fernando continue to shape my thoughts on Mennonite theology and witness.

The 2018 sabbatical also included a three-month stay at the Vrije Universiteit (VU) Amsterdam where I was hosted by Fernando Enns and benefited from almost daily discussions with Andrés Pacheco Lozano. Research presentations to the VU Ecumenical Theology group, the VU Faculty of Theology's Beliefs and Practices Department, and the Doopsgezind Seminarium helped me develop the project considerably. As did conversations with Henk Bakker, Daniël Drost, Cornelius van der Kooi, Marius van Hoogstraten, and many others. Kees and Nelleke Blokland's generous hospitality—and gorgeous garden apartment just off the Vondelpark—made Amsterdam feel like home. My sabbatical research fed directly into Chapter 3 in the present work. Mary Schertz and Rachel Miller Jacobs also commented on an early outline of what became Chapter 3. I developed the outline in a chapter on a volume on religion and care ethics and am thankful for recommendations from editors Maurice Hamington and Maureen Sander-Staudt and a peer reviewer.

In 2019, I developed Chapter 4 through presentations at the Second Global Mennonite Peacebuilding Conference (GMPC) in Elspeet, the Netherlands, and at a session of the Afro-American Religious History Unit at the American Academy of Religion Annual Meeting. I am particularly grateful for encouraging encounters at these events with Rachel Harding, Alle Hoekema, Harky Klinefelter, and Tobin Miller Shearer. Thanks also to the editors of the proceedings of the Second GMPC, Fernando Enns, Nina Schroeder-van 't Schip, and Andrés Pacheco Lozano, for their comments.

During the 2020/1 academic year, I again participated in AMBS's Scribes for the Reign of God collaborative research process, this time with a focus on ecology. Malinda Berry, Rachel Miller Jacobs, and I from AMBS were joined by Goshen College colleagues John Roth, Jan Bender Shetler, and Jonathon Schramm. My research and writing during the project resulted in a conference paper delivered at the 2021 Rooted and Grounded Conference, hosted by AMBS, and a publication in *Mennonite Quarterly Review*. This article is the basis of much of Chapter 2.

Throughout this period, I have met almost annually with a small group of Mennonite scholars in White Pigeon, Michigan. The group, convened by Mark Barker and John Roth, has also included Robert Brenneman, David Cramer, Ryan Schellenberg, and Luis Tapia Rubio. At White Pigeon we share our writings and our lives, and the counsel and prayers I have received there about this book project have been indispensable. I am especially glad for the moment at our 2021 or 2022 meeting when the group told me to stop taking on so many other writing projects and finish this one!

It took another sabbatical leave in the 2023/4 academic year to complete a draft of the book, and I am thankful to AMBS, especially President David Boshart and Academic Dean and Vice President Beverly Lapp, for the support, as well as to my in-laws, Brad and Lee Purlee, for time and space to write at their lovely home in southern Indiana. Studies in Anabaptist Theology and Ethics series editors Paul Martens and Laura Schmidt Roberts offered incisive feedback on the draft and I was able to complete the main revisions at the end of a lengthy trip through the western United States with my family. Chapter 5 was written mostly at the Paris Mennonite Center, in the gaps of an almost unbroken flow of deep conversation with Lane Miller, and completed at Sean Rowland's lovely Brussels apartment.

Many others have contributed to this book in ways large and small. I give thanks especially to Linda Thomas, for an important conversation at Panera—and much else. To Katerina Gea, Andrew Hudson, Steve Thomas, Marcus Winchester of the Pokagon Band of Potawatomi, and the leaders of the 2021 Indiana Master Naturalist course for conversations on ecology, theology, and Indigenous politics. To Nekeisha Alayna Alexis, Simon Barrow, Billy Funk, Fernando Sandoval Guzmán, Benjamin Isaak-Krauss, Andrés Pacheco Lozano, Jason Shenk, and Janna Hunter-Bowman for conversations around church and politics. To Angie Law for clarity. To Malinda Berry, David Cramer, Wess Daniels, Anicka

Fast, Drew Hart, Marius van Hoogstraten, Andy Brubacher Kaethler, Maxwell Kennel, Safwat Marzouk, Elizabeth Miller, Tyler Parks, Bharat Ranganathan, Gary Slater, Andrew Suderman, Laura Schmidt Roberts, and Luis Tapia Rubio for intellectual friendship and inspiration. To Luis also for excellent research assistance. To AMBS faculty and staff—and especially members of the History, Theology, and Ethics Department, the staff of Institute of Mennonite Studies, and Brent Graber—for their companionship during the years of writing this book. To students at the Elkhart campus and online, and in Ethiopia, Mexico, and Puerto Rico, for contributing more than they—or I—can possibly know. To Hively Avenue Mennonite Church for being a community of care, witness, and worship. To the Central District Conference and its minister Doug Luginbill for enabling me to see inside a regional church body during a term on the board. To Anna Turton and Jack Curtin at T&T Clark for their patience and dedication to seeing this book come to publication. To Paul Martens and Laura Schmidt Roberts for guiding me to the end. And to my family and friends in Texas, Indiana, Canada, Europe, and Latin America for their love and support. I dedicate this book to Brittany Purlee, gift, breath, love—and free spirit.

1

Picturing Spirit

Outside my window the St. Joseph River runs west. Two miles downstream it is joined by the Elkhart River, and later by the Dowagiac and Paw Paw Rivers. Eventually the St. Joseph opens into Lake Michigan, where it mingles with many waters on their way through the Great Lakes, out the St. Lawrence Seaway, and into the Atlantic Ocean. Depending on the wind, the river's surface can stand still or, like today, can appear to move eastward. The wind only rustles the trees in my vicinity, but on the other side of the river flags stand at attention. One of the flags features the logo of the City of Elkhart, Indiana. The other is a dark blue American flag with one bright blue stripe.

The complex entwinement of the global and the local that sociologists have sometimes termed "glocalization" is visible today from my window.[1] In addition to the Atlantic destiny of the waters of the St. Joseph River, I could mention the connection of the wind I observe to the global atmospheric circulation that, like our rivers and oceans, is currently being disrupted by climate change. I could also reference the relation between the wind and the air that gives breath to all living creatures—to the rabbit that hopped by earlier, to the bees that hover above clustered sedum flowers in my lawn, to me as I begin writing this book. I could further talk about the wind and the blue American flag that signals support for the police,

---

[1] Roland Robertson, "Glocalization: Time-Space and Homogeneity-Heterogeneity," in *Global Modernities*, eds. Mike Featherstone, Scott M. Lash, and Roland Robertson (London: Sage, 1995), 35–53; Victor Roudometof, *Glocalization: A Critical Introduction* (New York: Routledge, 2016).

for the "thin blue line" whose violence purportedly saves us from falling into chaos. Both Eric Garner and George Floyd cried out "I can't breathe!" as American police officers crushed their bodies for, respectively, selling unregistered cigarettes and (maybe) using a counterfeit bill. In Bogotá, Colombia, Javier Ordóñez uttered similar last words—"No puedo respirar"—as police subdued and then attacked him with tasers for, supposedly, breaking a Covid-19-related curfew. I could go on from there to discuss the histories of colonization and slavery, capitalism and militarism, ecology and health, and their mutual relations.

Is God, or the work of God, visible in some way in this glocally entangled landscape? Christian theologians have typically identified the Holy Spirit as God abidingly present to and active within creation. The Christian doctrine of the Spirit is rooted in the Hebrew concept of *ruach*, which brings together various images including breath, wind, and personal temperament or character. These images are used to describe God and what God does to create and give life to the world, and they are also used to name the breath that passes the lips of particular creatures, the wind that shakes trees at specific times and places, and the moods that swing this or that historical human. *Ruach* spans the intimate and the public, the local and the global, the creaturely and the divine. When the early Christians reflected on their experience of the *pneuma* that, according to John, Jesus had breathed on them (Jn 20:22) and, according to Luke, had been poured out upon them at Pentecost (Acts 2:1–4), they found that word in the Septuagint translating *ruach*.[2] So it is perhaps not surprising that they envisioned the Spirit of God (*pneuma theou*) as at once cosmically creative and "inside" each follower of Jesus and community of disciples. The Spirit makes the connections between God, the global, and the local. From this pneumatological vantage, then, I can witness God at work in wind and water, breath, and motion.

---

[2]This description of early Christian theological activity follows from a narrative advanced by McClendon in which the experience of Christ and of Christ's Spirit resulted in a process of "catachresis" or reinterpretation of existing theological language. See James Wm. McClendon, *Doctrine: Systematic Theology, Volume 2* (Nashville: Abingdon, 1994), 106–22. Coakley also highlights the experience of the Holy Spirit as driving early Christian theology. Sarah Coakley, *God, Sexuality, and the Self: An Essay "On the Trinity"* (Cambridge: Cambridge University Press, 2013), 100–151.

But what, exactly, do I see? How is God the Spirit at work before me? What kind of connections does the Spirit make? What difference does that make for victims of police brutality, the pandemic, and poverty? Some contemporary theologians have responded to such questions by suggesting that the Spirit is largely about forming Christian congregations that care for the brutalized, the sick, and the poor as part of the ordinary rhythm of congregational life. Other theologians insist that the Spirit defies death by calling forth movements of oppressed groups and their allies for justice. Still others argue that the Spirit shows up in fluid networks of friends and acquaintances where the life-giving gospel is shared. Although these responses point in significantly different directions, a common image or picture emerges from them of the Spirit as divine pastor or community organizer who gathers people together and mobilizes them for action. The influence of the Spirit is immediate and personal, requiring minimal organizational infrastructure, planning, or coordination. Much, if not all, of what the Spirit does occurs at the local level and concerns small, relatively informal groupings or communities. Mass movements perhaps arise as these communities converge more or less spontaneously. So is that what I see when I look out of my window, Spirit wind assembling communal witness?

Yes. But there is more to see. In this book I contend that the Spirit's creativity gives rise to social and material structures that are complex and dynamic and that are oriented to abundant life with God and creaturely solidarity. Creation's complex dynamism, or relationality, suggests that a variety of organizational forms might be available to pursue its normative ends. Small community organizations, social movements, and fluid networks are indeed valid organizational means of participating in Spirit organizing, but so are institutions that bridge locations and generations. Of course, actual institutions—like actual communities, movements, and networks—are beset by sin, so a formal argument in their favor does not take us very far. With that observation in mind, I further argue that institutional reform and the foundation of new institutions to further the goals of solidaristic social movements are potential ways to participate in the work of the Spirit. In short, the alternative picture of the organizing Spirit developed in this book indicates that when I look outside my window, I might also see Spirit-inspired institutions pursuing life, solidarity, healing, and justice.

Spirit and Organizations in Contemporary Theology

Contemporary theologians promulgate a picture of the Holy Spirit as organizing communities, movements, and networks, mostly if not exclusively in local contexts.[3] This section elucidates what I will refer to as contemporary theology's pneumatological-sociological picture—a picture that depicts the Spirit giving shape to particular social and organizational forms—through a discussion of several contemporary writings on the Spirit. In addition to describing the main lineaments of the picture, I assess reasons for its disregard for institutions.

The strongly communal character of the picture is evident in postliberal pneumatology. In his book *After the Spirit: Constructive Pneumatology from Resources outside the Modern West*, Eugene Rogers generates a pneumatological story oriented to the good of the body.[4] Rogers identifies a narrative antitype in the gospel stories of the Spirit resting on Jesus in his conception, baptism, transfiguration, and resurrection. Working his way up and down the analogical "ladder," he takes these stories to indicate both how the Spirit relates to Jesus and the Father in the eternal life of the Trinity, and how the Spirit rests on the bodies of those who

---

[3] I say more in the final section of this chapter about my reliance on the Wittgensteinian concept of "pictures" in both the critical and constructive arguments of this book.
I roughly define "contemporary theology" as academic theology published since the early 1970s. This definition makes most of the sources under consideration contemporary *to me* (I was born in 1980). But it also seems to me that a variety of shifts occurred in the theological scene in the early 1970s that continue to define how academic theology is done. These shifts include the proliferation of liberation theologies; the development of postliberal theology; and the rise of evangelical theology as a political and academic force. I touch on each of these strands of theology in what follows. Other important shifts include the rise of Pentecostal theology (in part through association with neo-evangelicals) and the greater interaction between Eastern and Western theologians. I touch on Pentecostal sources in some of what follows, but the discussion is largely limited to Western theologians who connect in some way pneumatology to the social shape of Christian witness.
[4] Eugene F. Rogers, *After the Spirit: A Constructive Pneumatology from Resources outside the Modern West* (Grand Rapids, MI: Eerdmans, 2005). In Chapter 3, I discuss aspects of Rogers' project that are friendly to the alternative picture I am developing.

constitute the church for their healing, justice, and eternal joy.⁵ The resting Spirit incorporates diverse bodies into the body of Christ, a liturgical community that forms bodies in and for commitments of marriage, friendship, and child-rearing—and thereby slowly "transfigures" society.⁶ The eucharistic community formed by the Spirit is, indeed, "a means to resist evil and victimage" and to care for the poor.⁷ Broad social transformation emerges from the quotidian practices of local congregations gathered by the Spirit.

Postliberal theologian Ephraim Radner shares Rogers's attention to communities while deflecting concern for social change. Radner's *The End of the Church: A Pneumatology of Christian Division in the West* develops an account of the Spirit's absence from the divided church. Accepting the Spirit's absence restrains ecumenical optimism and encourages a penitential posture expressed in ordinary, "antiprogrammatic" Christian practice shorn of any sense of its present capacity to affect reunification.⁸ In a more recent book, *A Profound Ignorance: Modern Pneumatology and Its Anti-modern Redemption*, Radner expands his critique of the church's strategic organizing and of attempts to associate such organizing with the Spirit.⁹ These attempts, he avers, stem from a flawed modern conception of the Spirit (or "the spirit") as the agent of unity amidst extreme cultural difference and as the agent of healing amidst limitless suffering.¹⁰ According to Radner, the Spirit rather points us to Christ and his broken body, not to a

---

⁵Rogers, *After the Spirit*, 104–11, 127–8. On the analogical ladder, see pages 56 and 111.
⁶Rogers, *After the Spirit*, 183–91.
⁷Rogers, *After the Spirit*, 129, 131–2.
⁸Ephraim Radner, *The End of the Church: A Pneumatology of Christian Division in the West* (Grand Rapids, MI: Eerdmans, 1998), 352–3.
⁹Ephraim Radner, *A Profound Ignorance: Modern Pneumatology and Its Anti-modern Redemption* (Waco, TX: Baylor University Press, 2019). (See page 422n57 for his account of his differences from Rogers.) Radner first worked out his pneumatological minimalism in his doctoral dissertation, later published as *Spirit and Nature: The Saint-Médard Miracles in 18th-Century Jansenism* (New York: Crossroad, 2002).
¹⁰Radner, *A Profound Ignorance*, chapters 1–5. See pages 112–16 on the shift from "Age of Spirit" to "spirit of the age" in Hume and other eighteenth-century philosophers.

strategy for cultural or medical transformation. Life in the Spirit is an impressionistic and wandering journey in the way of the suffering Christ that offers no maps for bettering life on Earth. After rejecting the modern pneumatological fantasy, our only task is to pursue a "normal" Christian life, bearing suffering in light of the inscrutable yet trustworthy divine plan.[11] Like Rogers, Radner deploys parental and marital images to portray the normal Christian life.[12] Both postliberal theologians strongly suggest that the Spirit's organizing work prioritizes local communities such as families and congregations.

Communities also come to the fore in liberation pneumatologies, though typically in connection to social movements. José Comblin's *The Holy Spirit and Liberation* was born out of the author's participation in Latin American base ecclesial communities, small groups of usually poor Catholics gathering for Bible study and social engagement.[13] In Comblin's eyes, impoverished Latin Americans depend completely on the Holy Spirit and therefore have a unique experience of the Spirit.[14] On the basis of this experience, poor Latin Americans act for their own liberation via community-building public testimony. They then experience the realization of liberated community as "life and resurrection, as newness of life. It is felt as new birth."[15] Describing this dynamic from the perspective of the Spirit, Comblin writes that "the Holy Spirit acts through the poor in history. When the poor succeed in becoming agents in history, then the Spirit of God is at work."[16] It is therefore only possible

---

[11] For a related argument aimed at liberation theology, see Daniel M. Bell, *Liberation Theology after the End of History: The Refusal to Cease Suffering* (New York: Routledge, 2001).
[12] Radner, *A Profound Ignorance*, 304–15. Cf. Rogers, *After the Spirit*, 189. Radner talks only about maternal parenting, whereas Rogers discusses adoption as an option for "all Christian couples," including same-sex ones. I discuss Radner further in Chapter 3.
[13] José Comblin, *The Holy Spirit and Liberation*, trans. Paul Burns (Maryknoll, NY: Orbis, 1989); Luiz Carlos Susin and Jon Sobrino, "Sage and Prophet: José Comblin 1923-2011," in *Lord and Life Giver: Spirit Today (Concilium)*, eds. Paul Murray, Diego Irarrázaval, and Maria Clara Bingemer (London: SCM, 2011), 148–53.
[14] Comblin, *The Holy Spirit and Liberation*, 23.
[15] Comblin, *The Holy Spirit and Liberation*, 42.
[16] Comblin, *The Holy Spirit and Liberation*, 54.

to say that "the church is born of the Spirit ... [when] it is born of the people."[17] As the name indicates, the local "base" communities are truly the basic form of Spirit-empowered ecclesiality.[18] Yet since poverty, and not theological confession, is the condition of Spirit experience and ecclesiality, the church can also be described as "the huge caravan of the rejected of the earth who call out, cry for justice, invoke a Liberator whose name is often unknown to them."[19] The Spirit connects poor Latin Americans by organizing them into base communities and then into a mass movement.

Other liberation theologians make similar use of community and movement language when discussing the work of the Holy Spirit. Gustavo Gutiérrez, for instance, highlights the Spirit's role in uniting poor Latin Americans to Christ and the Father.[20] This trinitarian life in the Spirit takes organizational form in a community of love and mutual service toward the end of liberation. It can also be described in terms of movement: "the spiritual journey is marked by a constant creative freedom under the action of the Spirit."[21] Karen Baker-Fletcher relatedly views God the Spirit as empowering Black women's survival and liberation. "The calling of the people of God, a community in union with the Spirit, is to embody more fully this empowering, liberating, sustaining Spirit."[22] Embodying the Spirit is a process that takes place "moment by moment, day by day" toward the fulfillment of "the apocalyptic vision of a new heaven and a new earth by being wise stewards of body, dust, and spirit, engaged in the task of healing."[23] This image of progressive transformation through quotidian communal practices is perhaps closer to postliberals like Rogers than to Comblin's image of an irruptive caravan of justice. Yet each of these liberation theologians

---

[17]Comblin. *The Holy Spirit and Liberation*, 87.
[18]See also Leonardo Boff, *Ecclesiogenesis: The Base Communities Reinvent the Church*, trans. Robert R. Barr (Maryknoll, NY: Orbis, 1986).
[19]Comblin, *Holy Spirit and Liberation*, 95.
[20]Gustavo Gutiérrez, *We Drink from Our Own Wells: The Spiritual Journey of a People*, trans. Matthew J. O'Connell (Maryknoll, NY: Orbis, 1985), 54–71.
[21]Gutiérrez, *We Drink from Our Own Wells*, 86.
[22]Karen Baker-Fletcher, *Sisters of Dust, Sisters of Spirit: Womanist Wordings on God and Creation* (Minneapolis: Fortress, 1998), 126.
[23]Baker-Fletcher, *Sisters of Dust*, 127.

emphasizes, in a way largely foreign to postliberalism, the Spirit's creation of communities of people who have experienced oppression based on some aspect of their identity (cultural origin, race, gender). At times liberation theologians turn from a positive account of how the Spirit shapes communities and movements to critical comments that describe what the Spirit does not do. Latin American feminist theologian Nancy Bedford shares many of the tendencies of the liberationists just described.[24] But she further argues that when a Spirit-led justice movement "becomes a fixed organization, possibilities for flexibility, creativity, and unconventional leadership decline."[25] Below I suggest that this juxtaposition between flexible, creative, unconventional, and above all *just* movements and inflexible, uncreative, conventional—and by implication *unjust*— "fixed organizations" sheds considerable light on central features of the contemporary picture. That is the case especially when "communities" are described in parallel terms to movements, as when Bedford advocates for "a community that is vigilant in the face of injustice, supportive of creative ways of pushing back against systemic inequities, and able to welcome the provisional and imperfect nature of our efforts."[26] Communities and movements are amenable to the Spirit's influence, but fixed organizations (whatever those may be) are not.

Some theologians push this perspective further toward a generalized posture of dissent. Queer theologian Marcella Althaus-Reid, for instance, writes that "a liberative Holy Spirit needs to be a Queer Holy Spirit, incarnated in our communities of resistance …, not to normalize but to support acts of defiance to structures of sexual and economic justice."[27] Althaus-Reid regards the persistence of homophobia in Latin American liberation theology as an effect of internalized colonialism. "To decolonize the Holy Spirit," she contends:

---

[24]See, for instance, Nancy Bedford, *La porfía de la resurrección: Ensayos desde el feminismo teológico latinoamericano* (Buenos Aires: Kairós, 2008), which draws on Latin American, feminist, and womanist theologies.
[25]Nancy Bedford, "A Narrow Gate? Proceeding along the Way of Jesus by the Spirit," *Mennonite Quarterly Review* 92, no. 4 (October 2018): 495.
[26]Bedford, "A Narrow Gate?," 493.
[27]Marcella Althaus-Reid, *The Queer God* (New York: Routledge, 2003), 127.

[W]e need to hear the ... voices among us which claim for themselves the right to transgress structures of oppression as part of the intervention of the Holy Spirit in our lives. We need a more ambivalent Holy Spirit, moving with flexibility in our lives and challenges, taking away our internalization of oppression ... while giving us back our voices of dissent.[28]

Here the Spirit and the communities formed by the Spirit are associated with resistance, defiance, transgression, and dissent.

Linn Tonstad has developed Althaus-Reid's "ambivalent" pneumatology in the direction of a "non-reproductive" ecclesiology.[29] On the one hand, the Spirit assembles a great "banquet" of individuals; on the other hand, the Spirit makes no attempt to unite these individuals in a way that would change their personal identities.[30] Rather than uniting with or "penetrating" Christ's body to cause it to reproduce, the Spirit comes alongside the different bodies that constitute it to "drive people wild" just as they are, in all their differences from each other.[31] Tonstad provocatively calls for an apocalyptic "abortion" of the reproductive church.[32] This emphasis on nonnormative difference is also visible in Ashon Crawley's description of the Spirit as "otherwise possibility" in homophobic and racist social spaces, including the church.[33] Although neither of these authors details the organizational shape of the banquet of difference or the pursuit of otherwise possibility, it is plausible that they (and Althaus-Reid) would join Bedford in opposing "fixed organizations" in the name of Spirit movements.

---

[28] Althaus-Reid, *The Queer God*, 127.
[29] Linn Tonstad, *God and Difference: The Trinity, Sexuality, and the Transformation of Finitude* (New York: Routledge, 2016). I discuss Tonstad further in Chapter 3.
[30] Tonstad, *God and Difference*, 235.
[31] Tonstad, *God and Difference*, 276. I owe the phrase "comes alongside" in this sentence to Gerard Loughlin's review of Tonstad's book in a *Syndicate* forum from May 22, 2017, https://syndicate.network/symposia/theology/god-and-difference/.
[32] Tonstad, *God and Difference*, 269.
[33] Ashon T. Crawley, *Blackpentecostal Breath: The Aesthetics of Possibility* (New York: Fordham University Press, 2016).

The non or anti-normative thrust of their arguments certainly makes identifying any stable organizational pattern difficult, and the image of the reproductive church's abortion would seem to cash out in the termination of ecclesial institutions designed to prolong or expand the church across time and space.

In his book *Liquid Church*, evangelical theologian Pete Ward does not commit to a liberationist political vision but does explicitly endorse a movement-based ecclesiology he connects to the Holy Spirit.[34] Ward is a skeptic about the value of traditional church organizations, which he describes as remnants of an outdated "solid church" model. He points instead to the networked relational possibilities of "contemporary media, business, and finance."[35] Taking advantage of these possibilities generates the new model of the "liquid church." In the liquid church, informal "connections, groupings, and relationships" are "a kind of network where the Holy Spirit is at work creating church."[36] The liquid church model "implies that a church might be something that we make with each other by communicating Christ, so it is not an institution as such."[37] Indeed, the "institution of the church, local or national, is largely irrelevant to ... creative and productive activities" such as evangelism, worship, and large occasional gatherings.[38] Ward sees the Spirit at work in such non-institutional, minimally planned activities. Since the Holy Spirit is the Spirit of life, all of life—and particularly its informal, spontaneous, and noninstitutional forms—can be seen as the arena of Spirit activity and so as the site of Christian participation in God, so long as this participation ultimately points to salvation in Christ.[39] Here the Spirit's alternative to "fixed organizations," "programmatic

---

[34] Pete Ward, *Liquid Church* (Eugene, OR: Wipf & Stock, 2013).

[35] Ward, *Liquid Church*, 2–3. Ward recognizes that not everything about these networks and their "consumerist environment" is compatible with the gospel, though only names the "illegal drugs trade" as an example (78).

[36] Ward, *Liquid Church*, 3.

[37] Ward, *Liquid Church*, 2.

[38] Ward, *Liquid Church*, 3.

[39] Ward, *Liquid Church*, 78–86.

practices," or "institutions" is not "ordinary" congregations or identity-based movements of oppressed groups, but rather fluid relational networks.[40]

Contemporary Theology's Pneumatological-Sociological Picture

Abstract expressionist paintings famously appear to many viewers as confusions of colors and lines, as energetic but incoherent messes. Perhaps some readers will have a similar response to my presentation of the above contemporary pneumatological writings. Given the striking differences and dissonances among these writings, it may not seem possible to discern any pattern emerging from them. However, just as careful scrutiny of an abstract expressionist painting can reveal, for instance, consistent (and sometimes quite conventional) patterns of color that tie the image together by providing a loose visual unity, so a careful examination of contemporary pneumatology catches sight of certain common themes.

"Community" is ubiquitous in contemporary pneumatology and appears to be the preferred term to describe the social consequences of the Spirit's influence. The Spirit forms eucharistic or liturgical communities where people can meet, marry, and raise children (Rogers, Radner); communities of poor Latin Americans organizing for their liberation (Comblin, Gutiérrez); the people

---

[40]See also Andy Lord, *Network Church: A Pentecostal Ecclesiology Shaped by Mission* (Leiden: Brill, 2012). Lord argues from Scripture and the history of pentecostalism for networks as the basic "middle structures" connecting churches for the purpose of church growth. He sees growth-oriented ecclesial networks as consonant with "the concept of movement [that] is central to pentecostal ecclesiology, as seen in a missionary narrative reading of Luke-Acts" (87). In other words, the structures of the church should reflect the "movement" character of the Spirit's work to form and spread the church. Lord is responding, among other targets, to Amos Yong's "ambivalence about institutions and networks" (72n65). Yong had written that "pentecostalism is first and foremost an ecumenical experience and spirituality rather than an organized network of institutions" (*The Spirit Poured Out on All Flesh: Pentecostalism and the Possibility of a Global Theology* [Grand Rapids, MI: Baker Academic, 2005], 144–5).

of God understood as a community inclusive of Black women who embody the Spirit through their daily practices of healing and liberation (Baker-Fletcher); and communities of resistance to sexual and economic injustice (Althaus-Reid). Bedford's caution that communities remain flexible, creative, and dedicated to justice; Tonstad's image of the Spirit-assembled banquet of difference; and Ward's liquid churches of friends and acquaintances all challenge any overly tight definition of community, but all still depict the Spirit as bringing people together for a common purpose.

Not every invocation of "community" necessarily recommends the formation of local organizations. The equation of community with the people of God or a vast banquet does not necessarily entail a *local* pattern of gathering. Congregations and base communities are local, if by local we mean something like "occurring in a determinate social and/or spatial context," taking place within a specifiable "here" rather than "there"[41] Generally speaking, congregations and base communities exist because relatively small groups of individuals who live more or less in the same region gather together somewhat regularly.[42] But the image of an eschatological banquet and the theological concept of the people of God are irreducible to particular gatherings. Rather, they trade on the wider sense of community included in phrases such as "the international community," "the LGBTQ community," or "the Taylor Swift fan community." These phrases again point to shared interests and perhaps to shared outlooks and ways of organizing life, and the communities they name may include a variety of organizations

---

[41]Arjun Appadurai argues that under conditions of globalization "localities" are defined socially and map loosely onto geographies. Appadurai, "The Production of Locality," in *Modernity at Large: Cultural Dimensions of Globalization* (Minneapolis: University of Minnesota Press, 1996), 178–99. With Ward in mind, we might also extend the language of local community to describe discrete digitally mediated social networks, similar to how we talk about the "digital commons" or "digital public sphere" (both phrases extend a "local" spatial concept to internet phenomena).

[42]This description of congregations is challenged today by "commuter churches" and "digital churches." I take it that these are still relatively exceptional and the general case mentioned in the text still usually applies. Still, commuters are apt to live somewhat close to their congregations (they are unlikely to fly in from across the world regularly) and digital communities might be understood as "local" in the sense mentioned in the previous note.

(from nation-states to online forums). At the same time, within contemporary pneumatology even this wider sense of community is often construed in local, especially congregational terms.

Baker-Fletcher articulates communal Spirit embodiment as a process that occurs "moment by moment, day by day." This language reflects contemporary pneumatology's tendency to imagine Spirit transformation as an ongoing "journey" (Gutiérrez, Radner) toward an eschatological horizon. Baker-Fletcher's language points to a "bottom-up" conception of social change, in which small, daily acts of healing and liberation by oppressed people add up, in the long run at least, to large-scale transformation. This outlook is shared by Rogers, with his promise of social "transfiguration" via ordinary congregational life, and perhaps Comblin, if his image of a continent-wide "caravan" is taken to project a mass movement of smaller communities (with each community as a car or wagon in the caravan).[43] Radner denies expectations of social change but likewise emphasizes the peripatetic character of life in the Spirit. The stress on ongoing (permanent?) resistance in Althaus-Reid strikes a similar note.

The image of the journey is one of many images of movement in contemporary pneumatology. Social movements follow Spirit empowerment (Comblin, Bedford) and the Spirit makes the church "liquid" to connect with today's culture (Ward). For many contemporary theologians, personal and group identities are at the heart of such movements of the Spirit. The liberation theologians discussed here name various groups as privileged agents of the Spirit: poor Latin Americans (Comblin, Gutiérrez), Black women (Baker-Fletcher), queer people (Althaus-Reid). Tonstad's banquet is (blessedly) nonreproductive just to the extent that it leaves personal identities alone—it does not try, the Spirit does not try, to create new and shared identities out of existing different ones. What Tonstad writes against is perhaps most visible in Rogers and Radner, both of whom make marriage and childrearing central to their pneumatological ecclesiologies. These postliberal theologians

---

[43]Jürgen Moltmann, *The Church in the Power of the Holy Spirit: A Contribution to Messianic Ecclesiology* (Minneapolis: Fortress, 1993), 317, similarly develops an account of bottom-up ecclesial reform. Reform, he argues, emerges from "the rank and file" and "the starting point [of reform] lies in the congregation and its form as fellowship."

are, at least from Tonstad's perspective, invested in the reproduction of Christian identity in a way that subsumes or effaces other identities.[44]

At this point several prominent features of contemporary pneumatology should be apparent. Contemporary theologians strongly associate Spirit formation with community and local communities (congregations, base communities), as well as movement and movements of various kinds (the everyday journey of healing and/or resistance; mass social movements; liquid church). They tend to imagine Spirit-inspired change as a bottom-up process, and to prioritize the informal and "ordinary" as arenas of Spirit activity—of course, what contemporary theologians regard as ordinary varies widely. Radner's reproductive congregations embody what he regards as the "normal" form of the Christian life, while Baker-Fletcher's people of God pursue healing and freedom in their daily lives. Even Tonstad's banquet could be taken as an appeal to the preservation of ordinary (i.e., typical and pervasive) identity-based differences.

Earlier I suggested that Bedford's division between Spirit-led justice movements and "fixed organizations" illuminates contemporary theology's central pneumatological-sociological picture. For Bedford, fixed organizations are the negative of creative, flexible, unconventional, and just movements. "Fixity" here is an organizational quality freighted with moral and political, not to mention theological, meaning. Fixed organizations, like Radner's "programmatic" churches and Ward's "solid churches," are out of step with the movement of the Holy Spirit. The Spirit *moves* and this movement forms, at maximum, communities and movements rather than what Ward also describes as "institutions." On one side there are communities and movements, on the other fixed organizations or institutions. Communities and movements are pliable before the Spirit, ready to go where the Spirit blows at moment's notice. Although, apart from Ward, none of the

---

[44]Most obviously, Radner's equation of "normal" Christian life with marriage and childrearing renders other forms of Christian life "abnormal" and undesirable. Rogers's advocacy for gay marriage and adoption in the church could also be seen as restraining and distorting queer identity. On the conservative politics of gay marriage, see Melinda Cooper, *Family Values: Between Neoliberalism and the New Social Conservatism* (New York: Zone, 2017).

theologians mentioned engages organizational sociology, the fluid image of communities and movements they promulgate requires highly personal and informal organizational structures. Communities would need to be relatively small and local to remain organizationally flexible, lest decision-making processes become slowed by cumbersome formalities. Movements, likewise, would need to be largely spontaneous aggregations of what communities are already doing, rather than the result of elaborate, perhaps centralized, organizational coordination and planning. The Spirit organizes small, local communities that at times may merge into larger movements.

In the remainder of this book, I employ Ward's term "institutions" to name the organizational form that is banished from (or at best neglected in) the contemporary theological pneumatological-sociological picture. I do so for two reasons. First, it seems to me that Ward's use of "institutions" as the negative (if not negation) of interpersonal, informal networks reflects common practice, at least among English speakers.[45] We commonly place institutions on one side and communities, movements, networks, families, friendships, and other purportedly more personal forms of organizing human relations on another side. Critical discussions of "institutions" frequently call out not only their inflexibility, but also the alienating anonymity that results from their divisions of labor and corresponding complex (and potentially large) structures, as well as the way that accumulating the capital required to start and run institutions makes them subordinate to powerful interests. Such criticisms can be sparked by the kinds of evangelistic or, broadly speaking, "mission driven" reasons that Ward has in mind. But they

---

[45]This ordinary usage of the term "institution" differs from its technical definition in sociology. Sociologists usually consider institutions to be the macro-level background norms, ideologies, and expectations that structure social life. All social life is "institutional" in this respect, insofar as its coherence as "social" depends on its sharing some common, binding features. By contrast, sociologists discuss the kinds of organizations I am concerned with in this book (and following ordinary usage am calling "institutions") as meso-level "formal organizations," visible structures in which individuals are regularly and intentionally grouped together for a common purpose. See Sadiya Akram, *Bourdieu, Habitus, and Field: A Critical Realist Approach* (Cham: Palgrave Macmillan, 2023), 142–4; Marc Garcelon, "The Missing Key: Institutions, Networks, and the Project of Neoclassical Sociology," *Sociological Theory* 28, no. 3 (September 2010): 328–9.

can also—and in recent public discussion regularly do—take the shape of moral and political complaints about institutions.[46]

Take the social media slogan, sometimes shared as a hashtag, "the institutions won't love you back." This slogan is deployed as a warning to individuals who might lovingly invest their time and energy into promoting an institution, e.g., to academics tempted to dedicate themselves to their universities. Institutions will not love you back, so the warning goes, because institutions are not individual or small groups of people capable of mutual relations of loving care. Institutions won't love you by seeking to understand you and adjusting policies and procedures for your benefit. They are inflexible or fixed. Even if institutional leaders respect you and your work, it is unlikely you will make much of an impact on the course of institutional development. If, say, you submit a proposal for the good of the institution through its normal channels, it may be "lost in paperwork" or be rejected because it was "filed incorrectly." The bureaucratic structures and processes of institutions are anonymous and are not shaped by love for you as a unique contributor to institutional life. These structures and processes will also work against you if for some reason you find yourself filing a complaint with the institution. Then anonymity may be wielded as a shield, not only to sideline your complaint on technical grounds but also (or instead) to disclaim the responsibility of present institutional leadership—"the responsible people do not work here anymore" or "we have new leadership" or even the classic "we were just following orders."[47] These and other institutional mechanisms may especially be brought to bear against you if your complaint offends the powerful politicians and investors whose support the institution depends on for its survival.

---

[46] I discuss examples of such critical (or "pessimistic") approaches to Spirit and institutions in Chapter 3.

[47] Each of these responses plays with the impersonality and interchangeability of positions in an organizational hierarchy in a different way. "The responsible people do not work here anymore" says both "moral responsibility is personal and attaches to the specific persons filling the positions at the time an infraction occurred" and "that responsibility does not attach to the position itself, which can be filled by any number of people hired by the institution." "We have new leadership" says something similar, this time applied to an entire leadership group. "We were just following orders" disclaims any responsibility for underlings in a hierarchical structure.

Institutions in the end only love themselves and will do anything to sustain themselves—"institutions care only for their own survival" has become another slogan in recent years.

This ordinary way of talking about institutions and their differences from more informal and personal organizational forms—forms in which you are liable to "be loved back"—is the main reason behind my choice to utilize the term "institutions" consistently for the kind of organizations relegated to the background (at best) of the contemporary pneumatological-sociological picture. Theologians, it seems, have taken the ordinary critical account of institutions on board when picturing the relationship between Spirit inspiration and human social organization. Implicit in this discourse, ordinary and theological, is a definition of institutions as organizations that are relatively stable, complexly and formally structured, and reliant on significant amounts of material resources. Some institutions are relatively small and local, while others are relatively large and translocal. Size matters to institutional critics, especially because scale, structural complexity and formality, and resource use often go together. The larger and more structurally complex the institution, the greater is the need for formal and usually centralized planning, administration, and leadership to ensure institutional coherence. Larger institutions also need a greater quantity of resources to sustain them. An institution's commitment to endure across some stretch of time—which may be a determinate period or may be open-ended—can also require considerable leadership and material resources. The entrenchment of this conception of institutions in ordinary and theological discourse recommends its critical discussion in this book. My interest is less in disputing the accuracy of how this discourse frames "institutions" and more in offering a rejoinder to the near unanimous perception that institutions so understood are pernicious and unhelpful.

The other reason to employ this ordinary concept of institutions is that quotidian anti-institutional discourse is similar in notable respects to dualistic accounts of organizations in modern social theory. The late-nineteenth-century German sociologist Ferdinand Tönnies, for example, produced a well-known theory of the distinction between "community" (*Gemeinschaft*) and "society" (*Gesellschaft*), with the former characterized by persons voluntarily united in intimate relationship and the latter by involuntary groupings mediated by impersonal bureaucratic structures.[48] Tönnies's contemporary Max Weber famously described bureaucratic societies as an "iron cage" that restricts individual freedom in the name of rational planning.[49] These views were taken up by philosophers at the Institute of Social Research in Frankfurt after the First World War as offering critical insights into the nature of modernity. The Frankfurt School in turn contributed to the growing critique of bureaucracy-induced anomie after the Second World War, the moment when massive factory-style governmental and business organizations began to dominate life in Europe and North America.[50] It is not a far leap from the

---

[48]Ferdinand Tönnies, *Community and Civil Society*, ed. Jose Harris and trans. Jose Harris and Margaret Hollis (Cambridge: Cambridge University Press, 2001 [1887]). Tönnies was developing Thomas Hobbes's account of voluntary and involuntary political organizations in *Leviathan*, ed. C. B. Macpherson (New York: Penguin, 1985 [1651]), that is, of forms of political organization described in terms of their basis in the unity of individual wills. For Hobbes, only an impersonal, machine-like state (the "Leviathan") can protect us from tearing each other apart in the name of our conflicting wills. Many modern critics of institutional bureaucracy have flipped Hobbes on his head, accepting his description of the nature of different organizational forms but rejecting his normative conclusions.

[49]Max Weber, *The Protestant Ethic and the Spirit of Capitalism*, trans. Talcott Parsons (New York: Routledge, 1992 [1920–1]), 123. At least, this is how Weber has typically been interpreted. See Jason A. Josephson–Storm, *The Myth of Disenchantment: Magic, Modernity, and the Birth of the Human Sciences* (Chicago: University of Chicago Press, 2017), 269–301, for an alternative reading of Weber.

[50]Max Horkheimer and Theodore W. Adorno, "The Culture Industry: Enlightenment as Mass Deception," in *Dialectic of Enlightenment: Philosophical Fragments*, ed. Gunzelin Schmid Noerr and trans. Edmund Jephcott (Stanford: Stanford University Press, 2002), 94–136; Charles Perrow, "A Society of Organizations," *Theory and Society* 20, no. 6 (December 1991): 725–62. Perrow expanded this argument in *Organizing America: Wealth, Power, and the Rise of Corporate Capitalism* (Princeton: Princeton University Press, 2002). Other influential social theories to consider in this connection are Turner's theory of *communitas*, MacIntyre's conception of virtuous community (contrasted with bureaucracies), and Foucault's exposure of the power/knowledge dynamic of quintessential modern institutions such as prisons and hospitals. Victor Turner, *The Ritual Process: Structure and Antistructure* (London: Routledge and Keegan Paul, 1969); Alasdair MacIntyre, *After Virtue: A Study in Moral Theory*, 2d ed. (Notre Dame, IN: University of Notre Dame Press, 1984); Michel Foucault, *Madness and Civilization: A History of Insanity in the Age of Reason*, trans. Richard Howard (New York: Routledge, 1989); Michael Foucault, *Discipline and Punish: The Birth of the Prison*, trans. Alan Sheridan (New York: Vintage, 1995).

theoretical division between bureaucracies and communities to the ordinary opposition between institutions and local, personal organizational forms.[51]

Although I will not examine the theoretical or social origins of the dualistic conception of organizational forms in the present work, it will be useful to keep that conception in mind since it in some sense dramatizes the terms in which anxieties about institutions are ordinarily expressed, including by contemporary theologians (some of whom may indeed have been influenced by dualistic social theories). In the book's conclusion, moreover, I draw tentative connections between contemporary theologians' dualistic pneumatological-sociological picture and the anti-institutional culture of neoliberal capitalism. More immediately, it is helpful to have the modern dualism in mind as, beginning in the next section, I converse with "postmodern" theory to sketch a different sociological picture of organizations and their relation to the Holy Spirit. In this alternative picture, the dualistic framing of "institutions versus community," "the local versus the non-local," and so forth is replaced by a more dynamic and relational view of organizing, organizational forms, and organizations. Though I call upon social theory to aid in the development of this picture, the picture's basis is an account of the relationality at the heart of the divine economy and of creation. This relationality, I suggest, characterizes the work of the organizing Spirit and should characterize humans' participatory responses to the Spirit.

---

[51]"Not a far leap" is a rhetorical turn of phrase indicating logical continuity, not a causal relation. Whether the theorists influenced popular discourse, inherited their distinctions from their broader cultures, or some combination of the two is not a matter I take up here. We should also be careful to note that we use the English-word "institution" in various other ways in ordinary speech, for instance to refer to a beloved individual, family, or local organization as an "institution in" (pillar of) their community. We also regularly use "institution" in a fairly neutral, descriptive way to talk about some organization or another. I have found it interesting to observe how the same people who criticize "institutions" in broad terms sometimes go on to start "institutes," "centers," and other formal organizations dedicated to their alternative, anti-institutional visions. It is an intriguing psychological and sociological question why and how such conflicting uses of "institution" can coexist—but this is of course the case for many ordinary terms and concepts.

Organizing Relations: Theological and Sociological Perspectives

One major contemporary theologian of the Holy Spirit who has engaged the pneumatological-sociological connection explicitly and done so in a relational direction is Sarah Coakley. In Coakley's *God, Sexuality, and the Self: An Essay "On the Trinity,"* she argues for a model of incorporation into the life of the Trinity that begins with the Spirit. Mystics and charismatics, as well as the history of trinitarian theology, strongly suggest that the Spirit takes the leading role in incorporating believers into Christ and his body so that they might enjoy his relation with his Father. Starting with the Spirit, according to Coakley, both affirms trinitarian orthodoxy (since the Trinity is the vector of the Spirit's work) and affirms the sometimes-untidy pneumatic experience associated with mystics and charismatics. Drawing on sociologist Ernst Troeltsch's tripartite ecclesiological typology—with its church-, sect-, and mystic-types—Coakley rejects any dualism that would place the Holy Spirit on the side of either established, "orthodox" ecclesial institutions or of the anti-institutional sects and mystics.[52] Instead, she contends that the experience-based innovations of mystical and charismatic communities are essential for the deepening and enlivening of the institutional guardians of orthodoxy.

This move breaks with the dualism undergirding much of the contemporary pneumatological-sociological picture yet affirms its general thrust. On the one hand, Coakley depicts ecclesial

---

[52]Coakley, *God, Sexuality, and the Self*, especially 157–62, 341–2. Moltmann, *The Church in the Power of the Spirit*, 314–36, also references Troeltsch while arguing for a dynamic relationship between ecclesial institutions (which he identifies with established denominations) and "grassroots communities." He proposes a "double strategy" that combines reforming efforts "from above" and "from below," and roots this strategy in "the committed congregation" that is open to both institutional direction and grassroots ferment (335). The latter move is continuous with the local emphasis of much contemporary theology. See also Jürgen Moltmann, *The Spirit of Life: A Universal Affirmation* (Minneapolis: Fortress, 1992), 247, for a brief affirmation of the role of regional and national churches in facilitating ecumenical community and political influence within the fellowship of the Spirit. Moltmann suggests that these structures should be federated rather than hierarchical to avoid fostering a "passive welfare mentality."

institutions as potentially subject to (re)organizational pressure from the Spirit insofar as they are open to the influence of mystical and charismatic communities. She identifies a productive sociological relation between seemingly dissident, anti-institutional pneumatic communities and seemingly Spirit-bereft institutions, a relation useful to the Spirit's organization of triune incorporation. On the other hand, Coakley still associates direct Spirit formation largely with relatively noninstitutional communities. The Spirit's connections to institutions are mostly indirect and mediated by communities described precisely in terms of their greater pneumatic pliability.[53]

If Coakley does not fully break with the reigning pneumatological-sociological picture, she at least points in a more helpful relational direction. Calling to mind my view from the window that started this chapter, we can see why a relational conception of organization is so essential, for example when conceptualizing the "local" character of organization and organizing.[54] The river connects to the Atlantic Ocean. The wind on the river is part of the global atmospheric circulation. These streams of water and air are in turn disturbed by global dynamics related to anthropogenic climate change. A flag in support of police is legible as part of a global struggle over police brutality. Recent phases of that struggle highlight inequalities related to the racial and economic legacies of colonialism and pandemic. A community or a movement formed to bear witness to the Spirit's presence here, in my local area, confronts the ecological and political reality that "here" is always in some way bound up with "there" on our globalized planet.

---

[53] I discuss Coakley's work further in Chapter 3, including her concept of "mixed-type" communities and individuals within institutions. This concept introduces additional nuance into her pneumatological-sociological picture, but still does not arrive at an account of institutions themselves as potentially participating in the Spirit. Coakley also persists in associating the Spirit with flexibility, change, subversion of norms, and so on, and not with stability or other attributes that she sees as characteristic of institutions.

[54] I focus on the contemporary pneumatological-sociological picture's emphasis on "the local" in the following paragraphs both to indicate the kind of work that a relational analysis affords and because I think that particular emphasis underlies some of the picture's other key features, e.g., the bias toward bottom-up change, informal and relatively fluid organizational structures, identity, and community. Some of these connections surface in the following discussion, others elsewhere in the book.

This relational reality strongly suggests that any conception of local organizations as narrowly and exclusively concerned with their immediate environments is unhelpful and misleading. It is unhelpful to the extent that it may encourage local organizers to neglect their wider entanglements. It is misleading insofar as it may distract us from seeing how organizational efforts in each locality are always in some way connected to other localities. But here an anxiety might surface—does an alternative, glocally entangled conception of local organizations rob the latter of their integrity and diminish the importance of the local focus of their work? Not necessarily. If we take local organizations to be constituent parts of the entangled world, then they have their own integrity within a larger, translocal context to which they are inherently related. This integrity can be conceived of practically, as pointing to the intelligibility and validity of concrete local organizations as instruments of human action in and on the world; it can also be thought of formally, as indicating specific organizational patterns that are comprehensible and legitimate (e.g., local congregations and activist organizations). This integrity, however, is also relational and depends on an acknowledgment of actual and potential connections to other localities.

The preceding statements reflect the outlook of contemporary social theory and the socioeconomic dynamics named by terms such as "glocalization" and "globalization." As we have seen, glocalization in particular names the mutual though uneven composition of "the local" and "the global" as a feature of late-twentieth- and early-twenty-first-century societies.[55] On the other hand, these statements also reflect theological judgments made in view of the dynamic unity

---

[55] See the previous citations of Appadurai, Robertson, and Roudometof. As an example, consider a global restaurant chain that launches a special item and appeals in marketing copy to its origins in a given local context (mozzarella cheese and olive oil from Italy, Kentucky bourbon, Thai street food). In the process, the chain generates production standards (ingredients, appearance, flavor profile) that local chefs may feel pressured to adopt—or deviate from—in order for their food to come across as "genuine" and "authentic." Other examples might highlight ways that global brands more or less invent some products they claim as originating in local contexts. Although such dynamics are global today, they are "uneven" insofar as not every locality is equally pervaded by or subject to global flows of information, finance, commodities, migrants, etc.; not every global flow draws equally or in the same way from localities (global ubiquity is also a selling point in many a marketing pitch); and the relative power of different localities and global flows will vary considerably.

of the divine economy and of God's creation.[56] If we imagine, for instance, creation as a web of interwoven threads, then pulling on one thread exerts more or less force on the rest of the web. Consider in this regard the scope of basic theological claims related to sin and God's response to sin via the election of Israel, the significance of Christ's ministry and death, and the mission of the church (from Jerusalem "to the ends of the earth"—Acts 1:8[57]). While each of these claims is anchored in a particular local geography, namely, that of the Ancient Near East and/or the first-century Mediterranean world, their ramifications are taken to be cosmic.[58] Here we have a series of theological "butterfly effects," seemingly discrete local events with global influence.[59] Or, to return to the web image, we have a set of local events that exert maximum force on the rest of the web, transforming it in the process. This description might be analogically extended to take in the activities of local organizations today that seek to join in the work of the Holy Spirit—these activities are pursued locally but may reverberate beyond their local

---

[56] By "divine economy" I mean the triune God's actions toward creation. The unity of the divine economy can be articulated on various grounds, such as the Barthian claim that God's single work is Jesus Christ (creation and election are internal to incarnation and redemption) and the classical trinitarian claim that work predicated of one "Person" of the Trinity can always be predicated of the other two "Persons." I.e., while biblical and historical theological language make it "appropriate" to associate the Father with creation and providence, the Son and Spirit create and preserve with the Father as acts of the one God. Language describing Christ and Spirit as "Creator" is not out of place. The main point I am making in the text is that all creation shares a status *qua* divine work, and that insofar as the various "parts" of creation share this status they are always already related to one another in a fundamental and definitive way. The following sentences begin to explore some practical implications of creation's relationality as derived from its createdness. I further elaborate these matters below and throughout the book.

[57] All biblical quotations in this book are from the New Revised Standard Version.

[58] Some caution with this language should be exercised with regard to the local "origins" of sin. In the case of sin we are dealing less with a determinate physical geography and period of time and more with an imagined, proto-historical context—yet even this context is anchored in a general way to the Ancient Near East (Gen. 2:10–14); this geography sets the context whether "sin" is seen to enter creation with the consumption of forbidden fruit in 3:1–24 or with Cain's slaying of Abel in 4:1–16.

[59] The contemporary notion of "the global" does not of course map on to either ancient or modern understandings of "the cosmic." I am using the terms somewhat interchangeably here to signal the encompassing scope of the local effects in question.

contexts. They are bound up with, find some of their significance in, their translocal reach.

But the *mutuality* of the dynamics described by social theorists cautions against any description that limits the direction of force unilaterally, from the local to the global or from the bottom to the top. Similarly, the unity of divine economy and of creation might also lead us to expect "top-down" effects, such as those found in theological claims about the universal availability of wisdom as part of creation's fabric, the encompassing reality of Christ as the one in whom "all things hold together" (Col. 1:17), or of God's reign as creation's formative *telos* or final cause. There are also strong theological grounds for regarding sin not merely as something that expanded from local origins, but as a cosmic force personified as the "principalities and powers." From this perspective, the specific qualities of each of creation's constituent "threads" are determined to some extent by the overall properties of the (fallen) creational web. What happens *here*, in this local setting, is irrevocably shaped by the universal dimensions of the divine economy and of sin. In that case, we can depict local contexts as subject to pressure from "global" or universal theological realities, such that any local organization can be assessed according to, for instance, its orientation to God's wise rule or its subjection to the powers' rule.[60]

Putting the "bottom-up" and "top-down" stories together requires sensitivity to the mutuality and entanglement of the local and the global, and to the particular ways in which developments at these scales interact with each other in given contexts. Although the breadth of the theological claims could be taken as recommending a maximal and totalizing account of mutual influence—such that *everything* that takes place at the local level shapes the *entire world*, and *each* global development shapes *all* localities equally— there are theological as well as sociological reasons for expecting

---

[60] This orientation or subjection might be regarded as intentional (in the positive case, the organization takes aiming at God's reign as its mission) and/or practical (regardless of its intentions, the organization does some things that resemble God's reign or that point in the direction of God's reign). Among the contemporary theologians discussed above, Ward emphasizes an organization's intentional orientation toward salvation in Christ, while Comblin emphasizes its practical orientation toward the liberation of poor Latin Americans.

mutual influence to be at times uneven and asymmetrical and therefore to require context-sensitive interpretation. Even the grandest theological claims about the influence of sinister "powers" or about the universal effects of Christ's crucifixion need to be qualified in practice by careful discernment of just how life in a given setting is marred by sin and/or exhibits signs of redemption.[61] A sociologist might add that social influences can also be relatively modest and local or regional in scope. The possibility of regional (neither strictly local nor global) influence introduces meso-level forces into the emerging picture, taking us beyond a local–global binary.[62] These perspectives provide further reasons for paying close attention to the actual play of forces within a given context, and for assessing the actual or potential shape of organizational activities accordingly.

The burden of this book is to develop what I have just referred to as an emerging nonbinary picture that contrasts with the dualistic tendencies of the contemporary pneumatological-sociological picture described in the previous section. The preceding paragraphs begin to draw out this contrast with reference to the relation between "the local" and other geographic and social contexts. Instead of fixating on the local as the privileged space of Spirit formation, with other spaces only influenced indirectly and perhaps spontaneously through local organizing, we can for theological and sociological reasons view "the local" as entwined with regional and global dynamics. Elsewhere in the book I make similar arguments with respect to the other common features of the contemporary pneumatological-sociological picture, especially the binary opposition between, on the one hand, communities and movements and on the other institutions.

The resulting alternative picture portrays the Spirit's role in the divine economy as organizing complex relations for life-giving ends. By describing the object of the Spirit's organizing in terms of "relations," I adopt the web-like conception of creation mentioned

---

[61] Here we might think of the differential treatment of specific congregational bodies in the letters of Paul or the beginning of Revelation.

[62] For one theological complement to this analysis, consider the concept of "names" and the "name above all names" in passages such as Eph. 1:21 or Phil. 2:9. Although some "named" figures, e.g., emperors, pretended to universality, other "names" (Herod Antipas, Pontius Pilate) had a more regional import.

above. To recapitulate, if creation is in some theological sense a single whole—it is what God creates, all that is not God, and is collectively subject to divine action and the power of sin—it is a complex whole with many parts.[63] These parts, moreover, are interrelated insofar as developments in any one of them can reverberate through the other parts, and insofar as global and regional (meso-level) developments can influence specific parts. Creation taken as a whole just is the organizational configuration of its parts; creation is a dynamic pattern of mutually (though unevenly) interacting parts. Each part, on the other hand, can only be understood through its relations to other relevant parts and to the whole. Given the relational constitution of each of these parts, a strain of philosophy and social theory suggests that the parts themselves should be thought of as relations.[64] That is, each part only exists as a node of relations to other parts and to the whole. Strip a part of its relations and the part disappears. Change a part's relations and the part changes too.

This relational ontology can also be affirmed on theological grounds at the most general (global or cosmic) level, since creation only exists in relation to God.[65] The web of creation depends on God for its being, it has no existence outside of this relationship. Creation cannot be stripped of its constitutive relation to God, or it would cease to exist.[66] Sin changes that relation and so changes creation. The language of fallen humanity's "sinful nature" reflects this change and the ontological implications for humanity *qua* creature of its changed relation to God. Yet these implications do

---

[63]In Chapter 2, I interpret Genesis 1 as portraying the divine act of creation as a Spirit-tended, dynamic process of complex structural differentiation.

[64]As I discuss below, the main figure I am drawing on here is Pierre Bourdieu. Bourdieu was self-consciously developing the philosophical ontology associated with Ernst Cassirer, Claude Lévi-Strauss, Kurt Lewin, and others. See Pierre Bourdieu and Loïc J. D. Wacquant, *An Invitation to Reflexive Sociology* (Cambridge: Polity, 1992), 96–8.

[65]I argue along similar lines in Jamie Pitts, *Principalities and Powers: Revising John Howard Yoder's Sociological Theology* (Eugene, OR: Pickwick, 2013), 27–30. I will reference this earlier work at times without drawing on its principal subject, Yoder, as a normative source. I discuss Yoder's sexual abuse at the beginning of Chapter 3.

[66]I am assuming that this dependence is unidirectional. God's existence does not depend on creation, else it would not make sense to describe God as "God."

not run all the way down, so any talk of sinful nature has to be strictly qualified by the enduringly graced "nature" of creation as created for and providentially tended toward consummate relation with God.[67] Sin's power is, with respect to creation, universal but not all-encompassing. It cannot encompass or relationally change creation's constitutive relation to its Creator—it can only distort that relation. Creation is a relational web that receives its basic orientation through its relation to God. This God-creation relation is creation's overall organizing principle, the fundamental dynamic that shapes the configuration of its internal relations. Sin's distortion of the God-creation relation thus has internal organizational consequences for creation. God redeems this sinful situation by reorganizing creation toward a fuller, undistorted relation to God. Creation and redemption are, from this perspective at least, a divine project of organizing and reorganizing the relations that make up creation.

The pneumatological dimension of the alternative picture I propose in this book is rooted in this relational account of the divine project toward creation, of what theologians call the "divine economy."[68] Throughout *Organizing Spirit* I offer detailed discussions of organizational developments within particular social contexts and suggest what difference it makes to see these developments as subject to creative and redemptive organizational pressure from the Holy Spirit. In other words, I repeatedly ask what difference it makes to see the Spirit as organizing complex relations. This difference, I argue, challenges normative attempts to narrow the scope of human responses to the Spirit to local, fluid, and relatively informal organizations. While these attempts are in

---

[67]Cf. John Milbank, *The Suspended Middle: Henri de Lubac and the Debate Concerning the Supernatural* (Grand Rapids, MI: Eerdmans, 2005).

[68]I could take a further step and suggest that the relational character of the divine economy reflects and is rooted in the relationality of the Trinity. Although I am not totally averse to "social trinitarianism," I am mindful of Karen Kilby's worry that it too easily projects desired sociopolitical arrangements into the Godhead. It moreover seems to me sufficient for the purposes of my argument to focus on the divine economy rather than speculate about its connections to divine ontology. See Kilby, "Perichoresis and Projection: Problems with Social Doctrines of the Trinity," *New Blackfriars* 81, no. 956 (October 2000): 432–45.

many cases understandable, emerging, for example, as reactions to institutional inaction and abuse, I warn against them precisely when the pursuit of justice is at issue. Whether the issue at hand is ecological justice (Chapter 2), gender justice (Chapter 3), or racial justice (Chapter 4), institutions have a significant role to play—notwithstanding their ongoing contributions to injustice. Although I at times appeal to pragmatic reasons for embracing institutions—challenges such as climate change seem to demand the kind of intentional planning and coordination enabled by institutions—my basic mode of argumentation is theological, insofar as I am consistently at pains to show how regarding contemporary struggles for justice in connection to the organizing Spirit challenges any dualism that would pit noninstitutional organizing against institutional organizing.

Since I am at odds with what I have called a dualistic pneumatological-sociological picture, I also make use of a nondualistic, relational sociology throughout the book. In particular, I engage sociologist Pierre Bourdieu's concept of social spaces or "fields" at various points in the following chapters to highlight the advantages of a relational conception of the social contexts I study. For Bourdieu, a "field" or social space is a set of interrelated positions defined by their relative quantities and types of capital.[69] Any given field shares its orientation to some type or types of capital rather than others. In Bourdieusian sociology, "capital" names not only material relations—say, ownership of the means of production—but also the social and cultural goods (family and professional contacts, educational qualifications) an individual or group has at their disposal.[70] All capital, moreover, has symbolic dimensions, through which they are perceived as valuable and worth pursuing. Bourdieu frequently depicts fields as four-dimensional spaces divided by a horizontal axis indicating

---

[69] I summarize Bourdieu's basic concepts, including "field," in Pitts, *Principalities and Powers*, 18–24. For an accessible introduction in Bourdieu's words, see Bourdieu and Wacquant, *An Invitation to Reflexive Sociology*, 94–115.
[70] Bourdieu, "The Forms of Capital," trans. Richard Nice, in *Handbook of Theory and Research for the Sociology of Education*, ed. John G. Robinson (Westport, CN: Greenwood Press, 1986), 241–58.

positions that hold relatively more cultural (left) or material (right) forms of capital, and a vertical axis indicating positions that hold more (top) or less (bottom) capital overall. Individuals who grow up or spend considerable time within specific fields are more or less formed to see specific forms of capital as important and to dedicate their lives to pursuing such capital. Bourdieu calls the embodied disposition to perceive and care about particular forms of capital due to prolonged participation in a field an agent's "habitus." Habitus is Bourdieu's smallest social unit. Although he mostly uses the term to describe individual human beings ("agents"), since he also plots organizations as capital-constituted positions within social fields some scholars extend the concept to speak of "organizational habitus."[71] Be that as it may, the main point for our purposes is to see that each position within a field—a person or an organization—is a capital relation and also a center of interpretive agency whose actions or practices shape the field. Agents' practices are likely to contribute to the reproduction of the fields that formed them, though Bourdieu stresses that social reproduction is never mechanical and always involves struggle and change.[72] What is reproduced is the overall structure of the field, with a tendency for dominant and subordinate agents to maintain their relative positions.

So far I have been describing the internal dynamics of fields, but it should also be said that Bourdieu regards fields as "microcosms" of larger social forces.[73] One way he develops this point is by describing a "field of power" operative in a given society, in which the most dominant agents from the most dominant fields struggle over the relative value of their capital. The results of this struggle can reverberate within the society's other fields in various ways, for instance by devaluing a type of cultural capital formerly

---

[71]Tim Hallet and Matthew Gougherty, "Bourdieu and Organizations: Hidden Traces, Macro Influence, and Micro Potential," in *The Oxford Handbook of Pierre Bourdieu*, eds. Jeffery Sallaz and Thomas Medvetz (Oxford: Oxford University Press, 2018), 273–98.
[72]Bourdieu and Wacquant, *An Invitation to Reflexive Sociology*, 139–40.
[73]Pierre Bourdieu, *Microcosmes: Théorie des champs* (Paris: Raison d'Agir, 2021).

dominant within a particular field and raising the value of a previously subordinate type of cultural capital in the same field.[74] In Bourdieu's sociology, therefore, we observe lines of force running both up from particular fields to the general field of power and down from the field of power to those other fields. Similar dynamics are also present within fields, as agents from various positions can influence the shape of a field. Indeed, it is the collective practices of all the agents constituting a field that give that field its shape. It may make sense in some specific cases to speak of especially transformative "bottom-up" or "top-down" influences, but in most cases we should expect to see a variety of positions involved in giving a field its current and emerging parameters.

Bourdieu's sociology of fields, therefore, contributes to the alternative pneumatological-sociological picture I am developing in this book by offering a finely grained account of the dynamic complexity of social organization. I accordingly deploy the concept of fields throughout the following chapters in two primary ways.[75] First, it shapes in a general way the detailed empirical descriptions or case studies in the next three chapters by leading me to highlight the relational character of the social contexts, organizations, and organizing activities under review. Second, it appears explicitly as an analytical resource when challenging theological tendencies to collapse the Spirit's work and human response to the Spirit into a dualistic framework. I repeatedly call upon the field concept to urge

---

[74]Think of the itinerary of the label "evangelical" during the presidency of Donald Trump. On the one hand, supporters of Trump's political movement increasingly claimed that label regardless of their religious affiliation. On the other hand, many Christians abandoned the label. The label's value increased among a certain fragment of the political field and decreased in the Christian field. In the latter field, the status of labels such as "exvangelical" and "deconstructing Christian" rose. Data analyst Ryan Burge regularly explores these phenomena on his blog, *Graphs about Religion*, https://www.graphsaboutreligion.com/.

[75]In addition to direct references to Bourdieu's development of the concept, I also make use of a considerable body of work in organizational studies that draws on it.

theologians to envision a more complex social reality in which exist a variety of organizational possibilities for joining the organizing Spirit to address historic injustices.[76]

Picturing Spirit

In this chapter I have argued that many contemporary theologians operate with an implicit pneumatological-sociological picture. I have also begun to put forward an alternative picture. This use of the concept of "pictures" draws from the philosophical tradition associated with Ludwig Wittgenstein. In his late writings *Philosophical Investigations* and "Philosophy of Psychology—A Fragment," Wittgenstein develops an account of the pictorial character of language. Whereas in his early work he imagined that the structure of propositions (truly or falsely) pictured states of affairs in the world,[77] he now suggests in a more general way that stretches of ordinary language at least implicitly picture a context in which it makes sense to use them. (The phrase "the sky is blue" assumes a world in which there is an object called "the sky" and there are colors that can be predicated of objects.) These pictures can go unexamined and can deceive us into thinking that such a context necessarily exists, or perhaps that its existence is more or less encompassing than it actually is (e.g., that everything above us is "sky" and therefore blue). We can, he writes, be held captive by

---

[76]The sociological character of the concept of "field" I am working with distinguishes it from Wolfhart Pannenberg's use of field theory in his theological work. Pannenberg is largely concerned to employ field theory as developed in physics to illuminate intra-trinitarian relations and to describe creation as a space-time field subject to divine action. Like Pannenberg, I closely associate the Holy Spirit with the creational field, but my objective is less to defend an account of divine action and more to describe organizational parallels between the Spirit's activities within the divine economy and human participation in those activities. As stated in a previous note, I do not explore questions of trinitarian ontology in this book. For an overview of Pannenberg's use of field theory, see Theodore James Whapham, "Spirit as Field of Force," *Scottish Journal of Theology* 67, no. 1 (2014): 15–32.

[77]Ludwig Wittgenstein, *Tractatus Logico-Philosophicus*, 2d ed., trans. David Pears and Brian McGuiness (New York: Routledge, 2001).

our language's pictures, hindered from seeing our situation clearly.[78] In such cases he indicates that we might look more closely—for example by studying alternative pictures that draw attention to overlooked ordinary possibilities for our words and actions—and hope for a shift in aspect, a shift in how we see and what we see as being the case.[79] An aspect shift may allow language to return from "holiday," where it lost touch with reality, and restore its traction on the "rough ground" of ordinary life.[80] In other words, seeing things anew may help us reevaluate our language and find ways to speak and think—and new guiding pictures—that meet the everyday challenges that face us.

This book is an attempt to "explore the picture"[81] embedded in common theological language about the Spirit's relation to certain sociological, and specifically organizational, forms such as "communities," "movements," and "institutions," and to recommend an aspect shift toward a fuller and truer picture of the organizational possibilities of life in the Spirit. Both pictures, the one I am challenging and the one I am proposing, are pneumatological in the sense that they advance doctrinal claims about the Holy Spirit and about what we should expect to see when the Spirit is

---

[78]The notion of being held captive by a picture comes from *Philosophical Investigations* §115: "A *picture* held us captive. And we couldn't get outside it, for it lay in our language, and language seemed only to repeat it to us inexorably" (emphasis original). This and the following quotations are from the revised fourth edition of G. E. M. Anscombe's translation of the *Philosophical Investigations*, prepared by P. M. S. Hacker and Joachim Shulte (Oxford: Blackwell, 2009).

[79]On "aspect-seeing" and shifts in aspect, see "Philosophy of Psychology—A Fragment," xi. This text is included in the version of the *Philosophical Investigations* cited above.

[80]The quoted words are from *Philosophical Investigations*: "Philosophical problems arise when language *goes on holiday*" (§38, emphasis original). "The more closely we examine actual language, the greater becomes the conflict between it and our requirement ... We have got onto slippery ice where there is no friction, and so, in a certain sense, the conditions are ideal; but also, because of that, we are unable to walk. We want to walk, so we need *friction*. Back to the rough ground!" (§107, emphasis original).

[81]Wittgenstein, "Philosophy of Psychology—A Fragment," vii.55: "our language describes a picture. What is to be done with the picture, how it is to be used, is still obscure. Quite clearly, however, it must be explored if we want to understand the sense of our words. But the picture seems to spare us this work: it already points to a particular use. This is how it takes us in."

present and active in creation. The pictures are sociological in the sense that they identify a specific set of organizational patterns that we should pursue in order to respond to the Spirit. The book's argument is that the contemporary pneumatological-sociological picture has an overly narrow view of how the Spirit organizes and, relatedly, a diminished conception of the range of organizational options available to those seeking to participate in the Spirit's work. The alternative picture of the Spirit built up in the following chapters calls attention to the complex and relational character of the Spirit's organizing and the correspondingly complex and relational organizational possibilities open to Spirit-oriented humans. Adopting this more expansive pneumatological-sociological picture, I argue, is a matter of faithfulness to the organizing Spirit and to the life that the Spirit seeks to foster in death-dealing situations. In this book I am particularly concerned to show how the formation and reformation of institutions might be compatible with life in the Spirit in situations defined to some extent by ecological catastrophe, sexism, and racism. These situations draw my focus both because of their urgency and because theologians have often taken them to defy an institutional response.

In the remainder of this section, I survey the content of the rest of the book's chapters to offer additional clarity about how I analyze the contemporary pneumatological-sociological picture and offer an alternative. Chapter 2 develops the image of the "hovering Spirit" who dynamically structures creation and orients it to life-giving solidarity. Contrary to the claims of some Anabaptist ethicists, environmental politics should not be limited to community organizing in discrete localities since—by virtue of the Spirit's hovering—every locality is related to other localities. This point is drawn out through a detailed relational account of a single watershed, the Elkhart River Watershed. Joining the Spirit's work for environmental justice in this watershed requires connections to other watersheds, connections that can be fostered by translocal institutions. The complex organization of such institutions is of a piece with creation's Spirit-gifted organizational complexity. These organizations, in turn, are subject to the same norms as creation—norms bestowed by the Spirit as Lord and giver of life.

Chapters 3 and 4 refine the treatment of institutions by discussing questions related to institutional reform and institutional connections to social movements. Chapter 3 takes up the reform question by engaging pneumatological writings (Rogers, Coakley) that associate Spirit sanctification with the progressive transformation of the church to include women and queer people. I deepen this association by examining women's movements within some Mennonite denominational institutions in North America. The relative success of these movements challenges "pessimistic" pneumatologies (Tonstad, Radner) and contributes to a picture of the "sanctifying Spirit" who brings about gender justice in part through the reform of ecclesial institutions.

Countering this pessimism does not involve the claim that *all* institutions are reformable or that *everyone* inspired by the Spirit should pursue a reform agenda. Chapter 4 affirms that departing unjust institutions can be a valid response to the Spirit but denies that such departures need be thought of as always rejecting institutions as such. Taking the life and writings of Vincent Harding as a guide, I focus on institutions that have arisen within racial justice movements—some of which have resulted from a break with dominant institutions. Harding's notion of "freedom institutions" gives rise to a picture of the "doubling Spirit" who encourages the sustenance and expansion of movements through institutions. This picture also clarifies how Christians might think of relations among ecclesial institutions and extra-ecclesial institutions dedicated to racial and other forms of justice, as well as how institutions might powerfully integrate identity politics and politics aimed at material conditions.

Finally, Chapter 5 recapitulates the argument of the book and draws some conclusions related to the pursuit of life-giving solidarity today in the name of the Spirit. Specifically, I am concerned with beginning to think through how a pneumatological political theology might provide critical legitimation for institutions in a neoliberal era pervaded by a thoroughly anti-institutional culture. I suggest that resources in this book open onto a global imagination in which ecclesial and other institutions play a crucial role in opposing and providing democratic alternatives to neoliberal institutions.

My construction of an alternative pneumatological-sociological picture is guided by three central methodological commitments. First, I am a Mennonite theologian and am committed to engaging Mennonite history and thought as a constructive resource in theology. The discussion of Anabaptist environmental ethics in Chapter 2 and the studies of North American Mennonite women's movements and Harding, who spent a decade as a Mennonite pastor and peace worker, all reflect this commitment.[82] Those two studies, moreover, not only exemplify and reinforce arguments made on theological grounds, but also supply additional normative criteria for depicting the Spirit and responses to the Spirit. That is because I take the subjects of those studies to be conversation partners within my own theological tradition, partners whose voices I am keen to learn from. This understanding follows from my view of Mennonite theology as guided by the interpretation of Scripture through and alongside careful listening to pressing voices within the theologian's context—voices such as those arising from the Mennonite tradition; from within the theologian's own community; from larger theological, intellectual, and cultural discussions; and from the theologian's own reflection on their convictions.[83] I differ from many fellow Mennonite theologians by regarding not only sixteenth-century Anabaptist thought as bearing normative theological weight, but also the extended conversations—conversations extended in many cases within ecclesial institutions—that have developed in the five hundred years since.[84] My decision to begin sketching the alternative picture with an engagement of biblical material, and to engage that material through the narrative hermeneutic favored by many Mennonite theologians and in conversation with an ecumenical variety of contemporary theologians, also reflects this methodological orientation.

The second guiding methodological commitment is inspired by Bourdieu's notion of "reflexivity." Bourdieu thought that the best way to account for and critically transform one's own subject

---

[82]"Anabaptism" names the sixteenth-century movements out of which Mennonites and Hutterites arose. It is commonly used today as an umbrella term for those traditions as well as the main other traditions that have split off from Mennonites (Amish, Mennonite Brethren, etc.) or that began under the (at least partial) inspiration of Anabaptist history and theology (Brethren in Christ, Church of the Brethren, the Bruderhof, etc.).

[83]I spell out this methodological approach to Mennonite theology in my unpublished manuscript *Love Seeking Integrity: An Introduction to Christian Theology in the Anabaptist Tradition* (2023, typescript).

[84]I discuss these methodological issues in my article with Luis Tapia Rubio, "Anabaptist Theology," in *St Andrews Encyclopaedia of Theology*, ed. Brendan N. Wolfe et al. (St Andrews: St Andrews University, 2022), article published October 19, 2023, https://www.saet.ac.uk/Christianity/AnabaptistTheology.

position as a scholar was to carry out sociological research on the conditions that gave rise to one's own habitus. That is why he focused many of his investigations on his home region of the Béarn in southwest France and on the Paris-centered French educational system in which he spent most of his life. The promise of reflexive sociology, according to Bourdieu, is that the exposure of the formational conditions of your habitus gives you an opportunity to reflect explicitly on those conditions and on what you see, experience, and do as a result and, through reflection, to begin to change your habitus.[85] Although I am not a sociologist, and do not pretend to be in these pages, my decision to employ case studies has been guided by reflexive considerations. A commitment to reflexivity has also guided my selection of empirical cases. Over more than a decade I have worked in the Elkhart River Watershed and have worshiped and worked in denominational institutions shaped by the Mennonite women's movement and the legacy of Vincent Harding. It seemed crucial for my self-understanding as a theologian situated in such a way to examine these "research objects," as Bourdieu would put it, and to allow that examination to illuminate and challenge how I conceive of and address questions related to institutions vis-à-vis environmental ethics, sexism, and racism. At times in this book, as at the start of this chapter, I make the process of reflexive thought transparent by referring to my personal situation in connection to the subject matter. As a theologian, I take reflexivity to be a component of the ongoing work of getting clear about the normative commitments and practical entanglements with which we approach the subjects we study.[86] Theological categories relevant here include the pursuit of truth, the avoidance of idolatry, repentance, and the renewal of our minds.

Those categories point to the third and final methodological commitment that shapes how I have gone about developing the alternative pneumatological-sociological picture in this book. This commitment is to a certain understanding of "participation" that

---

[85]Bourdieu and Wacquant, *An Invitation to Reflexive Sociology*, especially 174–215, 248–53.
[86]Jamie Pitts, "Christian Ethics, the Bible, and the Powers of Reading," in *Scripture, Tradition, and Reason in Christian Ethics: Normative Dimensions*, eds. Bharat Ranganathan and Derek Woodard-Lehman (New York: Palgrave Macmillan, 2019), 17–43.

distinguishes between what we can attribute to God and what we can attribute to ourselves. The theological language of participation acknowledges both that creatures can by grace join God's work and that the resulting creaturely efforts are still not to be confused with divine works.[87] I accordingly write throughout the book of Spirit organizing and the organizational dimensions of human responses to the Spirit. At best such responses participate in the Spirit yet are still not to be identified simply as works carried out by the Spirit. The hovering, sanctifying, and doubling activities of the organizing Spirit are not immanent causes giving rise to human organizational efforts. They inspire, encourage, and empower such efforts. Human organizing, for its part, can aim to participate in the Spirit, taking its cues as far as possible from the pneumatic revelation of the divine organizing impulse and destiny. But human organizing and organizations, including institutions, are creaturely and not divine activities. That means the "positive" picture rendered in the following pages of institutional formation and reformation as in some way participatory in the Spirit is in no way intended to offer a blanket blessing on all institutions. Institutions and other human

---

[87] The language of "participation" covers both creation's general dependence on God as its source and destiny and human actions that align with God's character and will, such as the pursuit of God's good in a creation marred by sin and evil. See Andrew Davison, *Participation in God: A Study in Christian Doctrine and Metaphysics* (Cambridge: Cambridge University Press, 2019). Strictly speaking, a participatory metaphysics insists that God does everything creatures do since creatures exist and take their character and capacities as gifts from God. God is in this way the primary cause of creaturely action, while creatures are the secondary causes. This distinction indicates that every creaturely action is caused wholly by God and wholly by creatures according to their respective natures or modes of being (219–38). To speak as I do in the text of human organizing as "not a divine work" is to highlight its practical basis in human action and therefore its finitude and fallibility. It is not to deny that human organizing is caused by God in the sense that God enables it, gives it its form, and draws it into ultimate communion with God. Consider in this connection Davison's summary statement that "creaturely being is from God, but God's own being is not given to the creature, just as the goodness of creatures is from God, but not such that we could say that God's own goodness performs the work of being the creature's goodness, in place of a derived creaturely goodness" (and, similarly, "God is the origin and giver of creaturely form, rather than being the creature's form for it") (90). So creaturely actions are caused by God, but not in such a way that God performs our actions in our place. That would remove our agency and responsibility, as well as the sense in which we must distinguish our work from God's in order to avoid idolatry.

organizations, we might say, are analogous to the "principalities and powers" mentioned repeatedly in the Pauline epistles—they may in a general way be rooted in the dynamic structural complexity of God's good creation (Chapter 2) yet they are marred by sin in contingent and specific ways that require discernment and creative action if those institutions are to participate in the organizing Spirit (Chapters 3 and 4).[88]

My alternative pneumatological-sociological picture is intended to serve discernment regarding what the Spirit is doing and how we might respond. In constructing that picture I have made several decisions and exercised my own discernment about what qualifies for inclusion and what can be left out. Some of the criteria for this discernment have already been mentioned, namely, that the content of the picture in some way results from an interpretation of relevant passages of Scripture and an engagement with relevant conversation partners in my context. A more substantive criterion comes from what I take to be an important, though frequently neglected, strand of Mennonite pneumatology, in which the Spirit is conceived as initiating discipleship, leading the new disciple into Christ's body through water baptism, and guiding disciples' collective practices (baptism, Lord's Supper, Bible study, material sharing, friendship, witness, etc.).[89] It is this pneumatological narrative, along with voices from Scripture and contemporary theology, that leads me to envision the Spirit as the organizing Spirit and to investigate the relation between the organizing Spirit and human organizations. A central argument of this book is that participation in the work of institutions—forming them, reforming them, leading them, working for them, or being a member of them—can be imagined as part of, and not antagonistic to, human participation in the Spirit's organization of collective discipleship.

---

[88]See Pitts, *Principalities and Powers*. The point could also be made in the idiom of the early Barth: human organizing is "historical" and possibly "religious." As such it points negatively to the grace that exceeds, enables, and conditions it and cannot be confused with that grace. Still, as historical it might be oriented more or less by faith. Karl Barth, *The Epistle to the Romans* (New York: Oxford University Press, 1933), 115–48.

[89]Jamie Pitts, "Pneumatology," in *T&T Clark Handbook of Anabaptism*, ed. Brian C. Brewer (London: T&T Clark, 2021), 373–86.

2

Hovering Spirit

A glance outside my window reveals a world in which wind and water here are connected to wind and water there, far away. It is also a world in which diseases travel abroad and political memes circulate among the international users of social media platforms. Does this world, in its material and social interconnectedness, bear witness in some way to the presence of the organizing Spirit? This chapter argues that it does, and how it does so cautions against taking an overly "localist" approach to organizing aimed at environmental justice. If the structurally complex, relationally entangled character of the world is a sign of the Spirit, of how the Spirit creates and sustains creation, then participating in the Spirit can include the work of the structurally complex, relationally entangled organizations we ordinarily call institutions.

The critical target in this chapter is a recent debate in Anabaptist environmental ethics in which most of the interlocutors assume or explicitly argue that the practical response to ecological catastrophe should take a local organizational form. The debate represents the politicization of Anabaptist environmental ethics.[1] Whereas previous generations of Anabaptists mostly occupied themselves with theological visions of creation care and stewardship, today's watchwords are ecological justice, decolonization, and land

---

[1] This chapter is an edited version of Jamie Pitts, "The Hovering Spirit, the Elkhart River Watershed, and Political Institutions," *Mennonite Quarterly Review* 96 (January 2022): 25–46. Thanks to David Cramer, John Roth, and Duane Stoltzfus for feedback during the publication process.

redistribution.² In his review of Anabaptist writings on ecology, Peter Dula celebrates this turn to the political as both pragmatically necessary and a theologically salutary recovery of the church's identity "as a social movement."³

Within this freshly politicized field, discussions of politics largely focus on congregations, community organizing, and protest movements. Local initiatives have priority, even if the definition of "local" is sometimes contested.⁴ As Ched Myers suggests approvingly in his foundational essay on "watershed discipleship," this priority on the local has deep roots within Anabaptist history and theology.⁵

One pragmatic lesson that can be drawn from successive global crises, however, is that the scale and complexity of our planet's economic and ecological systems call for functioning institutions, organizations whose own scale, complexity, and endurance enable effective political management and transformation. The financial crash of 2008, the coronavirus pandemic, and global climate chaos have exposed the weakness and injustices of political institutions, including church institutions, that have been hollowed out and corrupted by forty years of neoliberalism's fetishization of the market.⁶

While accusations against global capitalism abound in Anabaptist environmental ethics, there has been little discussion of the potential or actual contribution of institutions—and especially of institutions that operate translocally—to the political struggle for environmental justice. The work of national denominations, global church bodies,

---

²See Peter Dula, "Anabaptist Environmental Ethics: A Review Essay," *Mennonite Quarterly Review* 94 (January 2020): 7–36.
³Dula, "Anabaptist Environmental Ethics," 34.
⁴Here I have in mind Luke Beck Kreider's criticism of "watershed discipleship" as wrongly emphasizing bioregions over "a place's geography of privilege and its cycles of social power." Beck Kreider, "Varieties of Anabaptist Environmentalism and Environmental Racism," *Mennonite Quarterly Review* 94 (January 2020): 51.
⁵Ched Myers, "From 'Creation Care' to 'Watershed Discipleship': Re-placing Ecological Theology and Practice," *Conrad Grebel Review* 32 (Fall 2014): 272–5. Although it will not be my focus in this article to contest this claim, suffice it to say that I see additional political theological possibilities in the Anabaptist tradition.
⁶Peter Mair, *Ruling the Void: The Hollowing of Western Democracy* (New York: Verso, 2013). I discuss the relationship between neoliberalism and institutions in Chapter 5.

and international relief, development, and mission agencies is absent from most discussions of Anabaptist environmental ethics. Local community organizations, not translocal institutions, are the privileged agents in the Anabaptist ecologist's political imaginary.

This chapter explores the gap between Anabaptists' eco-localism and the potential contribution of translocal institutions to environmental politics, ranging from existing ecclesial, political, and social institutions to new ones that might better address emergent global challenges. After further fleshing out the organizational picture embraced by Anabaptist environmental political ethicists, I offer a contrasting picture of the Spirit whose hovering generates a dynamically structured eco-social field for the purpose of fostering life through creaturely solidarities. The hovering Spirit's organization of and within particular localities connects them in life-giving solidarity with other localities. Human organizing that seeks to participate in the Spirit might relate similarly to specific localities and thereby be open to the translocal organizational possibilities presented by institutions. I develop this point through an analysis of one locality or bioregion, the Elkhart River Watershed. Interpreting the watershed's overlapping physical and social geographies through the picture of the hovering Spirit highlights the relationships that constitute it as a locality. Political organizing for environmental justice within the watershed ought to take those relationships into account. Doing so, however, would require some engagement with institutions whose focus is translocal in scope. The picture of the hovering Spirit helps situate such engagement within the pursuit of the divine economy and its restoration of creation.

The Organizational Politics of Anabaptist Environmental Ethics

Dula's comprehensive review identifies three basic strands of Anabaptist environmental ethics: one that emphasizes the divine call for humans to steward the earth; a second that focuses—for eco-pacifist or agrarian reasons—on our spiritual interconnectedness with the earth; and a third that recommends watershed discipleship as a mode of eco-justice.[7] "With watershed discipleship," Dula writes, "the *politics* of environmental ethics starts to move closer to the foreground."[8] By politics, Dula explains, he means not merely state processes, but "the broader sense of deliberation and contestation among diverse constituencies about the creation and deployment of power to achieve the well-being of the collective." Dula contends that each of the three strands of Anabaptist eco-theology evades politics to some extent: defenders of eco-justice tend to appeal to a pre-political natural order that demands justice—in this case, watersheds; Christian stewards point to the Bible as a guiding resource above politics; and eco-spirituality claims both nonpolitical natural and theological warrants.[9] "We need to make sure," he concludes, "that whatever strategy we choose, we don't let it become de-politicizing."[10]

According to Dula, a politicized Anabaptist environmental ethics would enact "a recovery of a material and political description of theology's task." Drawing on the work of Willis Jenkins, Dula recommends the "prophetic pragmatism" found in postliberal and liberation theologies, which both acknowledge "the mutuality of action and reflection."[11] Dula sees something like prophetic pragmatism emerging in the work of Anabaptists Justin Heinzekehr and Luke Beck Kreider. While Heinzekehr reinterprets watershed discipleship in terms of a Marxist version of materialist politics, Beck Kreider points away from watersheds toward involvement in wider ecological justice movements.[12]

---

[7]Dula, "Anabaptist Environmental Ethics," 13–28.
[8]Dula, "Anabaptist Environmental Ethics," 28, emphasis original.
[9]Dula, "Anabaptist Environmental Ethics," 28, 31. Dula is talking at this point about wider currents in Christian environmental ethics, but advances his argument as if these claims apply to Anabaptist ethics.
[10]Dula, "Anabaptist Environmental Ethics," 31.
[11]Dula, "Anabaptist Environmental Ethics," 32. Here Dula is writing specifically about liberation theology. He goes on to discuss Stanley Hauerwas's postliberal ethics as sharing this view of the relationship between theory and practice. Dula cites Willis Jenkins, *The Future of Ethics: Sustainability, Social Justice, and Religious Creativity* (Washington, DC: Georgetown University Press, 2013), 81.
[12]Dula references two papers presented at the 2018 Rooted and Grounded conference (Elkhart, IN): Heinzekehr, "In Defense of a More Materialist Church: Marx, Mennonites, and Bioregionalism" and Beck Kreider, "Varieties of Anabaptist Environmentalism and the Challenge of Environmental Racism." The following citations of Beck Kreider's essay are to the published version, as cited above.

Dula ends his essay by endorsing a "radically democratic environmental movement from below," which he hopes will be effective in the long run. He takes the Sunrise Movement, an organization involving youth in nonviolent climate activism in cities across the United States, as possibly already fulfilling his longing for a prophetic, pragmatic ecological movement.[13]

During his concluding reflections on politics, Dula dialogues with the writings of Ched Myers, whose political vision and experience he admires.[14] The writings of Myers and others on watershed discipleship do emphasize the politics of community organizing and social movements, key strategies in a politics "from below." Myers, for example, focuses on congregational practices, arguing that "the [foremost] task is ... re-inhabiting the church's own location."[15] Todd Wynward's treatment of watershed discipleship similarly centers on personal food consumption and organizations providing local alternatives to the industrial food system.[16] Cherice Bock introduces ecclesial watershed disciples as contributors to an "ecotopia" insofar as they plant gardens, partner with ecological organizations, get involved in activism, transform their buildings, and experiment with communal living.[17]

Beck Kreider, as mentioned, dissents from bioregionalism as an adequate framework for Anabaptist eco-theology. In an extended example, he discusses his congregation's discovery that

---

[13] Dula, "Anabaptist Environmental Ethics," 35, 36.
[14] Dula, "Anabaptist Environmental Ethics," 35.
[15] Myers, "From 'Creation Care' to 'Watershed Discipleship,'" 271.
[16] Todd Wynward, "Practice Watershed Discipleship," in *Rewilding the Way: Break Free to Follow an Untamed God!* (Harrisonburg, VA: Herald Press, 2015), chapter 18.
[17] Cherice Bock, "Watershed Discipleship," in *An Ecotopian Lexicon*, eds. Matthew Schneider-Mayerson and Brent Ryan Bellamy (Minneapolis: University of Minnesota Press, 2019), 307-8. Bock offers some examples that include gardening, protest, and Wynward's food organization (312-14). Although not employing the phrase "watershed discipleship," Matthew Humphrey also writes from an Anabaptist perspective about watersheds as the primary context of discipleship in his essay "Lived Theology in the Little Campbell River Watershed: A Primer on Bioregional Discipleship," in *Rooted and Grounded: Essays on Land and Christian Discipleship*, eds. Ryan D. Harker and Janeen Bertsche Johnson (Eugene, OR: Pickwick, 2016), 112-23. He suggests that bioregional discipleship "could begin in a community garden, a riverside cleanup, a march to save the wetlands, or a protest against a pipeline" (121).

they were located in a different watershed than the nearby city of Charlottesville, Virginia, where they were becoming involved in an antiracist protest movement. This created a dilemma for the congregation, which was then preparing to host a conference on watershed discipleship: church members could ignore the protest movement out of commitment to their own watershed or abandon the watershed for the protest movement. Beck Kreider resolves the dilemma by decisively coming down on the side of protest movements. Moreover, he discounts the ethical claims of watersheds by describing them as pre-political hydrological features; the claims that matter most for white Christians, according to Beck Kreider, are those arising from the historical geographies of ecological and racial injustice and from resistance movements formed within those geographies.

Although Beck Kreider disputes the tendency of watershed disciples to construe the local arena of politics in geographical terms, he shares their and Dula's sense that politics is largely a matter of involvement in local organizing and protest.[18] His example pits watershed discipleship against participation in a protest the next watershed over. The question was not, for instance, whether the congregation should put their energy into some form of local organizing or into supporting international anti-imperial struggles.[19]

The choice between local and translocal politics should not be overemphasized, and Myers and others do at least gesture toward solidarities across bioregions.[20] Sarah Thompson, in particular, has insisted on "connecting the dots" among struggles around the

---

[18] In a later conference paper, Beck Kreider further specified that Christians ought to prioritize Indigenous-led decolonial ecological movements. The argumentative framing and examples still presumed an orientation to politics as local engagement. Beck Kreider, "Stewardship, Settler Colonialism, and Solidarity" (paper presented at the Rooted and Grounded Conference on Land and Christian Discipleship, Anabaptist Mennonite Biblical Seminary, Elkhart, IN, October 15, 2021).

[19] For example, they might have discussed how to support the work of the Alianza Global de Comunidades Territoriales, a coalition of Indigenous communities in eighteen countries working to protect forests. See https://alianzaglobal.me/.

[20] Myers, "From 'Creation Care' to 'Watershed Discipleship,'" 274 (assuming "confederation" refers to coalitions across, and not only within, watersheds).

world.[21] Her slogan "Same Struggle Different Place" (SSDP) affirms the importance of both local organizations and efforts to tie them together. Nevertheless, on the whole Anabaptist ecological ethicists give little sustained attention to the organizational shape of those efforts, much less to developing a theological rationale for them.

The need for a prophetic pragmatic theology of institutional environmental politics is pressing. As Brazilian academic and organizer Rodrigo Nunes contends, the scale of climate change defies fantasies that bottom-up, locally oriented organizing will prove sufficient.[22] If, as he also suggests, "building a single global force" is likewise fantastical, then "to tackle a problem of that magnitude and complexity, the most plausible alternative seems to be some kind of distributed action combining organization at different levels and scales."[23]

Interestingly, Dula's favored Sunrise Movement does work at different levels and scales. Although more than 400 semi-autonomous local "hubs" are essential to its work, its national office in Washington, DC, provides guidance and cohesiveness to the movement.[24] Sunrise also has a DC-based political action committee that raises funds for political advertising and campaign

---

[21]Sarah Thompson, "An Ecological Beloved Community: An Interview with Na'Taki Osborne Jelks of the West Atlanta Watershed Alliance," in *Watershed Discipleship: Reinhabiting Bioregional Faith and Practice*, ed. Ched Myers (Eugene, OR: Cascade, 2016), 104. In the same volume, essays by Katerina Friesen, "The Great Commission: Watershed Conquest or Watershed Discipleship?" (26–41) and Lydia Wylie-Kellerman, "God's Gonna Trouble the Water: A Call to Discipleship in the Detroit Watershed" (75–87) helpfully situate specific watersheds in wider international contexts.

[22]Rodrigo Nunes, *Neither Vertical nor Horizontal: A Theory of Political Organization* (London: Verso, 2021), 39. Also Ewa Majewska, *Feminist Antifacism: Counterpublics of the Common* (London: Verso, 2021), 319: "preoccupation with the small scale and local actions" are "insufficient in the current state of global ecological catastrophe."

[23]Nunes, *Neither Vertical nor Horizontal*, 39.

[24]For a picture of how the national office relates to the hubs, see Brian Sitwell, "Sunrise General Movement Update: September 2021," *Sunrise Movement* (September 17, 2021), https://www.sunrisemovement.org/movement-updates/sunrise-general-movement-update-september-2021/.

donations.[25] The tenth of the Sunrise Movement's "principles" summarizes this facet of its organizational strategy: "We aim to abolish or reimagine institutions that degrade our communities and our climate. That requires working together to win and hold power at every level of government and society. We work with movements who share our values of transforming our country."[26]

While this language does align with Dula's definition of politics as "deliberation and contestation among diverse constituencies about the creation and deployment of power to achieve the well-being of the collective," its frank commitment to "abolishing or reimagining institutions" through multilevel, coalitional organizing cuts against the localism of Anabaptist environmental ethics. If movements like Sunrise are indeed heralds of a new age of ecological politics, then Anabaptists will need to reimagine prophetic pragmatism to include institutions. The following sections take steps in this direction by rendering translocal, institution-based organizing as a possible mode of participation in the hovering Spirit.

Hovering Spirit

The Bible begins with a cosmic scene of God creating through Word and Spirit. The Spirit of God (*ruach elohim*) hovers over the watery

---

[25] Open Secrets, "PAC Profile: Sunrise PAC," accessed August 23, 2024, https://www.opensecrets.org/political-action-committees-pacs/sunrise-pac/C00674697/summary/2020.

[26] Sunrise Movement, "Sunrise's Principles," accessed August 24, 2023, https://web.archive.org/web/20211009114812/https://www.sunrisemovement.org/principles/?m s=Sunrise%27sPrinciples. The quotation is from the version of the principles I read in October 2021. Sunrise has since revised its principles and dropped the language of "reimagining institutions." The only reference to institutions in their current statement of principles is negative: "We are fighting to turn the tide against racism and the institutions built on it" (principle 5). The overall language of the principles now aligns more closely with the vision of Dula, Myers, and the contemporary theologians discussed in Chapter 1 of this book: "building a mass movement of ordinary people" (principle 1); "we tell our stories about race, class, where we're from, and who we are" (principle 2); "we are all on a journey" (principle 3); "we transform ourselves" and "getting there is a lifelong journey" (principle 5); "a movement of everyday people" (principle 7); "we ground our work locally" (principle 8). Sunrise Movement, "Our Principles: Who We Are," accessed August 24, 2024, https://www.sunrisemovement.org/about/.

chaos, like a circling bird watching over her young.[27] Although the text does not identify the source of the primordial waters, they are portrayed as under Spirit's supervision—and with the catalyst of God's informing Word added to the mix, they soon produce the physical and temporal structures that define our cosmos.[28]

The Jewish authorship of Genesis 1 reminds us that *ruach* should not simply be identified with the divine "third," the Holy Spirit confessed by Christians. The ordinary translations of *ruach* as "wind" or "breath" have their place here, too.[29] Our imaginations are expanded by picturing a mighty wind from God stirring primeval chaos or the first Artisan's warm breath as he readies his materials.[30]

The creative movement of the Spirit in Genesis 1 can be sketched in three narrative arcs. First, we find the Spirit involved in creation's *dynamic structuring*. The Spirit does not remain with chaos, but rather partners with the Word to midwife chaos into cosmos.[31] The cosmos is defined to a significant extent by its divinely intended order—its classes of creatures, physical differentiations, and regular temporal sequences. Yet God also apparently intends for creation to give rise organically to creation, as the earth "puts forth vegetation" (Gen. 1:11) and the waters "bring forth swarms of living creatures"

---

[27]Basil of Caesarea, "Homily 2," *Hexaemeron*, para. 6, accessed August 23, 2024, https://www.newadvent.org/fathers/32012.htm. William P. Brown, *The Seven Pillars of Creation: The Bible, Science, and the Ecology of Wonder* (Oxford: Oxford University Press, 2010), 253n9, sees an inexact parallel with the "hovering" of a nesting eagle in Deut. 32:11. Brown suggests rather a raptor riding the wind, but his own exegesis of Gen. 1:2 discourages a violent interpretation of the image: the fruitful, beneficent relationship of *ruach elohim* and watery chaos contrasts sharply with chaos' sinister character in some ANE creation stories (chapters 2 and 3). If the circling raptor is no predator, and ultimately teams with Word to bring cosmos from chaos, then Deuteronomy's imagery of life-giving nurture and protection seems to fit Gen. 1:2.

[28]Brown, *Seven Pillars of Creation*, chapter 3; Elizabeth A. Johnson, *Ask the Beasts: Darwin and the God of Love* (London: T&T Clark, 2014), 131. As described below, I am treating the Holy Spirit as a character in the Bible's narrative, so occasionally drop the definite article and speak of "Spirit."

[29]Major translations including the NRSV, NJPS, and CEB translate *ruach* as "wind" in Gen. 1:2.

[30]On the "Artisan" image, see Brown, *Seven Pillars of Creation*, 47, drawing on the parallel with Bezalel in Exod. 31:3. I use male pronouns in light of this reference.

[31]Cf. Ps. 22:9.

(Gen. 1:20).[32] Each plant and animal, moreover, reproduces in its diverse and diversifying way.[33] Cosmos is chaos organized by Spirit and Word, heaving, formless oblivion crafted into dynamic structure.

Randy Woodley suggests that Indigenous notions of "harmony" are an illuminating parallel to the vision of Genesis 1. In both Genesis and an important Keetoowah Cherokee creation story, the emphasis is on the beneficent "interconnectedness" of diverse creatures: "Each part of the created whole comes from the unique mind of the Creator. Each works in relationship with the other, connected through their common origin and location in the universe, with the well-being of all at the center."[34] Another apt metaphor comes from Karen Baker-Fletcher, who probes the echoes between the dance of creation and the divine dance,[35] the latter represented in Genesis 1 by the twinned movements of Word and Spirit. For Baker-Fletcher, creative dancers move in freedom, yet their freedom takes place "within the limits of physical, spiritual, divine structure."[36] These images of harmony and dance evoke organization—musical notes and dancers ordered in some, even wild, relation to one another—enlivened by movement and change.

Harmony and dance also suggest that creational structures are enlivened by spiritual purpose. Creation is infused with its Artist's delight[37] and hope for creaturely thriving. We will come to the moral implications of this insight later, but first notice the spiritual reality it implies. As Spirit tended chaos, so Spirit tends cosmos.

---

[32]See Brown, *Seven Pillars of Creation*, 44–6, on the active role of creatures in divine creation. McClendon's "synergetic" ecological doctrine of creation can be seen as developing this insight. James Wm. McClendon, *Doctrine: Systematic Theology, Volume 2* (Nashville: Abingdon, 1994), 166–8. A theology of creation's agency could form one strand of a response to Beck Kreider's worry that watershed disciples valorize "pre-political" hydrology.

[33]See Brown, *Seven Pillars of Creation*, chapter 6, on creation's diversity.

[34]Woodley, "Early Dialogue in the Community of Creation," in *Buffalo Shout, Salmon Cry: Conversations on Creation, Land Justice, and Life Together*, ed. Steve Heinrichs (Harrisburg, VA: Herald Press, 2013), 98.

[35]Baker-Fletcher, *Dancing with God: The Trinity from a Womanist Perspective* (St. Louis: Chalice, 2006), chapter 3.

[36]Baker-Fletcher, *Dancing with God*, 79.

[37]See Brown, *Seven Pillars of Creation*, chapter 6, on God's delight in creation as portrayed in Ps. 104.

A pneumatological doctrine of providence finds its origins in the image of the hovering Spirit. The Spirit is God "effectually present"[38] to creation through all its, and all our, changes, lovingly turning our repeated drifts—and leaps—into chaos toward harmony. Here the figure of Lady Wisdom emerges, divine *Sophia* teaching wayward Israel and all humans to live at peace with ourselves and our fellow creatures (Prov. 8). The fact that *Sophia* has been interpreted as both Spirit and Christ[39] points back to that original partnership between Word and Spirit, to the dialectic of form and change at creation's heart. The double reading also points forward to creation's end, the acceptance of Spirit's invitation to renewed heaven and earth,[40] the return of Wise Jesus's rule[41]—the realization of "the Harmony Way."[42]

The hovering Spirit who collaboratively organizes and watches over the dynamic structuring of creation is *the Spirit who gives life*. This is the second arc to describe in our eco-pneumatological picture. The Spirit organizes for life; structures formed by the Spirit are intended to sustain diverse forms of life. The structures depicted in Genesis 1 include, of course, plant and animal life, with the former given to the latter—"everything that has the breath of life" (*nephesh hayyah*)—as sustenance (1:30). The parallel creation story of Genesis 2 portrays God directly blowing the breath of life (*nishmat hayyim*) into human-shaped dust (2:7). Throughout the Hebrew scriptures *ruach* and its synonyms repeatedly reference God's animating gift of life.[43]

---

[38] McClendon, *Doctrine*, 288.
[39] Jaroslav Pelikan, *The Christian Tradition: A History of the Development of Doctrine*, Volume 1: *The Emergence of the Catholic Tradition (100–600)* (Chicago: University of Chicago Press, 1971), 191–2.
[40] Rev. 22:17. See Peter Scott, *A Political Theology of Nature* (Cambridge: Cambridge University Press, 2003), 205–6, for discussion of the need to maintain a sense of the eschatological character of the Spirit's work.
[41] Cf. Rev. 22:20.
[42] Woodley, "Early Dialogue in the Community of Creation," 98.
[43] See discussion of various passages below. I am engaged in a Christian narrative theological reading of *ruach/pneuma* as a "character" in the unfolding biblical narrative, and so am identifying continuities across diverse texts and testaments. This approach necessitates caution, of course, and I am limiting my references to cases where *ruach* is evidently a God-sent power. Thanks to Ryan Schellenberg for conversation on this point. On narrative theological hermeneutics, see McClendon, *Doctrine*, 34–41.

The status of breath as a gift of Spirit entails the fragility of animality: We animals are dependent on God for our breath. Spirit is life's first cause, the sine qua non of animal being in its wild proliferation.[44] Breath is granted and also sustained by Spirit. This insight is given full expression in Ezekiel's vision of the valley of dry bones. God brings Ezekiel to the valley and tells him to prophecy to the bones that God "will cause breath [*ruach*] to enter" them (Ezek. 37:5). After Ezekiel's prophecy results only in the bones' enfleshment, in their reorganization as bodies, God tells Ezekiel to "Prophecy to the breath [*ruach*] ... : Come from the four winds [*ruchot*], O breath [*ruach*], and breathe upon these slain that they may live" (Ezek. 37:9).[45] This time Ezekiel is successful and is met by "a multitude" of breathing bodies (37:10). The point is evident: Like the valley of dry bones, broken, exiled Israel will stand again in the promised land—and this restoration will be accomplished by God's own "spirit" (Ezek. 37:14, *ruchi*).

Ezekiel's vision of spirit-filled Israel flourishing in the land after exile recalls an earlier part of the Bible's narrative, in which God promises a land to Abram so that his descendants would bless "all the families of the earth" (Gen. 12:1-3)—and this blessing, in turn, is reminiscent of God's first blessing of humans to serve as creation's caretaker (Gen. 1:28-31).[46] It is the Spirit who, throughout the narrative of the formation of God's people, ensures that the vital blessing will be attained. God-sent *ruach* lowers the flood waters so that Noah and his menagerie can repopulate the violence-corrupted earth (Gen. 8:1; cf. 6:13); carries and removes a plague of locusts (Exod. 10:13, 19) and parts the Reed Sea (Ezek. 14:21) to liberate

---

[44]Cf. Johnson, *Ask the Beasts*, 145–50, on Aquinas, Creator Spirit, and ecology.

[45]The image of wind-blown breath of course conflates the two primary translations of *ruach*.

[46]McClendon points to a theology of election centered on creation's blessing (*Doctrine*, 184–5). On the exilic context of Gen. 1:28-31, see Ellen Davis, *Opening Israel's Scriptures* (Oxford: Oxford University Press, 2019), 10–11. The command to "have dominion" (Gen. 1:28—Davis prefers "conquer") should be read in light of an exilic community dispossessed from their land. The character of dominion, as Davis and other interpreters suggest, is shaped by God's example as loving creator and provider. Johnson, *Ask the Beasts*, 264, reads the dominion passages in Gen. 1:28 and Ps. 8:6 critically, but argues that Genesis 2, Job, Psalm 104, and other passages "enfold ... the dominion [passages] into a more mutual pattern of relationship."

enslaved Israel.[47] *Ruach* brings quail to hungry Israelites wandering in the desert (Num. 11:31). The Spirit organizes and sustains a people to live well in and with a specific land, for the sake of all life that dwells on the earth.[48]

The particularity of election signals the third ecological characteristic or narrative-pictorial arc: *the hovering Spirit forms bonds of creaturely solidarity*. Israel is liberated from slavery and fed in the wilderness by God's *ruach* with the goal of establishing a shalom polity in which humans, animals, and land thrive. Jubilee practices of liberation and redistribution are intended to restore shalomic solidarity after inevitable periods of creep toward internal relations of domination and subordination.[49] Within the pentateuchal narrative, the drive toward creaturely solidarity occurs against the backdrop of the Genesis creation stories, which as Ellen Davis suggests portray humans and land as kin.[50] From this perspective, the basis of creaturely solidarity is our common status as shaped and enlivened by divine *ruach*.[51] This status is universally shared, and thus has global implications—the blessing of *all* the earth's "families." And yet the specificity of ecological regions and of living families (microbial, plant, animal) requires local organization. "Election" names the divine option for the realization of global shalom through, not in spite of, local particularities.[52] Israel's

---

[47]Note the relationship between *ruach* and water in both the flood and exodus stories, harkening back to Genesis 1's depiction of life emerging out of *ruach*-tended watery chaos.

[48]Davis, *Opening Israel's Scriptures*, 28–9, suggests that the phrase "families of the earth [*adamah*]" references the Genesis 2 creation story. "The fact that here blessing is evoked especially in the families' relation to *adamah* hints at something that will become clearer as the biblical story continues beyond Genesis—namely, that the Bible does not envision human flourishing apart from the flourishing of the fertile earth on which all life depends."

[49]Lev. 25; Deut. 15:1–18; Isa. 61; Lk. 4:16–30; Acts 2:44–5; 4:32–7.

[50]Davis, "Land as Kin: Renewing the Imagination," in *Rooted and Grounded: Essays on Land and Christian Discipleship*, eds. Ryan D. Harker and Janeen Bertsche Johnson (Eugene, Ore.: Pickwick, 2016), 5. Davis is discussing Gen. 2:7, which she translates, "And the Lord God formed the human being [*adam*], dust from the fertile-soil [*adamah*]." Also Johnson, *Ask the Beasts*, 263–4.

[51]The biological sciences affirm a similar point, insofar as soil, plants, and animals are in a constant, interdependent exchange of carbon dioxide and oxygen. Humans and other animals breath oxygen released by plants and moved around by (or as) wind. See Brown, *Seven Pillars of Creation*, 109–10.

[52]McClendon, *Doctrine*, 182–5.

narrative is the story of God pursuing shalom with one human "family" in one terrestrial region. Divine Spirit begins the story and keeps the search for local and translocal creaturely solidarity alive in spite of the challenges.

In the New Testament, Jesus is born of the Spirit's hovering over Mary. In Eugene Rogers' interpretation, "in the womb of Mary, the Spirit takes the lost cause of human flesh to be her own cause," thereby fulfilling "God's initial cause and intention ... nature's elevation."[53] Jesus embodies restored creation and forms a Jubilee community whose trust is rooted in attention to God's provision for plants and animals (Lk. 12:22-34). Paul calls this community the "Israel of God," whose members—drawn from all who "receive the promise of the Spirit through faith" (Gal. 3:14)—are "ruled" by the new creation reached through Christ's cross (Gal. 6:12-16). This translocal organization is also Christ's eschatological "bride," who joins the Spirit in inviting all to drink the renewed earth's "water of life" (Rev. 22:17). In these and similar passages, the hovering Spirit organizes dynamic socioecological structures to sustain a planetary solidarity of creatures.

Creation, Election, and Hovering Spirit

The hovering Spirit can therefore be pictured as dynamically structuring creation, giving it life and forming life-giving solidarities among creatures. This picture results in a relational conception of creation in two senses. First, the picture portrays creation as relationally constituted by the "economic" activities of the triune God. God is the source of creation's being and enduring existence. Creation depends on God and is constituted by its relation to God as Creator. The picture of the hovering Spirit emphasizes those activities that can be appropriated to the Creator Spirit's work in the divine economy. Those activities point to a second, "internal" sense in which creation can be conceived of as relational. If from an "external" or transcendent perspective creation is a simple unity—it is one as God's handiwork, one in its origin and destiny in God—an

---

[53]Eugene F. Rogers, *After the Spirit: A Constructive Pneumatology from Resources outside the Modern West* (Grand Rapids: Eerdmans, 2005), 101.

internal examination of creation, such as that presented in Genesis 1, reveals complexly interrelated physical and temporal structures. Divisions of space and time structure the cycles (solar and lunar) and directional processes (the ongoing creativity of distinct creaturely agents) that lend creation its dynamism. Creation's spatiotemporal dynamic also structures human and other animal sociality. Creation's cycles order our common lives and we contribute our collective agency to creation's progressive transformation. Our agency is collective in the sense that it is social, it is a project that inherently involves other creatures. We structure and restructure, organize and reorganize, our lives together as part of what it means to be creatures. Intentional organization is part of our form of life. It is not an "artificial" addition to creation but natural to our being as creatures.

Here the Pauline concept of "principalities and powers" becomes relevant, with its implication that basic material structures such as "heights and depths" (Rom. 8:39) as well as social and political ones including "names" (Eph. 1:21), "thrones" (Col. 1:16), and "authorities" (Rom. 13:1) have some basis in creation even if the shape in which we know them is disfigured by sin and death.[54] (A "height" is a beautiful, awe-inspiring mountain and a ledge to fall from.) If the Reformed debate over whether "government" would have existed "without the fall" is fanciful, it at least poses the question about the status of organization in God's good creation.[55] Whatever can be said about the "original" or ultimate goodness of hierarchical organizational patterns, of structures that enable some to have power over others, the pneumatological picture essayed in this section affirms the possibility that a range of organizational patterns could be oriented to the Creator Spirit's pursuit of life and creaturely solidarity. Insofar as humans are inherently social creatures, moreover, those patterns are constitutive of *our* life and the forms of creaturely solidarity that *we* can pursue. Yet the

---

[54]See Jamie Pitts, *Principalities and Powers: Revising John Howard Yoder's Sociological Theology* (Eugene, OR: Pickwick, 2013). I am grateful to Andy Brubacher Kaethler for encouraging me to connect my previous research on the powers to this project on Spirit and institutions.
[55]Richard J. Mouw, *Politics and the Biblical Drama* (Grand Rapids: Eerdmans, 1976), 32–6.

qualifications are necessary—we must speak of the *possibility* of *a range* of patterns corresponding to Spirit organizing because sin prevents unmediated access to any organizational form that we could denominate *tout court* as produced by the Spirit. The grammar of participation also implies reticence on this score, as do related considerations of creaturely agency—we are created to organize, not to be passive recipients of divine organization. Thus, we speak of organizing that *aims to participate* in the hovering Spirit.

Election brings these reflections together as a central example of the divinely intended differential structuration of creation. Election furthers the project of organizing creation by conferring a special status on a specific group. This status articulates the dialectic of particularity and universality, in which group existence "for itself" (a group's pursuit of its own sense of vocation) has integrity to the extent that it also and at the same time exists for (all) others, is dedicated to universal well-being. Promulgators of "localist" and "bottom-up" social solutions are correct to the extent that they emphasize local or small group integrity, but wrong insofar as they minimize universality as a component of integrity. To have integrity, local organizing needs to keep its universal horizon in mind, though what that "keeping in mind" looks like will differ according to historical context. Keeping in mind the universal cannot lead to the elimination of the particular, a process that would end in creation's homogenization or disorganization.[56] Difference and similarity across localities and local organizing have to be continually negotiated according to the extent that they

---

[56]William Cavanaugh forcefully argues that the modern nation-state, and civil society institutions subordinate to it, homogenize space in order to discipline citizens. Globalization extends this homogenizing project to the entire world. Cavanaugh is right to worry about the effacement of the local by the state and capitalist market, and I hope my remarks about the integrity of the local indicate my sympathy with his concerns. Yet Cavanaugh's alternative reinstantiates a kind of localism even as it seeks to overcome the local-universal dualism. For Cavanaugh, local congregations are the site of the universal insofar as in the eucharist their (theoretically) diverse members are "absorbed" into Christ's one body and thereby enact the church's catholicity. There is no positive account of the ecclesiality of translocal institutions in Cavanaugh's vision. William T. Cavanaugh, "The World in a Wafer: A Geography of the Eucharist as Resistance to Globalization," *Modern Theology* 15, no. 2 (April 1999): 181–96.

serve the Spirit's goal of life-giving solidarity. Questions related to the maintenance of a set of local differences or the construction of translocal alliances based on mutual interests are ultimately questions about the organizational shape of participation in the Spirit. Translocal organizations such as institutions can be important forums for discerning and coordinating such participation.

If the doctrine of election endorses formal organizational differentiation and gives it a general normative orientation toward the Spirit's universal organizing, further reflections on election fill out the normative picture. Election is the context in which the specific content of God's Word is given flesh, first in the formation of Israel and then in the incarnation and the church. Scripture emerges as the writings of God's elect peoples and exists as a record of those peoples' formative conversations and as a living Word that continues to form their common lives. Israel, Christ, the church, and Scripture—these sources offer details as to the quality and kind of "life" and "solidarity" pursued by God's Spirit. Although this book does not include a systematic accounting of these terms, I do build up several criteria for discerning the Spirit's organizing—and so for discerning what kind of organizing and organizations we might aim at as participants—drawn from and compatible with these sources in this and the following chapters.

In Chapter 1 I employed the image of creation as a web made up of interrelated threads. Election can be conceived of as a divine pulling on some localizable threads in a way that permanently reverberates and reforms (reorganizes) the rest of the web. It does so by generating enduring social differentiations through which creation's universal *telos* is clarified. If, as Willie James Jennings has argued, part of the besetting sin of the Christian tradition has been its attempt to eliminate the particularity of Christ's Jewish flesh,[57] a corollary of this sin is the false universalism constructed on its basis. *False* universalism erases difference and subjugates those whose flesh is deemed stubbornly or atavistically different. But the erasure of the universal, its abandonment in the name of the integrity of local difference, disintegrates creation by sundering the threads that compose it. Viewing creation as a relational web organized and

---

[57]Willie James Jennings, *The Christian Imagination: Theology and the Origins of Race* (New Haven: Yale University Press, 2010).

reorganized by the Spirit draws attention both to creation's universal status within the divine economy and its constitutive particularities. Activities aimed at participation in the Spirit, activities inspired by Spirit organizing and its goal, rightly range across creation and its multiple physical and social scales. If "institution" names a more or less stable mode of organizing, often across localities, then there is no reason to rule out the formation and reformation of institutions as a participative response to the organizing Spirit.

The Elkhart River Watershed

Earlier in this chapter I discussed watershed discipleship as a major recent development in Anabaptist environmental ethics. Advocates of watershed discipleship implicitly and explicitly favor organizing within local geographies for ecological justice. Local communities and especially congregations are the primary organizations promoted within the literature. Congregations are to learn about and from the individual watersheds in which they are located and organize for justice in solidarity with their watersheds. Although I noted Beck Kreider's dissent over the location of ecojustice organizing—he emphasizes geographies marked by histories of racial domination instead of bioregions—I suggested that both he and watershed discipleship share a focus on local geographies and organizing.

This section offers a rejoinder to these discussions through a relational portrait of a single watershed. The portrait casts considerable doubt on the localism of watershed discipleship ethics, insofar as it presents watersheds as constituted by complex physical relations to other watersheds, relations that result from large-scale processes of geographic formation. Conceiving of watersheds as inherently relational entities (or creatures) invites organizing activities that seek to work across the various relations that make up the watershed. The portrait sketched here also emphasizes the relational character of social-historical developments within the watershed, lending credence to Beck Kreider's objection to watershed discipleship yet pushing that objection toward the recommendation of translocal organizing and organizations. On the other hand, the portrait also affirms the watershed's integrity—albeit not its exclusive priority—as a site of local organizing nested within organizing taking place at a variety of bioregional and social scales. This portrait is therefore offered as additional evidence countering the localism of recent Anabaptist environmental ethics, evidence that supplements or extends the pneumatological picture developed above. The relationally complex, dynamic structuration that characterizes creation as the product of the hovering Spirit ought, in other words, to be visible in a given watershed. Allowing for the distorting effects of sin, the watershed's orientation to life and solidarity among creatures should also be visible in some way. The watershed's relational constitution comes to the fore when that watershed is viewed as an organizational fruit of the hovering Spirit.

The Elkhart River Watershed is the largest drainage area into the St. Joseph River, which is itself the third-largest watershed draining into Lake Michigan. Most of the watershed's 447,000 acres are devoted to agricultural use, and precipitation and irrigation run-off make their way into the headwaters of the river's north branch in LaGrange County, Indiana, and south branch in Noble County, Indiana.[58] Some of the southern headwaters are within the boundaries of the Merry Lea Environmental Education Center, owned by Goshen College since 1980. Over the past forty years, Goshen College biologists at Merry Lea have experimented with restorative land management practices, while hosting students of all ages in educational programs.[59]

Fifteen thousand years ago the watershed was under ice. As the Ice Age came to end, the watershed's contours took shape. A series of glaciers scraped and slid across the land, slowly withdrawing to the north.[60] Possibly the most significant contour left by glaciation was the St. Lawrence River Divide. Rivers north of this divide, such as the Elkhart, flow into the Great Lakes system and out into the

---

[58]Indiana Department of Environmental Management, "Elkhart River WMP 6–177," accessed August 23, 2024, https://www.in.gov/idem/nps/resources/watershed-management-plans/elkhart-river-wmp-6-177/.
[59]Goshen College, "Merry Lea Environmental Center of Goshen College," accessed August 23, 2024, https://www.goshen.edu/merrylea/.
[60]Wilton T. Melhorn, "Indiana on Ice: The Late Tertiary and Ice Age History of Indiana Landscapes," in *The Natural Heritage of Indiana*, ed. Marion T. Jackson (Bloomington, IN: Indiana University Press, 1997), 15–27.

Atlantic Ocean via the St. Lawrence Seaway. The Eel River, around fifteen miles south of the Elkhart's Noble County headwaters, is on the other side of the divide, and runs south toward the Mississippi through the Wabash and Ohio Rivers. A short portage crossing the divide, between the Maumee and Little Rivers, was the site of Kekionga, the headquarters of the Miami Indians, the region's major native group in the seventeenth and eighteenth centuries. These eight or so miles were the shortest land passage between the Great Lakes and the Mississippi River systems, and so were a target for colonial military conquest. In 1794, General Anthony Wayne captured Kekionga and established an American fort there—Fort Wayne, now the largest city in northern Indiana.[61]

On both sides of the St. Lawrence River Divide are rich soils and abundant waterways. The last glaciers stopped just south of present-day Indianapolis, the capital city in the state's center, and their creeping departure left central Indiana flat and fertile. The northern landscape is also largely level, but glacial deposits created hilly areas and left many wetlands and lakes. All of this land was heavily forested prior to Euro-American settlement, though native peoples tended the forests, turning some of the land into prairies.[62] In the early nineteenth century, white settlers quickly cleared the forests to build homes and plant crops, rolling thousands of unwanted logs into valleys for burning.[63] By removing habitat and hunting, settlers soon had driven the native black bear, American bison, white-tail deer, and many other species from the state.[64] Today, most of the wetlands have been drained and the forest appears only in fragments, with small concentrations in the state and county parks that dot the watershed.[65]

---

[61] James H. Madison, *Hoosiers: A New History of Indiana* (Bloomington, IN: Indiana University Press, 2014), 27–9.
[62] David Horst Lehman, "Common Ground: Potawatomi and Europeans on the Elkhart Prairie" (unpublished, 2011, typescript). Lehman has used ArcGIS software to map his research: https://univofillinois.maps.arcgis.com/apps/MapSeries/index.html?appid=8e8c73dffbe14ef8ad45d17a8f203290.
[63] Marion T. Jackson, "Perspective: The Indiana That Was," in *The Natural Heritage of Indiana*, ed. Jackson (Bloomington, IN: Indiana University Press, 1997), xxiii.
[64] Jackson, "Perspective," xix–xx.
[65] These include Chain 'O Lakes State Park, Ox Bow County Park, and several wetland conservation areas.

In addition to the Miami and the Potawatomi, other Native American peoples inhabited the region prior to colonization. According to Elan Pochedley, the Potawatomi thrived by living harmoniously alongside the Elkhart River and other area streams, which supplied pike and wild rice (*mnomen*) in abundance.[66] In the early nineteenth century, many Indigenous peoples united under the Shawnee leader Tecumseh and his brother, the Prophet Tenskwatawa, to resist white encroachment into their lands. American forces under General William Henry Harrison defeated Tecumseh at the Battle of Tippecanoe (1811), fought at Prophetstown in northeastern Indiana, and during the War of 1812.[67] Over the next decades, spurred especially by the federal Indian Removal Act of 1830, most remaining native communities in northern and central Indiana were removed through treaties—whose agreements were often reached after supplying the Indigenous signatories with whiskey—and coercion.[68] The most infamous example of the latter involved the 1838 removal of the Yellow River Band of Potawatomi, whose Chief Menominee rejected American treaties. A militia marched Menominee and his people at gunpoint from their northern Indiana village to Kansas. In 1861, most of this group accepted US citizenship in exchange for moving to private allotments in Indian Territory (Oklahoma). The group became known as the Citizen Potawatomi Nation, while the group that remained in Kansas is called the Prairie Band Potawatomi Nation.

The lands of the Elkhart River Watershed were ceded to the United States in treaties of 1821 and 1826.[69] In spite of American terror and duplicity, members of the Pokagon Band of Potawatomi

---

[66]Elan Pochedley, "Restorative Cartography of the Theakiki Region: Mapping Potawatomi Presences in Indiana," *Open Rivers: Rethinking Water, Place & Community* 18 (Spring 2021): 13. I am grateful to Katerina Gea for sharing this article with me.

[67]Madison, *Hoosiers*, 35–44. Harrison would use his victory over Tecumseh's federation as the cornerstone of his successful presidential run in 1840. His slogan "Tippecanoe and Tyler Too" and rally at the Tippecanoe Battle site were central to his campaign (41).

[68]Madison, *Hoosiers*, 118–24.

[69]These were the Treaty of Chicago (1821) and the Treaty of Mississinwas (1826). Devon Ezra Miller, *Changing Landscapes: Ambiguity, Imaginations, and Amish Settlers in Northern Indiana, 1825–1850* (PhD diss., Michigan State University, 2017), 61.

managed to remain in the region by adopting settler agricultural methods and converting their communal lands into parcels of private property.[70] After receiving federal recognition as a tribe in 1994, the Pokagon Band has developed its governance structures and economy considerably. Through its headquarters in Niles, Michigan, and South Bend, Indiana, the Pokagon Band provides legal and social services to tribal members throughout the St. Joseph River Watershed, including to those living in the Elkhart River valley. The tribe's Four Winds Casinos, with four locations across the region, generate significant funding for its health clinic, financial services provider, and business investment firm.[71] In 2003 the Pokagon Band enrolled over 1,000 acres of land in the largely drained Grand Kankakee Marsh into the US Department of Agriculture's Wetland Reserve Program, and later obtained a grant from the US Fish and Wildlife Service to begin wetland restoration.[72] Since 2011, the tribe has obtained state and federal permits to re-meander a section of the Dowagiac River (another tributary of the St. Joseph).[73]

Merry Lea's owner, Goshen College, was founded by Swiss-German Mennonites at the beginning of the twentieth century. Mennonites began to arrive in the region in the 1840s, shortly after the Native removals, purchasing sections of the Elkhart River Watershed for agricultural use and homesteading.[74] Elkhart County has an especially large number of Amish and Mennonites, one

---

[70]John N. Low, "Pokégnek Bodéwadmik, the Pokagon Band of Potawatomi Indians, Keepers of the Fire: A History and Introduction to the Community through Text and Images" (2015), https://johnlowpokagon.files.wordpress.com/2015/11/keepers-of-the-fire.pdf, 81; Mark R. Schurr, Terrance J. Martin, and W. Ben Secunda, "How the Pokagon Band Avoided Removal: Archaeological Evidence from the Faunal Assemblage of the Pokagon Village Site (20BE13)," *Midcontinental Journal of Archaeology* 31 (Spring 2006): 143–63.

[71]See statements on the tribe's business site, *Mno-Bmadsen*, https://mno-bmadsen.com/.

[72]US Fish and Wildlife Service, "We Support the Pokagon in Restoring and Enhancing Their Land," April 6, 2016, https://www.fws.gov/midwest/news/PokagonRestoration.html.

[73]Pokégnek Bodéwadmik/Pokagon Band of Potawatomi, "Dowagiac River Re-meander Project," accessed August 23, 2024, https://www.pokagonband-nsn.gov/dowagiac-river-re-meander-project.

[74]Miller, *Changing Landscapes*, chapter 5.

reason that many of its agricultural lands remain family farms—bucking a national trend of large-scale consolidation.[75] Although Amish farms are easily distinguished by the simplicity of their buildings and the absence of power-lines, Amish and Mennonite farmers resemble their neighbors in the intensity of their farming and their participation in the region's globally oriented agricultural economy, which is centered on corn, soybeans, and dairy products. At peak growing season, most fields have placards advertising the seeds sown in them. Many of the featured seeds were initially genetically engineered by Monsanto, an agricultural firm purchased in 2018 by the German company Bayer.[76]

Many Amish and other farms in the watershed also house long sheds where chickens or ducks are raised for slaughter. Culver Duck Farms, headquartered just outside of Middlebury, Indiana, and about a mile from the Elkhart River, is the nation's second-largest duck meat processor and has around 100 growing contracts with area farmers.[77] Culver specializes in white Pekin ducks, originally from China, and its products are largely aimed at Asian restaurants and markets in the United States. According to research by PETA, the company ships 30,000 pounds of duck feathers to China weekly for use in down products.[78] The Pekin duck was brought to American shores in the mid-nineteenth century and was quickly bred by Culver's founder, Herbert R. Culver, for large-scale meat

---

[75]United States Department of Agriculture, National Agricultural Statistics Service, "2017 Census of Agriculture, County Profile: Elkhart County, Indiana," 2017, https://www.nass.usda.gov/Publications/AgCensus/2017/Online_Resources/County_Profiles/Indiana/cp18039.pdf. On the development of agrobusiness in Indiana, see Madison, *Hoosiers*, 187.

[76]Seeds sold by companies such as LG and Beck's include Monsanto technologies. See https://www.lgseeds.com/technology and https://www.beckshybrids.com/Products/Technologies/Corn. Pioneer, another commonly advertised seed, is owned by Corteva, a seed and pesticide corporation spun out of DowDuPont in 2019. Corteva operates throughout the world. See https://s23.q4cdn.com/505718284/files/doc_downloads/feature_content/2021/2020-Corteva-Annual-Report.pdf.

[77]Food & Drink International, "Culver Duck Farms," accessed October 16, 2021, https://www.fooddrink-magazine.com/sections/producers/1687-culver-duck-farms.

[78]Michelle Kretzer, "Do You Believe Culver Duck Farms' Claims?" *PETA*, October 28, 2016, https://www.peta.org/blog/do-you-believe-culver-duck-farms-claims/.

production.[79] Other nonnative animals in the Elkhart River Watershed are concentrated at the Black Pine Animal Sanctuary, also near the river's headwaters. The sanctuary provides a "retirement" home for exotic animals discarded by pet owners and recovered from roadside attractions in the region. Its over sixty species include bears, wildcats, reptiles, and birds from around the world.[80] Sanctuary staff use feeding tours, a blog, and social media to draw attention to the horrors of the exotic pet trade and to mobilize its constituency to press for better regulations.[81] The presence of exotic animals in the watershed is directly tied to defaunation in Southeast Asia, Central America, and other regions.[82]

Many of the area's Mennonites are congregated in the watershed's urban environments, especially the Elkhart County towns of Middlebury, Goshen, and Elkhart. Some Mennonite churches—in particular, the Waterford and Benton congregations, just south of Goshen—have ministries focused on the health of the Elkhart River. The Waterford church cares for fifty-five acres of biodiverse wetland, and the Benton church participates in the Hoosier Riverwatch citizen science program.[83] Benton Mennonite Church's river ministry arose in part as it reflected on its long practice of baptizing new members in the Elkhart River. One of Benton's pastors, Doug Kaufman, is also a leader in the Mennonite Creation Care Network, which provides resources and consulting for Mennonite congregations engaging ecological issues.[84] Other Mennonite institutions, such

---

[79] Food & Drink International, "Culver Duck Farms."
[80] Black Pine Animal Sanctuary, "Our Animals," accessed August 23, 2024, https://www.bpsanctuary.org/about/animals/.
[81] E.g., Black Pine Animal Sanctuary, "What Is the Big Cat Public Safety Act?," September 2, 2021, https://www.bpsanctuary.org/blog/what-is-the-big-cat-public-safety-act/.
[82] See Rosemary-Claire Collard, *Animal Traffic: Lively Capital in the Global Exotic Pet Trade* (Durham, NC: Duke University Press, 2020).
[83] Waterford Mennonite Church, "Wetlands," accessed August 23, 2024, https://waterfordchurch.org/wetlands/; Benton Mennonite Church, "Creation Action," accessed August 23, 2024, https://bentonchurch.org/creation-care/.
[84] Mennonite Creation Care Network, https://mennocreationcare.org/. A related effort is led by the Mennonite Men organization, engaging congregations and men's groups to plant trees to mitigate the impact of climate change. See Mennonite Men, "JoinTrees," https://www.mennonitemen.org/jointrees.

as Goshen College and Anabaptist Mennonite Biblical Seminary, in Elkhart, contribute to the watershed's biodiversity through the maintenance of campus prairies.

The watershed's cities are also the centers of what is likely the world's largest recreational vehicle (RV) industry. Elkhart County's economy is heavily reliant on RVs, a luxury item vulnerable to wild market cycles in sales. During the financial crash of 2007 to 2009, factory owners shed workers in response to rapidly declining demand, at one point in 2009 leading the county to an unemployment rate of over 20 percent.[85] The start of the coronavirus pandemic had a similar result, but RV corporations were soon posting record sales numbers thanks to a massive surge of interest on the part of Americans in outdoor recreation.[86]

The local RV industry is well integrated into global capitalism. The nation's most successful RV company, Thor Industries, is traded on the New York Stock Exchange and owns the German RV manufacturer Erwin Hymer Group. Multinational holding conglomerate Berkshire Hathaway, led by billionaire investor Warren Buffet, owns another major Elkhart-based manufacturer, Forest River. Although publicly traded Winnebago Industries is based in Iowa, its towable trailer division is located in Middlebury. Together, these three manufacturers control 80 percent of the American RV market.[87] The RV industry also includes multinational corporations dedicated to building component parts, such as portable refrigeration specialist Dometic. Based in Stockholm, Sweden, Dometic relocated all of its US RV operations to Elkhart

---

[85]See historic unemployment rate statistics at the US Bureau of Labor Statistics website, https://www.bls.gov/.
[86]Sophia Cai and Michael Tobin, "RV Travel Was on Its Way Out. Then Came the Pandemic," *Fortune*, July 15, 2020, https://fortune.com/2020/07/15/coronavirus-summer-travel-rvs-road-trips/; Nicholas Jasinski, "RV Sales Have Soared during the Pandemic. These Stocks Could See More Gains Ahead," *Barron's*, October 3, 2020, https://www.barrons.com/articles/recreational-vehicle-stocks-could-see-further-gains-51601671189.
[87]Vince Martin, "5 RV Stocks Hoping for More Summer Travel: Pandemic Fears Have Stirred a Wave of RV Buying—and These 5 Stocks Could Benefit," *InvestorPlace*, July 7, 2020, https://investorplace.com/2020/07/5-rv-stocks-hoping-for-more-summer-travel/.

in 2019.[88] Meanwhile, estimates suggest that automation could eliminate 76 percent of RV and related jobs in the city of Elkhart alone.[89] The threat of automation and the vulnerability of the industry to market shifts create a precarious economic situation for many of the Elkhart River Watershed's human inhabitants.

On the Amtrak passenger train from Chicago to Elkhart, I have occasionally met RV delivery drivers. These individuals come to Elkhart County, pick up an RV or other vehicle, and drive it across the country to a dealer. Then a transport company pays their train fare back to Elkhart to start the process over.[90] Their travel relies on the dense network of highways and railroads that crosses the watershed. State and county roads connect watershed businesses with Interstates 80 and 90, which run contiguously for a time through northern Indiana as part of the Indiana Toll Road. The highways lead both west to Chicago, and then on to the West Coast, and east to Boston and New York City. The Indiana Toll Road, built with public funds in the 1950s, is integrated into the national highway system established in that decade to facilitate American military defensive preparations following the Second World War.[91] In 2006, the Indiana Toll Road was leased to a consortium of Spanish and Australian private transportation firms, Cinta-Macquarie, to raise funds for other state construction projects. After the consortium filed for bankruptcy in 2014, the lease was awarded to Australian investment manager IFM Investors, which drew on equity from over seventy US pension funds to finance the deal.[92]

---

[88] Ben Quiggle, "Dometic Announces New Location for HQ in Elkhart," *RVBusiness*, August 22, 2019, https://rvbusiness.com/dometic-announces-new-location-for-hq-in-elkhart/.

[89] City of Elkhart, "City of Elkhart Economic Diversification Study," December 2017, https://elkhart2040.com/research-studies-and-reports.

[90] The website *RVTransport Life* maintains an incomplete list of transport companies, https://rvtransport.life/rv-transport-carriers/.

[91] Richard F. Weingroff, "Federal-Aid Highway Act of 1956: Creating the Interstate System," *Public Roads* 60, no. 1 (Summer 1996), https://www.fhwa.dot.gov/publications/publicroads/96summer/p96su10.cfm.

[92] Robert Puentes, "The Indiana Toll Road: How Did a Good Deal Go Bad?," *Forbes*, October 3, 2014, https://www.forbes.com/sites/realspin/2014/10/03/the-indiana-toll-road-how-did-a-good-deal-go-bad/?sh=68075bc82087; Business Wire, "IFM Investors Completes Acquisition of Indiana Toll Road Concession Company," May 17, 2015, https://www.businesswire.com/news/home/20150527006535/en/IFM-Investors-completes-acquisition-of-Indiana-Toll-Road-Concession-Company.

The city of Elkhart is situated at the confluence of the Elkhart and St. Joseph Rivers. Early white settlers harnessed the power of the rivers for industry and business transportation. By the late nineteenth century, the railroads had displaced the rivers as the primary mode of moving people and goods. Early railroads had to be serviced about every 100 miles, and since Elkhart is 100 miles east of Chicago, it became the site of a major rail service center.[93] Tracks from throughout the eastern United States run through Elkhart and on to Chicago. During the early twentieth century, African Americans from Kentucky, Tennessee, and other Southern states arrived in Elkhart, escaping the Jim Crow South for a chance to work for higher wages on the railroad or in domestic service.[94] In the 1930s the growing Black community was forced into a segregated neighborhood, south of the tracks and west of the Elkhart River.[95] Upstream, Goshen remained a "sundown town," effectively off limits to African Americans after sunset, through the 1970s.[96] During that decade's nationwide wave of "urban renewal" efforts, Elkhart cleared its Black neighborhood, despite community resistance and with seemingly few ideas regarding the location's future—almost fifty years on, little redevelopment has taken place.[97] Black families were relocated, often to inferior housing in the city's South Central neighborhood. Today, African

---

[93] David Harnish, "Respectability and Reciprocity: How African Americans Formed a Community in Elkhart, Indiana," 2012, Mennonite Historical Library (Goshen College), 8.
[94] Harnish, "Respectability and Reciprocity," 9–11, 13–19.
[95] Harnish, "Respectability and Reciprocity," 12, 19–30.
[96] Harnish, "Respectability and Reciprocity," 12; Dan Shenk, "Portrait of a 'Sundown Town': Coming to Terms with Racism in a 'Mennonite' Community," *Mennonite World Review* (January 14, 2014), 1, 12–13. See Richard Rothstein, *The Color of Law: A Forgotten History of How Our Government Segregated America* (New York: Liveright, 2017), especially chapter 5, for broader background.
[97] John W. Bynum, "Ye Will Know Them by Their Fruits: The Story of Herbert M. and Ruth Tolson and the Tolson Community Center and Youth Center," *The Village Note* 1, no. 1 (Elkhart, Ind.: Tolson Community and Youth Center, City of Elkhart Parks & Recreation, March 2015): 8–9. The primary "achievement" of redevelopment is a government housing project, Washington Gardens. Much of the cleared neighborhood is still abandoned. On the wider national trends, see Rothstein, *The Color of Law*; Keeanga-Yamahtta Taylor, *Race for Profit: How Banks and the Real Estate Industry Undermined Black Homeownership* (Chapel Hill, NC: University of North Carolina Press, 2019).

American, Latino, and white residents of South Central live in one of the city's poorest areas.[98] The railroad tracks are now owned by Norfolk Southern Railroad, a publicly traded company based in Virginia. Among its major investors are global investment firms the Vanguard Group, BlackRock, and the Government Pension Fund of Norway.[99] Norfolk Southern and other major railroad freight companies are heavily reliant on the business of the coal industry and form a powerful lobby against climate science and policy.[100]

The mouth of the Elkhart River opens into the St. Joseph River in downtown Elkhart. Although heavily polluted by industry in the nineteenth and twentieth centuries, both rivers have been cleaned up in recent decades, particularly following the federal Clean Water Act of 1972.[101] In 2008 the Elkhart River Restoration Association, a nonprofit corporation, developed a watershed management plan, which received federal Environmental Protection Agency funding through a state agency to work in concert with the Elkhart County Soil and Water Conservation District. The management plan identifies various problems facing the watershed—from harmful agricultural runoff to biodiversity loss—and outlines steps to address these challenges.[102]

---

[98] City of Elkhart Community & Redevelopment, *2021–2025 Neighborhood Revitalization Strategy Area (NRSA) Plan (DRAFT)*, March 28, 2021, https://elkhartindiana.org/wpfd_file/city-of-elkhart-draft-2021-2025-neighborhood-revitalization-strategy-area-nrsa-plan/.

[99] CNN Business, "Norfolk Southern Corp," accessed August 23, 2024, https://www.cnn.com/markets/stocks/NSC. The Norwegian pension fund invests in the country's North Sea oil revenue. See Norges Bank Investment Management, "About the Fund," accessed August 23, 2024. https://www.nbim.no/en/the-fund/about-the-fund/.

[100] Robinson Meyer, "A Major but Little-known Supporter of Climate Denial: Freight Railroads," *The Atlantic*, December 13, 2019, https://www.theatlantic.com/science/archive/2019/12/freight-railroads-funded-climate-denial-decades/603559/.

[101] City of Elkhart, "The St. Joseph River: It's Health from a Historical Perspective," *YouTube*, August 18, 2017, https://www.youtube.com/watch?v=ww5ZTdErCoM&ab_channel=CityOfElkhartIN; "Summary of the Clean Water Act," *United States Environmental Protection Agency*, accessed August 23, 2024, https://www.epa.gov/laws-regulations/summary-clean-water-act.

[102] V3 Companies, *Elkhart River Watershed Management Plan*, March 6, 2008, https://ecm.idem.in.gov/cs/idcplg?IdcService=GET_FILE&dID=83085669&dDocName=83085602&Rendition=web&allowInterrupt=1&noSaveAs=1.

The Spirit Hovers over the Watershed

The Spirit hovers over the Elkhart River Watershed, dynamically structuring it, giving it life, forming bonds of creaturely solidarity within and beyond its bioregional boundaries. The Spirit's dynamic, life-giving structuration of creation is evident in the complex organization of the watershed's ecology—grinding glaciers reorienting the land, with flora and fauna flourishing in the wake of their retreat. The complex human social ecology visible in the watershed also echoes the hovering Spirit to some degree. Witness, for instance, ongoing histories of Indigenous peoples tending land and one another, forming, in solidarity, organizations for care, resistance, and repair. A diversity of settler organizations can also be seen preserving, protecting, and educating for environmental sustainability, drawing on resources from various church, university, civic, and government institutions. Yet the settler presence is also a sign of sin, bound up as it is with the displacement of original peoples, the clearance of forests and the dredging of wetlands, the exhaustion and pollution of waterways, and the production of disposable goods and workers for the global economy.

The relational web that makes up the watershed might be thought of as an ecological-social, or eco-social, field of relations. This field owes its material existence to the partnership of hovering Spirit and divine Word, and its ecological materiality is therefore inherently social—it only exists as related to the triune God. Since God gives creatures their own creative agency, the watershed is also an eco-social field to the extent that the complex and dynamic structures that make it up interact with one another to produce new forms of material and social organization. Humans are one form of creaturely participant in the eco-social field of the watershed. Human agency shapes and is shaped by watersheds. As political scientist Paulina Ochoa Espejo has argued, watersheds are "places" in which human and other creaturely agencies intertwine: "place, as part of the natural world, intervenes in human designs, actively participates in the creation of institutions, and transforms a geographic site into a place. As an area defined by space as well as human interactions, place is part of the political process rather than its neutral background."[103] The picture of the hovering Spirit further suggests that space and human interactions are accompanied by a variety of agency-laden creaturely exchanges and processes. This account cautions against any designation of watersheds as simply "pre-political," even if we humans have a tendency to silence and forget other creatures in our deliberations over creation's future. As an eco-social field, the watershed's rivers and winds and flora and fauna exercise agency along with and in interaction with its human inhabitants. Part of what watershed discipleship is calling for is a politics that incorporates these other creatures as contributing members of the watershed-as-polis.

Ochoa Espejo assists us in conceptualizing how a watershed is a place constituted by a confluence of human and other, "natural" creaturely agencies. The anthropologist Arjun Appadurai, however, offers the reminder that in conditions defined by globalization "localities" are constructed by differential global flows of people, goods, information, and other assets.[104] These localities do not neatly line-up with the physical, bioregional "space" of places. Recall that the Elkhart River Watershed hosts agricultural and industrial production integrated into global markets. Recall also that the watershed has been shaped, physically and otherwise, by human social histories that cannot be delimited to the watershed—histories of regional and global migration, religion, warfare, and politics, not to mention economics. The watershed may be a place with relatively definite spatial boundaries, even if those boundaries are also connection points where, for instance, one stream empties into another. But the watershed is also a locality with much more diffuse boundaries—boundaries that are in many cases global rather than "local" in any ordinary sense of that word.

Given the relational character of the watershed, it is unsurprising that organizations operating there work at a variety of scales. There are local organizations, including congregations, businesses, and ecological organizations. These organizations, nevertheless, are in many cases connected in some way to regional, national,

---

[103] Paulina Ochoa Espejo, *On Borders: Territories, Legitimacy, and the Rights of Place* (Oxford: Oxford University Press, 2020), 132.
[104] Arjun Appadurai, "The Production of Locality," in *Modernity at Large: Cultural Dimensions of Globalization* (Minneapolis: University of Minnesota Press, 1996), 178–99.

or international organizations. A host of organizations that primarily work on those larger scales are also directly involved in the watershed. It is difficult (and would perhaps be impossible) to find organizations that are strictly local if that means they are in some way dedicated exclusively to the watershed and cut off from developments beyond the watershed. The organizations are related, not just to each other and the watershed, but to people, events, funding, and other organizations in many places around the world. These relations, it should be underscored, are not only sources of the watershed's degradation. Indigenous political alliances, religious denominations, and ecological justice networks are, at the very least, not simply describable as opposed to the watershed's good. Under conditions of sin the import of these organizational forms may be ambiguous, but they are not wholly negative.

Conceptualizing the watershed as an eco-social field engenders a relational perspective on the watershed that attends to the kinds of constitutive relations just described—relations that are material as well as social, local as well as regional and global. Extending the field image would also enable an analysis of the various forms of capital that are present in the watershed and of social spaces structured through the pursuit of that capital. A formal sociological analysis is beyond the scope of this book, but a general or formal comment can be made with the book's overall theological argument in mind. We might say that eco-social fields are "naturally" oriented to life and creaturely solidarity, that is, they exist as creatures to pursue that purpose. This creaturely orientation can and has been disturbed by sin, leading to the ostensible replacement of life and solidarity with other goals, from the domination of land to the accumulation of money, from the maintenance of racial and gender hierarchies to the triumph of humans over and against other creatures. These goals, however, only ostensibly or partially replace life and solidarity, since without these goods the watershed—as place and locality—ceases to exist. The portrait of the watershed offered above, furthermore, provides abundant evidence of the persistence of life and solidarity-seeking even in degraded conditions. Organizing aimed at the pursuit of life and solidarity among creatures within watersheds participates to some degree in the work of the hovering Spirit.

As does organizing that seeks to work across watersheds, for instance by providing fora for deliberating about and means for facing common challenges and opportunities, working across watersheds in a sustained way requires complex organizations, which we typically describe as institutions. At least some of the regional, national, and international Indigenous, ecclesial, and eco-justice organizations mentioned earlier seem to take seriously the need to remediate harm within watersheds. They do so as institutions with complex personnel structures and funding models, budgets and long-term goals, and aims that include but are not limited to specific local contexts. These institutions can be thought of as tending to some of the relations that more locally focused organizations are not able to focus on, relations that constitute the watershed but are not limited to it, relations that endure across generations, relations that require intensive amounts of coordination and often money to repair and reorient to life and solidarity. These institutions, too, can be thought of as more or less participating in the hovering Spirit.

3

Sanctifying Spirit

Over the past decade my denomination, like many others, has begun to face the reality of gender-based and sexualized violence in our homes, congregations, and institutions. In the case of my denomination, Mennonite Church USA, this process has been spurred in part by the long-overdue reckoning with the abuse perpetrated by our most famous theologian, John Howard Yoder. This reckoning began with a June 2013 social media post by survivor advocate and activist Barbra Graber in response to yet another positive review of a Yoder-related book in a denominational magazine.[1] Graber raised concerns about the ongoing, typically uncritical promotion of the theological legacy of a person who was well known in Mennonite circles for perpetrating abuse. The overwhelming response to Graber's post led the denomination to form a discernment group to determine next steps. As a result of the group's work, over the next two years previously sealed archives related to Yoder's conduct were opened and the historian Rachel Waltner Goossen was commissioned to research and publish an article detailing failed, often half-hearted, attempts to prevent further abuse by Yoder. Goossen's article was published in a Mennonite academic journal

---

[1] For a detailed timeline of these events, see Mennonite Church USA, "John Howard Yoder Digest," accessed August 23, 2024, https://www.mennoniteusa.org/resource-portal/resource/john-howard-yoder-digest/.

in January 2015.² In March of that year, Anabaptist Mennonite Biblical Seminary (AMBS)—where Yoder had worked until 1984—held a "Service of Lament, Confession, and Commitment" led by President Sara Wenger Shenk. Another service of "lament and hope" was held at the denominational convention in July 2015. The convention also saw denominational moderator Elizabeth Soto Albrecht introduce a "Churchwide Statement on Sexual Abuse" that was approved by the vast majority of delegates. The discernment group concluded its work shortly after the convention.

This progression of events can be seen, among other things, as a remarkable culmination of over a century of women's organizing in Mennonite churches. The reach of Graber's voice, the power of Goossen's scholarship, and the effectiveness of Shenk's and Soto's institutional leadership are fruits of a long labor of "women talking" and acting for their safety, well-being, and power in an ecclesial and social context dominated by men.³ The fact that institutions such as Mennonite Church USA and AMBS were in any way responsive to the concerns raised by Graber, and the fact that women like Goossen, Shenk, and Soto were in academic and institutional positions to shape that response, testifies to the real, even if partial, victories won by women through generations of struggle. That struggle had successfully changed the institutions, not fully of course, but to the extent that they were able to take some important steps to redress a significant injustice.

---

²Goossen, "'Defanging the Beast': Mennonite Responses to John Howard Yoder's Sexual Abuse," *Mennonite Quarterly Review* 89, no. 1 (2015): 7–80. Ruth Krall, a retired Mennonite psychologist and theology professor, had already published an analysis of Yoder's conduct and institutional responses in a book posted to her website in 2012. Significant attention was given to this book after Graber's 2013 post. See Krall, *The Elephant in God's Living Room*, volume 3: *The Mennonite Church and John Howard Yoder, Collected Essays* (n.p.: Enduring Space, 2013), https://ruthkrall.com/books/the-elephants-in-gods-living-room-series/volume-three-the-mennonite-church-and-john-howard-yoder-collected-essays/.

³The phrase "women talking" references Miriam Toewes's novel *Women Talking* (New York: Bloomsbury, 2018), which depicts a discernment process among a group of women facing a (very real) rape epidemic in the Manitoba Colony of Old Colony Mennonites in Bolivia. The novel was made into a film of the same name by Sarah Polley (Universal Pictures, 2022).

The present chapter develops a picture of the Spirit as sanctifying the church through the reform of its institutions. The sanctifying Spirit inspires movements to transform ecclesial institutions so that the church might promote the well-being of all its members. Shared well-being is here understood as an index of holiness, of the "set-apartness" of the church that rejects conformity to worldly patterns of exploitation, domination, and marginalization. Movements that promote shared well-being through institutional reform can therefore be conceptualized as participating in the work of the sanctifying Spirit.

This chapter's argument is developed in three sections. In the first section, an account of the Spirit's sanctifying work is built up through an examination of Eugene Rogers's and Sarah Coakley's writings on the Spirit, gender, and sexuality. This area of pneumatological research provides a helpful test case, given the strong association of "holiness" and "sanctification" discourse with conservative positions on these topics. Examining the work of theologians who view Spirit sanctification as potentially transformative of standard gender/sex norms and practices provides a narrative arc for our picture of the Spirit who sanctifies in part by reforming established institutions. This narrative arc is then developed in the second section by elaborating on the story of North American Mennonite women, tracing in some detail their efforts since the nineteenth century to transform ecclesial institutions. Connecting these efforts to feminist pneumatology clarifies how the sanctifying Spirit works with movements to reform institutions. Identifying a place for institutions in the process of sanctification is not intended to validate any particular set of (Mennonite) institutions or to offer a blanket approval of institutions as such, under the illusion that they in theory can all be reformed. To expand on this point, I look in a third section at more "pessimistic" theologies (Linn Tonstad, Ephraim Radner) that caution against the kind of socially and politically transformative pneumatologies discussed in the previous two sections, particularly when these are coordinated with optimistic accounts of institutional reform. Drawing on the picture of the sanctifying Spirit developed here, as well as on Bourdieu's notion of social reproduction and Wittgenstein's analysis of rules, I seek to make room for a variety of responses to ecclesial institutions.

The Sanctifying Spirit, Gender, and Sexuality

Roman Catholic theologian Nicholas Lash maintains that confessing God's Spirit as "holy" entails a recognition of the sacredness of creation as divine gift. This recognition, in turn, leads to a "preferential option for the poor," to solidarity with creation under assault.[4] From this view, sacredness is a property of life insofar as life is a gift from God. That sacredness can be attacked by forces of sin and death, but not finally obliterated. The work of sanctification—the Spirit's and ours—is the work of honoring life even, or especially, in its marginal forms. As the Methodist theologian Joerg Rieger puts it, "sanctification is based on the alternative justice of the kingdom of God, which implies new relationships both to the neighbor ... and to the world."[5]

Although terms such as "holiness" and "sanctification" have often been wielded as cudgels against women as well as gender and sexual minorities, some theologians have tried to recover their conceptual substance so as to endorse the sacredness of gender, sexuality, and the body and to depict their place within the divine economy. These attempts unsurprisingly impinge upon questions concerning ecclesial organization. Does claiming the sacredness of women and gender and sexual minorities demand the transformation of standard organizational patterns, or can those patterns stand as they are? How does the associated movement toward "inclusion" of women and gender and sexual minorities in the church's ministry relate to the institutional church? Does God's solidarity with those oppressed for reasons of gender and sexuality abolish the church as an institutional reality? This latter possibility may correspond with the standard pneumatological-sociological picture described

---

[4]Nicholas Lash, *Holiness, Speech and Silence: Reflections on the Question of God* (Burlington, VT: Ashgate, 2004), 36, 44.
[5]Joerg Rieger, "Sanctification," in *The Cambridge Dictionary of Theology*, eds. Ian A. McFarland et al. (Cambridge: Cambridge University Press, 2011), 459. Cf. Bonhoeffer's discussion under the rubric of "sanctification" of the church's communal "political ethic" and its "struggle" to be the church—a struggle that manifests in part through the church's "bearing the troubles" of the attacked "least of the people." Dietrich Bonhoeffer, *Discipleship* (Minneapolis: Fortress, 2001), 261–2, 285.

in Chapter 1. If the Spirit breaks purportedly traditional gender and sexual norms, then perhaps the Spirit also leads us to break with institutions.

This section begins to advance a counter picture via a discussion of two Anglican theologians, Eugene Rogers and Sarah Coakley, both of whom coordinate the Spirit's sanctification of gendered and sexed bodies with ecclesial reform. Although, as noted in Chapter 1, Rogers primarily describes the church as a "community" and Coakley typically identifies noninstitutional ecclesial organizations as the engines of reform, both provide the lineaments of a picture of the Spirit who sanctifies in part by reforming church institutions. I expand on institutional reform as a potential mode of participation in the sanctifying Spirit in subsequent sections of the chapter.

Rogers shares Lash's traditional emphasis on the Spirit as "gift," developing the themes of "gratuity," "superfluity," and "excess" as properly pneumatological.[6] These terms should not be taken to indicate that the Spirit is dispensable from our descriptions of God or the divine economy. Rather, they underline grace as definitive of God's character and relation to creation. Through a narrative pneumatology—in which the Spirit's depiction within biblical and liturgical narratives is read as disclosing the Spirit's identity—Rogers suggests that the Spirit incorporates bodies into the body of Christ and sacramentally distributes the universal body of Christ to bodies. This activity works toward the healing and restoration of wounded bodies, justice for wronged bodies, and a final eschatological joy for all bodies.[7]

One of Rogers' signature arguments concerns God's "excessive" inclusion of the Gentiles in the plan of salvation.[8] Paul compares this inclusion in Rom. 11:24 to grafting a "by nature" (*kata physin*) wild olive tree (the Gentiles) onto a cultivated olive tree (Israel). This grafting is "contrary to nature" (*para physin*)—the same phrase Paul used earlier in Romans to describe Gentile same-sex sexual practices (1:26). Rogers suggests that this phrase might be better translated as "beyond nature" or "in excess of nature," and

---

[6] Eugene F. Rogers, *After the Spirit: A Constructive Pneumatology from Resources outside the Modern West* (Grand Rapids, MI: Eerdmans, 2005).
[7] Rogers, *After the Spirit*, 104–11, 118, 127, 128, 145.
[8] Rogers, *After the Spirit*, 99–101; Eugene F. Rogers, *Sexuality and the Christian Body: Their Way into the Triune God* (Malden, MA: Blackwell, 1999), 63–6.

reads its repetition as setting up a typological relationship between the same-sex-practicing Gentiles and the Gentile-including God. The excessive God brings in the excessive Gentiles. God does not change the Gentiles' nature (they remain "wild olive trees") but rather reforms their wildness through incorporation into God's plan of salvation, eliciting a form of virtue particular to their nature as Gentiles. Although Rogers recognizes that Paul was not speaking to the modern preoccupation with same-sex marriage, he takes Paul as offering a typology for divine action that can be applied to the present. Just as Gentiles are welcomed, preserved in some way as Gentiles (they do not have to become Jews), and made righteous by uniting with Jews in the body of Christ, so are same-sex couples welcomed, preserved in some way as same-sex couples (they do not have to become straight), and are oriented to virtue through the church's sacrament of marriage.

In *After the Spirit*, Rogers develops the pneumatological dimensions of this argument.[9] After recapitulating his interpretation of Romans 1–11—"God shows solidarity with the Gentiles' own characteristic of excess"[10]—he reads fifth-century liturgical poet Romanos the Melodist as indicating the trinitarian shape of the divine excess. The language of divine excess is "governed" by God's gracious preferential option for humanity, the extreme *philanthropia* of the incarnation—and "the Spirit conceives and keeps faith with *this* excess."[11] The virgin birth is the paradigm for the Spirit's work, a "paraphysical" (*para physin*) work that "is physical, in that it proceeds alongside, in solidarity with nature, and *para*, in excess of nature: a companion to nature, befriending, restoring, consummating, and exceeding it."

The terms of this companionship are elaborated throughout *After the Spirit*'s narrative pneumatology, which consistently highlights the Spirit's "resting" on bodies. The Spirit's resting on Jesus at his baptism, for instance, witnesses to the reality that the love between Father and Son is meant to be shared broadly, thereby inviting participation in the baptismal ritual. Here we learn that "it is characteristic of the Spirit to take up and render holy concrete,

---

[9]Rogers, *After the Spirit*, 99–104.
[10]Rogers, *After the Spirit*, 100.
[11]Rogers, *After the Spirit*, 103.

physical, sociological structures."[12] When the Spirit rests, the Spirit sanctifies, and sanctification gives rise to community:

> The Spirit renders the body liturgical, a site from which, by the Spirit's gift, God gives Godself to be perceived, and a site in which, by the Spirit's gift on gift, God gives Godself to be met ... Because the Spirit witnesses—indicates—points out, the finger of God applies to human beings a seal, it incorporates each one into a body, a community, not only of the Church, but of God's own life, into the virtuous circles in which God is known by God and partaken by God, so that human reception of God is not passive but participant.[13]

In short, the Spirit rests on bodies to create a collective terrestrial and eschatological body.

Among those incorporated by the Spirit into Christ's body are those who are being further sanctified by marriage. "Marriage," Rogers writes, "is primarily a structure for the transformation of the human being by the grace of God, which is to say by the Holy Spirit."[14] Marriage reminds us, and indeed enacts the reality, that "holiness is never an individual achievement or possession."[15] Given its sacramental, sanctifying character, Rogers argues that marriage should not be denied to same-sex couples. These couples benefit from marriage as a means of sanctifying grace—how then can the sacrament be denied them?[16] Non-procreative same-sex couples, moreover, are well positioned to "imitate God's own work of adoption" by adopting children. "Adoption bears witness to the Spirit that works by grace alongside nature"; the inclusion of the Gentiles can therefore also be described in terms of adoption.[17] The point here, though, is that same-sex couples further participate in the Spirit's community-building work of sanctification when they adopt children.

---

[12]Rogers, *After the Spirit*, 137.
[13]Rogers, *After the Spirit*, 137.
[14]Rogers, *After the Spirit*, 188.
[15]Rogers, *After the Spirit*, 189.
[16]See also Rogers, *Sexuality and the Christian Body*, 67–85, for an extended argument in favor of marriage as sanctifying same-sex couples.
[17]Rogers, *After the Spirit*, 189.

Rogers continues to spell out the connection between the excessive, paraphysical work of the Spirit, the Spirit of adoption, and same-sex marriage in a coauthored article. In that article, Rogers and coauthors shift their focus from the Spirit's sanctification of same-sex couples to the Spirit's sanctification of the church through the inclusion of such couples in its sacrament of marriage and common life. They first elaborate on Rogers's argument that the excessive logic of Rom. 11:24 fits the pattern of "the Spirit of adoption" from Rom. 8:15 and 23.[18] The Gentiles can be included despite any moral qualms because God the Spirit adopts those who "by nature" are not children and grafts in what is "by nature" wild. Rogers and coauthors deploy an argument from analogy to contend that "marrying same-sex couples comports with the mission of God celebrated by the Spirit in the body of Christ, even though it seems to exceed the marriage practices assumed by Scripture and honored by tradition."[19] Later, the authors put the point even more strongly, arguing that "in refusing to celebrate same-sex weddings we [the church] cut ourselves off from the Spirit's invitation to the feast and out of the Spirit's movement of adoption. Refusal to bear witness to and keep faith with love refuses participation in the work of the Spirit."[20]

The picture that emerges from these discussions depicts the Spirit as sanctifying individuals by drawing them into the church's sacramental life and as sanctifying the church and its sacraments by opening them to individuals (and couples and families) previously thought worthy of exclusion on moral or other purportedly "natural" grounds. The Spirit's sanctification of individuals respects their "nature"—it does not force Gentiles to become Jews or same-sex couples to become straight. Yet Spirit sanctification also transforms individuals (and couples and families), binding them into durable communities where they can be challenged to grow in virtue and

---

[18] Deirdre J. Good, Willis J. Jenkins, Cynthia B. Kittredge, and Eugene F. Rogers, "A Theology of Marriage including Same-Sex Couples: A View from the Liberals," *Anglican Theological Review* 93, no. 1 (Winter 2011): 57, 79–81.
[19] Good, Jenkins, Kittredge, and Rogers, "A Theology of Marriage," 57.
[20] Good, Jenkins, Kittredge, and Rogers, "A Theology of Marriage," 76. They develop the point about "love" through a discussion of the parable of the wedding banquet from Mt. 22.

bear witness to the love of God in Christ through the Spirit. This sanctifying process, however, also changes the church. When the church community lowers its barriers of access in response to the Spirit's invitation of Gentiles and same-sex couples—a process that involves hermeneutical, doctrinal, and liturgical innovation—it experiences and demonstrates how the Spirit not only "renders holy" individuals but also "concrete, physical, sociological structures." Though Rogers does not mention church institutions, presumably they are among the structures amenable to Spirit sanctification.

Sarah Coakley develops a similar picture from a different set of arguments in her writings on sexuality.[21] Coakley attempts to rehabilitate the Neo-Platonic strand of Christian theology by returning to its insight that all human desire in some way aims at God. In this tradition, the spiritual life is a process of purifying desire, including sexual desire, so that we might be wholly oriented to God. Coakley seeks to recover this approach to desire without embracing its tendency to censure desire and sexuality as such or desiring bodies (bodies that are often associated with women). Instead, she views spiritual purgation as "channeling," refining, and transforming desire—intensifying it, even—not eliminating it or the bodies that bear it.[22] The purgative journey is directed by the Holy Spirit in what Coakley describes as a "Spirit-leading" account of incorporation into the life of the triune God.[23] The Spirit draws us through our desire into Christ's body so that we might enjoy the relationship shared between Son and Father. Coakley views contemplative and charismatic prayer as privileged practices for

---

[21]Coakley, *God, Sexuality and the Self: An Essay "On the Trinity"* (Cambridge: Cambridge University Press, 2013); Coakley, *The New Asceticism: Sexuality, Gender, and the Quest for God* (London: Bloomsbury, 2015). Coakley finds Rogers's superfluity and resting arguments unconvincing. Coakley, *God, Sexuality and the Self*, 24, 56, and Coakley, "Review of *After the Spirit: A Constructive Pneumatology from Resources outside the Modern West* by Eugene F. Rogers," *Journal of the American Academy of Religion* 75, no. 2 (2007): 429–32.

[22]Coakley, *God, Sexuality and the Self*, 8–9; Coakley, *The New Asceticism*, 39–51 (on "re-channeling" desire). Rogers, *After the Spirit*, 101, also uses the language of "channeling" in a description of Thomas Aquinas on human passion: "for Aquinas, passion comes to provide the animal energy that it is the point of grace to channel or habituate into virtue, the energy without which the human being could do nothing at all."

[23]Coakley, *God, Sexuality and the Self*, 102; Coakley, *The New Asceticism*, 86.

initiating the incorporative journey, a practice in which we submit to the Spirit's "protoerotic pressure" so that our erotic "groaning" might be taken up and reformed by the Spirit's intercessory "sighs too deep for words" (Rom. 8:23, 26).[24] At this point Coakley somewhat controversially suggests that, by the Spirit, human desire participates in and responds to the divine desire that shapes the Trinity.[25]

Coakley describes her method as a *théologie totale* that attempts to do justice to the variety of ways—discursive and nondiscursive—we encounter and make sense of God.[26] This approach leads her to engage standard resources in systematic theology (Scripture, classic theological texts, church history, philosophy) as well as art, mysticism, and the social sciences. One source that animates her theology is the work of the sociologist Ernst Troeltsch, and especially its suggestions of symmetries between doctrine and social forms.[27] Troeltsch's famous threefold ecclesiological typology in particular guides Coakley's understanding of the church, past and present. Troeltsch distinguishes between a "church-type"—the church as a large, politically conservative, public institution integrated with other ruling class institutions—and a "sect-type," in which the church tends to be small, is often antagonistic to power, and has a rigorously committed membership largely drawn from the lower classes.[28] Alongside these types of churches, Troeltsch also identifies a "mystic-type," embodied in individuals seeking direct contact with the divine.[29] Whereas in medieval Christianity mystics often operated within church-type structures (including

---

[24]Coakley, *God, Sexuality and the Self*, 13–15, 55–6.
[25]Coakley, *God, Sexuality and the Self*, 308–39. Paul Daffyd Jones pushes Coakley to clarify her claims about divine desire in his review essay "On the 'Loving Mutations' of God, Sexuality, and the Self," *Syndicate*, November 11, 2015, https://syndicate.network/symposia/theology/sarah-coakley-god-sexuality-and-the-self/.
[26]Coakley, *God, Sexuality and the Self*, 33–65.
[27]Coakley, *God, Sexuality and the Self*, 118, 142, 157–62, 185, 341–2. Coakley's first book was on Troeltsch: *Christ without Absolutes: A Study of the Christology of Ernst Troeltsch* (Oxford: Clarendon, 1988).
[28]Ernst Troeltsch, *The Social Teaching of the Christian Churches*, vol. 1, trans. Olive Wyon (Louisville: Westminster/John Knox, 1992), 331–43.
[29]Ernst Troeltsch, *The Social Teaching of the Christian Churches*, vol. 2, trans. Olive Wyon (Louisville: Westminster/John Knox, 1992), 693, 729–802.

religious orders), Protestant mystics and their secular successors have generally eluded institutions as well as communal "sects" in favor of an individualistic spiritual journey.

Although Coakley mostly adopts Troeltsch's typology, she is interested in the enduring, and sociologically transformative, presence of mystics within both church institutions and sects, as well as the presence of sects within institutionalized churches. Regarding the early history of Christian doctrine, for example, she contends that a version of trinitarianism arose giving experiential priority to the Spirit not only in sectarian movements outside of the institutionalizing "church," e.g., Montanism, but also within the nascent ecclesial institutions.[30] Coakley presents "mixed-type" figures such as Irenaeus and Tertullian who advanced a Spirit-first doctrine of incorporation into the Trinity within those institutions (Tertullian of course also dallied with Montanism for a time), rather than an "institutional theology" that combined technical orthodoxy with a functional subordination of the Spirit to ordering Father and Son/Word, or a "sectarian" tendency to deviate from orthodoxy.[31] The mixed-type theologians root their orthodoxy in the contemplative or charismatic experience of being drawn by the Spirit into the Son to enjoy his relationship with the Father—the unity of the Godhead is here "discovered" through prayer, our own and the Spirit praying within us. This tradition "has tended to sit somewhat uneasily" within institutional churches, since it grants mystical "loss of control" as a goal of the spiritual life—rather than subordination to institutional or community order—and, perhaps unsurprisingly, has also frequently upset ecclesiastical binaries pertaining to gender and sexuality.[32] The history of Christian mysticism, according to Coakley, indicates that orthodoxy—as rooted in the experience of prayer—has also been bound up with the upsetting of such binaries.[33] The institutional church's tendency to subordinate the Spirit is no accident—it has often been a defensive response to pneumatic claims to authority by women and the "blurring" of sexual and spiritual desire. Yet the fact that

---

[30] Coakley, *God, Sexuality and the Self*, 118.
[31] Coakley, *God, Sexuality and the Self*, 123–5, 127, 142, 153–4.
[32] Coakley, *God, Sexuality and the Self*, 118, 127–8, 278, 293.
[33] Coakley, *God, Sexuality and the Self*, 331; Coakley, *The New Asceticism*, 75.

figures such as Irenaeus and Tertullian (and to some degree Origen, Gregory of Nyssa, and Augustine)[34] perpetuated a "Spirit-first," mystical trinitarianism within the institutional church indicates, on Coakley's view, the possibility of some kind of rapprochement between destabilizing mysticism and ordering institutions.

Coakley further complicates Troeltsch's typology with studies of two contemporary English charismatic communities, one more easily categorized as a "sect" but the other continuing within an Anglican denominational setting. Disassociating the mystic-type from individualism, Coakley sets out to discern traces of "a slightly subversive variation" exhibiting "a great commitment to personalized religious *depth*-within-community," a phenomenon that "does not withdraw, but more commonly disturbs and galvanizes the more settled social patterns of its surroundings."[35] This pattern is especially evident, according to Coakley, in the Anglican charismatic community that combines elements of sectarian egalitarianism with episcopal hierarchy ("including some cautious use of women in positions of authority") and charismatic phenomena with contemplative prayer.[36] Here Coakley finds another "mixed-type," a convergence of mysticism, set-apart community, and ecclesial institutions.

Although Coakley does not draw on her modified Troeltschian typology in her essay "Ecclesiastical Sex Scandals," possibly her most direct treatment of questions related to same-sex marriage and desire, it and related arguments can be seen as connected to the position she puts forward there. Coakley avers that the current scandals are beset by a series of "cultural contradictions," in which celibacy is at the same time widely regarded as "repressive" and forcibly enjoined on some; in which celibacy and marriage are seen as opposites, and in which a fixation on same-sex desire combines with a disregard for the evident disorders among "heterosexuals."[37] From Coakley's perspective, these contradictions can only be resolved through a renewed theology of desire. Rehabilitating Freud, whom she thinks is wrongly associated with the view that

---

[34]Coakley, *God, Sexuality and the Self*, 127–32, 277–95; Coakley, *The New Asceticism*, 48–53.
[35]Coakley, *God, Sexuality and the Self*, 159, 160 (emphasis original), 161.
[36]Coakley, *God, Sexuality and the Self*, 167–8.
[37]Coakely, *The New Asceticism*, 34–9. The quotation marks are Coakley's.

any attempt to modify sexual desire is repressive, and connecting him to the older tradition of ascetic Christian Platonism, she sets forth a vision in which both the celibate–married and heterosexual–homosexual binaries are undermined via prayer practices. As ascetic prayer aims at the purifying transformation of desire, all who submit to its discipline are subject to the Spirit's leading toward greater faithfulness to God and others. That submission, which "re-channels" *eros* toward *agape* and defies the modern dualism that pits repression against libertinism, is the starting place for celibate and married, gay and straight. When this argument is combined with her pneumatological-sociological writings, we have another picture of the Spirit expanding and changing the church (including its institutions) as it draws in those formerly excluded, transforming them, too, in the process.

The picture that emerges from Rogers's and Coakley's pneumatological writings is that of the Spirit sanctifying individuals and communities, which sanctification leads in some cases to changes within church institutions. This picture partakes of the standard contemporary pneumatological-sociological picture insofar as it strongly connects the Spirit with individuals and communities and hesitates to name institutions as an arena for participation in the Spirit. At the same time, Rogers and Coakley do at least open the possibility that participation in the Spirit can lead to institutional reform. In Rogers's own writings, he stresses the sanctifying potential for same-sex couples when the church opens the sacrament of marriage to them. Although the accent is still communal and familial, the implication is that the church cooperates with the Spirit when it changes its policies to better support the work of holiness. This outlook becomes explicit in Rogers's coauthored article, where the church's affirmation of love via the extension of marriage to same-sex couples is figured as a mode of participation in the Spirit. Although Rogers's writings do not explore institutional matters related, for instance, to the mechanisms of policy change or other organizational reforms necessary to support same-sex couples, he does point in the direction of institutional reform as a fruit of participation in the Spirit.

Coakley's nuanced sociology of ecclesial organizations offers additional specificity as to how Spirit-led sanctification might result in institutional reform. In her account, pneumatically inclined individuals and communities can influence church institutions from various distances. Sometimes the influence comes from solitary mystics or independent communities, but sometimes it comes from the inspiration of individuals and communities within institutions. Coakley's recognition that communities can exist within institutions or, in Troeltschian terms, that sects may exist within churches, is a significant step beyond the standard picture's sociological dualism. Her concept of the "mixed-type" in particular highlights relations between different kinds of organizations, and construes these relations as conduits of institutional transformation. This concept will be useful to keep in mind in the next section, which describes the reforming impact of women's movements within some denominational institutions. But it will not be sufficient to categorize only the movements as "mixed-type," but also the institutions themselves. In other words, the lines between institution and movement are often organizationally blurry, as the movements proceeded in part by reorganizing the institutions, for instance, by starting new denominational ministries. The history, we will see, calls for a more relational understanding of organizing and organizations than that provided by either Rogers or Coakley.

The Sanctifying Spirit and Institutional Reform: The Case of North American Mennonite Women

This section narrates how North American Mennonite women organized over a period of one hundred years, turning their subordinate care work into organizational power that resulted in the reformation of Mennonite denominational institutions, so that there are now women at nearly every level of denominational and congregational leadership.[38] This history contributes in multiple ways to the development of a relational picture in which institutional reform is a potential mode of participation in the sanctifying Spirit. First, it corroborates the basic idea that meaningful change can result

---

[38] As of 2024 a woman had not served as chief executive of any of the denominations discussed below. Women had headed denominational ministries, regional conferences, and congregations, and had served as denominational moderators at various points.

from movements operating mostly within institutions. Yet in doing so it also complicates the sociological division between movements or communities and institutions. After telling the history, I suggest that the concept of an organizational field better captures what is going on in the history. This concept enables denominational institutions, for example, to be conceived of as constituted by various dynamic organizational structures rather than simply opposed as "stable institutions" to upstart movements and communities. As some of the women involved in this history explicitly claimed inspiration from the Holy Spirit in their reform efforts, their story also expands our view of how Spirit sanctification can encourage institutional progress toward gender justice. Participation in the reformation of an organizational field can, in some circumstances, be figured as participation in the sanctifying Spirit.

A brief overview of North American Mennonite institutions will help the reader follow the story. Mennonites and their Anabaptist ancestors are usually regarded as one of the classic "sect-type" traditions, but in North America as elsewhere they have created a variety of denominational institutions since the nineteenth century. North American Mennonites who are descended from European Anabaptist communities tend to identify either as "Swiss-German" or as "Russian."[39] Due to the differences in their historic experiences and migration patterns, these two groups of Mennonites have different theological emphases and initially organized into two main bodies: the (Old) Mennonite Church (MC), made up largely of Swiss-German Mennonites, and the General Conference Mennonite Church (GC), made up largely of Russian Mennonites.[40] Increasing collaboration over the twentieth century eventually led to the composition of a shared confession of faith and an institutional

---

[39] This paragraph and much of the rest of this section are adapted from Jamie Pitts, "Mother Eberly's Coin: Care Ethics, Democratic Politics, and North American Mennonite Women's Movements," in *Care Ethics, Religion, and Spiritual Traditions*, eds. Maurice Hamington and Maureen Sander-Staudt (Leuven: Peeters, 2020), 334–42.

[40] There are many other Mennonite bodies in North America, though most of these continue to restrict women's participation in church ministry. Since my focus is on successful reform movements, I am limiting my discussion to the denominations named in the text. For an overview of North American Mennonite history see Royden Loewen and Steven M. Nolt, *Seeking Places of Peace: Global Mennonite History Series: North America* (Intercourse, PA: Good Books, 2012).

merger. The merger, however, was also the occasion for a division on national lines, and Mennonite Church Canada (MC Canada) and Mennonite Church USA (MC USA) were born in 2002. In what follows I tell and interpret some of the story of women's movements in the MC, the GC, and their successor denominations, to gain a clearer picture of the organizational dynamics of ecclesial reform. I tell this story in three overlapping stages, reflecting the development of women's organizing activities from domestic and congregational caring (stage 1) to service and mission organizations (stage 2) to social activism and academia (stage 3).

Stage 1: Domestic and Congregational Caring

Veronica Ulrich Eberly and her six children migrated in 1727 from the Palatinate area in the German Rhineland to Pennsylvania. Born in Switzerland in 1685, Eberly and her husband Heinrich planned a new life for their family free from the persecution that they experienced as Mennonites in Switzerland and southwest Germany. But after changing ships in Rotterdam, Heinrich claimed he needed to go to shore for something. He never returned. Mother Eberly, as she came to be known, was left to tend to her family during the Atlantic crossing and later in Lancaster County, Pennsylvania.

Mother Eberly's son Jacob, married and dedicated to farming his mother's land, occasionally visited the village of Lancaster for supplies. One day Mother Eberly drew from her few funds and gave Jacob a small coin to purchase molasses for her at the village store. He took the coin but used it instead to purchase a cowbell, which he "rang ... exuberantly as he approached home." His mother, though, "was so disappointed that she wept bitterly."[41]

Mother Eberly's story illustrates some persistent features of Mennonite women's experiences in North America. Mother Eberly was a migrant, a landowner and head of her household, and a woman whose goods and desires were vulnerable to the whims of men. Migration has defined Mennonite life in North America for generations, and Mother Eberly was, in the early eighteenth century,

---

[41]Elaine Sommers Rich, *Mennonite Women: A Story of God's Faithfulness, 1683–1983* (Scottdale, PA: Herald, 1983), 30–1.

among the first waves of Swiss-German migrants. A later wave of Mennonite migration, this time from the Russian Empire after the Second World War, would see an entire generation of women who, like Mother Eberly, migrated without husbands, fathers, or other adult men, as many had been killed in Stalin's gulags or during the war.[42] These women were responsible for the survival of their families as they crossed the ocean and created homesteads in difficult conditions. Their responsibility, in turn, gave them significant authority in day-to-day decision-making and in the education of their children, including in spiritual education.

Historian Marlene Epp observes that this pattern—in which Mennonite women take religious leadership in migrant communities that are dependent on families for social reproduction—repeated in communities with or without men, including in late-twentieth-century Canada among refugees from Central America and Southeast Asia.[43] However, she contends, the centrality of family in North American Mennonite history has been both empowering and limiting for women.[44] Mennonite families, whether in rural villages or urban neighborhoods, have typically been patriarchal, resulting in gendered divisions of labor and the susceptibility of women's authority to male prerogative. Elaine Sommers Rich further describes how a historic Mennonite ideal of marriage as a partnership between equals with different roles developed into a gendered separation of spheres during the early twentieth century, as pressures of urban assimilation and fundamentalist theology took hold.[45]

---

[42]Marlene Epp, *Women without Men: Mennonite Refugees of the Second World War* (Toronto: University of Toronto Press, 2000).
[43]Marlene Epp, *Mennonite Women in Canada: A History* (Winnipeg: University of Manitoba Press, 2008), 172–3.
[44]Epp, *Mennonite Women in Canada*, 61–2, 174.
[45]Rich, *Mennonite Women*, 41, 43. This conception of marriage can be seen as an effect of rural life, in which "the Mennonite family, either nuclear or extended, was a central institution for organizing community life and transmitting beliefs. A family functioned as an economic unit, and was the building block for village and settlement formation" (Epp, *Mennonite Women in Canada*, 61). It also has roots in the Anabaptist theological conviction that marriage is a partnership between two committed disciples of Christ. See C. Arnold Snyder, *Anabaptist History and Theology: An Introduction* (Kitchener, ON: Pandora, 1995), 275–98.

If the authority Mennonite women have gained in and through the home should accordingly be viewed with some ambivalence, the nature and shape of that authority should not be overlooked either for its immediate or later contributions to the story of women's movements. Rich suggests that a Mennonite women's "heritage" has been passed down from the early homesteading experience, a heritage of working with one's hands, offering hospitality, frugality, and community service.[46] The next section will show how women leveraged that heritage to create a variety of service organizations in the late nineteenth and early twentieth centuries, as well as to take leading roles in the burgeoning Mennonite missionary movement. At this point it is sufficient to note some of the concrete forms taken by that heritage, especially as they shaped Mennonite congregational life.

For Mennonite women on rural homesteads, working with one's hands has involved, among other activities, sewing, quilting, gardening, cooking, and canning, and of course bearing and raising children.[47] By taking on—and being made to take on—these basic responsibilities of care, Mennonite women have sustained and reproduced Mennonite life. Though twentieth-century sociological transformations would lead many Mennonite women and their families off farms and into cities, the importance of domestic handiwork continues to be affirmed, for instance, by popular cookbooks written by and for Mennonite women.[48] Mennonite women past and present have, moreover, taken central roles in their congregations through their work of cooking and sewing for events and charity auctions.

Mennonite women's hospitality and home management have taken a variety of notable forms. Elaine Sommers Rich tells the story of two Pennsylvania women who harbored Native Americans fleeing settler violence in 1767.[49] Another woman settled tensions

---

[46]Rich, *Mennonite Women*, 35.
[47]Rich, *Mennonite Women*, 77.
[48]Doris Janzen Longacre, *More-with-Less Cookbook*, 2d ed. (Scottdale, PA: Herald, 2003); Lovella Shellenberg et al., *Mennonite Girls Can Cook* (Harrisonburg, VA: Herald, 2011).
[49]Rich, *Mennonite Women*, 32.

between her nonresistant husband and the soldiers who showed up unannounced at their farm by inviting the men to dinner.[50] In the late nineteenth and early twentieth centuries, Susan Ressler Good Hostetler wrote a regular column in the Mennonite press advising women on housekeeping; one column counseled ministers' wives on gentle ways of guiding their husbands' theology.[51] The related impulse and effort to foster social connections among rural homesteads led not only to the women's organizations described below, but in several cases to the establishment of congregations.[52] Congregations were also birthed out of some urban boarding homes for Mennonite girls working as domestic servants, homes that were largely led by women.[53]

The patriarchal character of most Mennonite congregations meant that, even if women founded and sustained them, they typically did not have formal roles in congregational decision-making or leadership until the mid-to-late twentieth century.[54] As Epp details with respect to Canadian congregations, women's quest for participation in decision-making processes was long and often arduous.[55] Women's formal participation only became widespread in the 1960s, partially in response to sociological

---

[50] Rich, *Mennonite Women*, 34–5.
[51] Rich, *Mennonite Women*, 47–8.
[52] Rich, *Mennonite Women*, 180.
[53] Epp, *Mennonite Women in Canada*, 45–8.
[54] It is, again, important to note that I am limiting my discussion to those Mennonites that would later form Mennonite Church Canada and Mennonite Church USA. Many conservative Mennonite congregations and conferences do not recognize women pastors. It is also worth noting that by focusing on women's movements within Mennonite communities, I am not discussing women who left those communities altogether. Their lives, including their relations to Mennonite women's movements and their own organizing efforts beyond the church, are an important topic for further study. For related studies of queer Mennonites, some of whom left the church at least for a time, see J. Alicia Dueck, *Negotiating Sexual Identities: Lesbian, Gay, and Queer Perspectives on Being Mennonite* (Berlin: Lit, 2012); Rachel Waltner Goossen, "'Repent of the Sins of Homophobia': The Rise of Queer Mennonite Leaders," *Nova Religio* 24, no. 3 (2021): 68–95.
[55] Epp, *Mennonite Women in Canada*, 132–44.

changes in North American culture toward more horizontal and inclusive organizational structures, and toward the involvement of women in the waged labor force. When women began financially supporting the church out of their own incomes, it became difficult to justify excluding them from decision-making.[56] Women, moreover, had gained leadership experience in women's and missionary organizations, and were prepared to agitate for their own inclusion.

Epp and Anita Hooley Yoder further describe the influence, in both Canada and the United States, of feminism on these debates. Women, and some men, began to contest the patriarchal character of the church itself, arguing on biblical and theological grounds for gender egalitarianism.[57] The goals of this contest were not only the right to participate in congregation-wide votes and committees, but also to serve in official pastoral roles. Explicitly feminist theological arguments to this end overlapped with personal testimonies from women who felt they had been called by God to serve as pastors. In Epp's view, this attempt to root women's access to pastoral ministry in divine vocation enabled women to advance toward formal equality with men while perpetuating the image of women as submissive and obedient.[58] Furthermore, Epp notes that the opening of ordination to women at the end of the 1970s coincided with the devaluation of ordination, as theologians argued for a more horizontal conception of church leadership.[59]

---

[56]Epp, *Mennonite Women in Canada*, 141.
[57]Epp, *Mennonite Women in Canada*, 123; Anita Hooley Yoder, *Circles of Sisterhood: A History of Mission, Service, and Fellowship in Mennonite Women's Organizations* (Harrisonburg, VA: Herald, 2017), 57–70. See also Lois Y. Barrett and Dorothy Nickel Friesen, eds., *Proclaiming the Good News: Mennonite Women's Voices, 1972–2006* (Elkhart, IN: Institute of Mennonite Studies, 2023).
[58]Epp, *Mennonite Women in Canada*, 127.
[59]Epp, *Mennonite Women in Canada*, 123–4.

Stage 2: Women's Service Organizations and Mission Activity

A significant strand in the argument for women's participation in congregational decision-making and leadership drew on women's experience in mission and service organizations. The nineteenth century has been called the "Great Century" of Protestant mission, and during this period "progressive" North American Mennonites vigorously participated in a variety of missionary activities.[60] Here "mission" meant not only issuing evangelistic calls to conversion to Christian faith, but also attempts to address hunger, poverty, illiteracy, and other modern social issues. Both major Mennonite denominations created mission agencies in the mid-to-late nineteenth century, and in 1920 these and related denominations formed Mennonite Central Committee to focus on relief, development, and refugee resettlement. Mennonite women, shut out at this point from official leadership, founded their own organizations to promote mission and meet concrete needs.

Many of these organizations began as "sewing circles," groups of women meeting regularly to sew bedsheets and clothing, make quilts, can food, and otherwise prepare materials for people in need. Some of these materials were for local needs—a family whose house burned down, a nearby community destroyed by natural disaster—and some were for Mennonite mission projects in North America and abroad. In Gladys Goering's terms, for many women, participating in such activities was an extension of their ordinary, domestic care work—they were "just being neighborly."[61] The circles also served the women's own social and spiritual needs, as described by Anita Hooley Yoder: "In their organizations, women came together to work, to meet the needs of others, often with amazing dedication. But they also came together to work—to meet their own needs of fellowship and community."[62]

---

[60]By "progressive" I mean Mennonites who saw engagement with other communities and the "modern" world as a positive good, in distinction from "traditionalist" Mennonites who sought relative isolation in rural settings. These terms are employed throughout Loewen and Nolt, *Seeking Places of Peace*.
[61]Gladys Goering, *Women in Search of Mission: A History of the General Conference Mennonite Women's Organizations* (Newton, KS: Faith and Life, 1980), 23.
[62]Yoder, *Circles of Sisterhood*, 28.

The developing circles often collaborated, and eventually organizations emerged in each denomination to coordinate their work. These organizations raised considerable funds for their activities and were able to hire staff, support missionaries, and issue publications. As such, they were crucial institutions for generating solidarity and training women for organizational leadership.[63] Writing about (Old) Mennonite Church sewing circles, Sharon Klingelsmith suggests that, while sewing and related activities were "the foundation upon which the work could be built," ultimately the circles' leaders viewed them as "a stepping stone to more significant work."[64] That work was full participation in their churches' mission.[65]

Men, and some conservative women, resisted the women's organizations. The most extreme act of resistance occurred during the 1920s, when the MC mission board unilaterally dissolved the Woman's Missionary Society (WMS) and created new leadership and funding structures for the denomination's sewing circles.[66] Later organizational struggles have included the challenge of incorporating Black, Latina, and Indigenous women as participants and leaders;[67] criticisms from feminists that the organizations were too conservative;[68] and a general decline in participation after the 1970s.[69]

A paradoxical contribution to the organizations' decline was their own success. Although feminist critique of patriarchal church structures stood in some tension with the traditional women's organizations, as will be explored below, the combination of both

---

[63] Gloria Neufeld Redekop, *The Work of Their Hands: Mennonite Women's Societies in Canada* (Waterloo, ON: Canadian Corporation for Studies in Religion, 1996), 61; Yoder, *Circles of Sisterhood*, 42, 58, 86.

[64] Sharon Klinglesmith, "Women in the Mennonite Church, 1900–1930," *Mennonite Quarterly Review* 54, no. 3 (1980): 189.

[65] Cf. Goering, *Women in Search of Mission*, 105, writing on the GC women's organizations: "Not all groups sewed. The term 'our mission and sewing societies' in the first year indicated a difference of approach."

[66] Klingelsmith, "Women in the Mennonite Church," 199–201; Rich, *Mennonite Women*, 201.

[67] Felipe Hinojosa, *Latino Mennonites: Civil Rights, Faith, and Evangelical Culture* (Baltimore: Johns Hopkins University Press, 2014), 149–73.

[68] Yoder, *Circles of Sisterhood*, 90–8.

[69] Redekop, *The Work of Their Hands*, 103–10; Yoder, *Circles of Sisterhood*, 143–55.

resulted in the opening of denominational boards and committees to women's participation.[70] In many cases, the first women to serve in the church-wide structures were in fact the leaders of the women's organizations.[71]

Anita Hooley Yoder suggests that, although the women's organizations have declined, they remain important sources of social and especially spiritual connection for their members.[72] The spiritual character of the organizations is also highlighted by Gloria Neufeld Redekop, who contends that the Canadian organizations historically "functioned as a parallel church for Mennonite women."[73] As evidence, Redekop points to the structural similarities between typical Mennonite worship services and the schedules of the conferences and other gatherings hosted by the women's organizations. Yet in doing so women were not merely imitating services designed by men; they were contesting the normative shape of Mennonite worship—Redekop reports that one woman wrote publicly that the women's gatherings were more likely to model the New Testament pattern for worship than were male-led congregations.[74] Similarly, Felipe Hinojosa tells the story of how two women, Gracie Torres and Seferina de León, introduced music influenced by the Civil Rights Movement and popular styles from South Texas into Latina Mennonite conferences during the 1970s. This music was eventually taken up by many Latino Mennonite churches, becoming an identity marker for Latinos within the white-dominated church.[75]

Even as priorities have shifted during the past several decades of decline, both Redekop and Yoder argue that mission and service remain important features of Mennonite women's organizations.[76] Yet Mennonite women's understanding of mission began to change in the 1970s, when it became increasingly common to criticize traditional mission work as culturally imperialistic.[77] Prior to that

---

[70] Epp, *Mennonite Women in Canada*, 169.
[71] Yoder, *Circles of Sisterhood*, 119–22.
[72] Yoder, *Circles of Sisterhood*, 135–42.
[73] Redekop, *The Work of Their Hands*, 73, 98–9; Epp, *Mennonite Women in Canada*, 161.
[74] Redekop, *The Work of Their Hands*, 73.
[75] Hinojosa, *Latino Mennonites*, 168–71.
[76] Redekop, *The Work of Their Hands*, 129; Yoder, *Circles of Sisterhood*, 174, 207.
[77] Yoder, *Circles of Sisterhood*, 138.

decade, it was common for women's organizations to support many women missionaries. Since the beginning of the mission movement in the nineteenth century, becoming a missionary was "a way in which [women] could effectively function as religious leaders but far away from the watchful eye of church authorities."[78] Missionary women were some of the first women to be ordained and to preach in North American congregations.[79] Male leaders gave women some leeway in missionary roles because they saw traditional feminine virtues, such as nurture and self-denial, as beneficial on the mission field.[80] Once again, women found ways to leverage their identification with care work into space for the development of their interests and capacities.[81] It therefore came as a surprise when, in the late 1970s, they began to find that their sponsoring women's organizations were losing interest in their work.[82]

Stage 3: The turn to social activism and academia

As Anita Hooley Yoder points out, it is possible to see the Mennonite women's organizations as shifting their focus from traditional mission and service work to issues they had previously neglected, such as domestic violence and sexual abuse.[83] When the women's organizations began addressing those issues in the 1980s, they were catching up to feminists who had been busy writing and organizing around them for over a decade.

The primary institutional vehicle for Mennonite feminists was the Committee on Women's Concerns, formed in 1973 under the

---

[78]Epp, *Mennonite Women in Canada*, 145. For broader patterns, see Dana L. Robert, *American Women in Mission: A Social History of Their Thought and Practice* (Macon, GA: Mercer University Press, 1996).
[79]Epp, *Mennonite Women in Canada*, 147–8.
[80]Epp, *Mennonite Women in Canada*, 149–50.
[81]Although I do not expand on the significance of this point further here, it is the main theme of Pitts, "Mother Eberly's Coin." Care and care ethics could be related to the present argument by exploring the image of the Spirit as Paraclete in John 15–16. "Paraclete" can be translated as "Advocate" (NRSV, NIV), "Helper" (NASB, NKJV), or "Comforter" (KJV).
[82]Yoder, *Circles of Sisterhood*, 138.
[83]Yoder, *Circles of Sisterhood*, 138–9.

auspices of Mennonite Central Committee's Peace Section. In Yoder's analysis, the Committee served needs that were not being met by the traditional women's organizations.[84] A major part of the Committee's work was the publication of a *Report*, which for over thirty-one years featured regular articles criticizing the exclusion of rape, child abuse, domestic violence, and related topics from typical Mennonite peace theology. The articles, however, were not merely critical. Carol Penner describes how *Report* authors developed a distinctive interpretation of Jesus based on their understanding of their Anabaptist tradition, their personal stories, and their feminist commitments.[85] In place of the Jesus of male Mennonite theology—a Jesus who emphasized redemptive suffering and nonresistance—this Jesus was dedicated to radical equality and nonviolent resistance to patriarchy and other forms of oppression. In early issues of the Report, authors also advanced a feminist pneumatology, in which the pouring out of the Spirit onto both "sons and daughters" (Acts 2:17) and the distribution of the Spirit's gifts to all members of the church were taken as liberating women from role restrictions.[86] In summary, "writers asked vital questions and wrestled with God. They had suggestions about how followers of Jesus"—and those who dwell in the Spirit—"could work for change in church and society."[87]

This shift to consider how the historic Anabaptist-Mennonite peace witness might extend beyond the church to counter violence in "society" participates in a wider movement among Mennonites after the Second World War. As the story is usually told, many North American Mennonite men, after being mocked and humiliated by their fellow citizens for refusing military service, felt a sense of

---

[84]Yoder, *Circles of Sisterhood*, 67–8.
[85]Carol Penner, "Jesus and the Stories of Our Lives," in *Liberating the Politics of Jesus: Renewing Peace Theology through the Wisdom of Women*, eds. Elizabeth Soto Albrecht and Darryl W. Stephens (London: T&T Clark, 2020), 38–47.
[86]Peace Section Task Force on Women in Church and Society, "Current Developments," *Report* 1 (August 1973): 4–5; Peace Section Task Force on Women in Church and Society, "Restoring Wholeness," *Report* 3 (December 1973): 1; Miriam L. Weaver, "The Status of Widows in the Church," *Report* 4 (February 1974): 6.
[87]Penner, "Jesus and the Stories of Our Lives," 35.

restlessness and responsibility to get involved in social change.[88] Since the Second World War was quickly followed by the Cold War arms race, the Civil Rights Movement, and the Vietnam War, Mennonite men had plenty of opportunities for nonviolent activism in the coming decades. However, as historian Rachel Waltner Goossen has detailed, many Mennonite women also lived and worked in alternative service camps during the war, experienced abuse from their militaristic neighbors, and were motivated by their experience to engage in social service and peace activism after the war.[89]

Likewise, the story of Mennonite peace theology typically tracks the postwar shift from traditional theologies of nonresistance toward theological justifications of active nonviolence—all as written by men. The publications of the women's organizations and the Committee on Women's Concerns represent an alternative tradition, one focused on the concrete needs of women, children, and communities around the world. This tradition is perhaps most clearly seen in the ongoing series of Women Doing Theology (WDT) conferences, which began in 1992. Carol Penner describes how these conferences have integrated worship, academic and ordinary women's theological reflection, and creative dialogue among an increasingly diverse set of participants.[90] Penner suggests that this format is rooted in Mennonite women's feminist reclamation of their Anabaptist heritage, yet shares significant features with the Catholic Women-Church gatherings that began in the early 1990s.[91] This interpretation strikingly places the WDT conferences in continuity with earlier gatherings of Mennonite women's organizations which,

---

[88]Royden Loewen, "Privilege, Right, and Responsibility: Peace and the North American Mennonites," in *From Suffering to Solidarity: The Historical Seeds of Mennonite Interreligious, Interethnic, and International Peacebuilding*, ed. Andrew P. Klager (Eugene, OR: Wipf and Stock, 2015), 66–9.
[89]Rachel Waltner Goossen, *Women against the Good War: Conscientious Objection and Gender on the American Home Front, 1941–1947* (Chapel Hill, NC: University of North Carolina Press, 1997).
[90]Carol Penner, "Mennonite Women Doing Theology: A Methodological Reflection on Twenty-Five Years of Conferences," in *Recovering from the Anabaptist Vision: New Essays in Anabaptist Identity and Theological Method*, eds. Laura Schmidt Roberts, Paul Martens, and Myron Penner (London: T&T Clark, 2020), 59–64.
[91]Penner, "Mennonite Women Doing Theology," 64–75.

as discussed above, have been viewed as creating a parallel church structure.

The presence of women academics at the WDT conferences reflects the growing number of Mennonite women who have obtained advanced theological degrees and academic positions since the 1980s. Mennonite women have made significant contributions to a variety of theological disciplines, including biblical studies, church history, ethics, practical and pastoral theology, and systematic theology. The numerous academic publications by Mennonite women include studies of power in communal biblical interpretation;[92] suffering, forgiveness, and Christ's death on the cross in light of violence against women;[93] and the central role of women in Anabaptist-Mennonite history.[94] After the public exposure of the most famous twentieth-century Mennonite peace theologian, John Howard Yoder, as a serial sexual abuser,[95] Mennonite women theologians have engaged in a full-scale reevaluation of what it means to follow Jesus.[96]

A full-scale evaluation of life in the Spirit by Mennonite women has yet to appear, though this fact perhaps follows the historic tendency in Mennonite thought to focus on Jesus over the Spirit.[97]

---

[92] Lydia Neufeld Harder, *Obedience, Suspicion, and the Gospel of Mark: A Mennonite-Feminist Exploration of Biblical Authority* (Waterloo, ON: Canadian Corporation for Studies of Religion, 1998); Lydia Neufeld Harder, *The Challenge Is in the Naming: A Theological Journey* (Winnipeg: Canadian Mennonite University Press, 2018). These and the following citations are intended to be indicative, not exhaustive.

[93] Gayle Gerber Koontz, "Seventy Times Seven: Abuse and the Frustratingly Extravagant Call to Forgive," *Mennonite Quarterly Review* 89, no. 1 (January 2015): 129–52; Susanne Guenther Loewen, "Can the Cross Be 'Good News' for Women? Peace Theology and the Suffering of Women," *Anabaptist Witness* 3, no. 2 (December 2016): 109–21.

[94] C. Arnold Snyder and Linda A. Huebert Hecht, eds., *Profiles of Anabaptist Women: Sixteenth-century Reforming Pioneers* (Waterloo, ON: Canadian Corporation for Studies in Religion, 1996); Kimberly D. Schmidt, Diane Zimmerman Umble, and Steven D. Reschley, eds., *Strangers at Home: Amish and Mennonite Women in History* (Baltimore: Johns Hopkins University Press, 2002).

[95] See discussion and references at the beginning of this chapter.

[96] Elizabeth Soto Albrecht and Darryl W. Stephens, eds., *Liberating the Politics of Jesus: Renewing Peace Theology through the Wisdom of Women* (London: T&T Clark, 2020).

[97] Jamie Pitts, "Pneumatology," in *T&T Clark Handbook of Anabaptist Theology*, ed. Brian Brewer (London: T&T Clark, 2020), 373–86.

But there are promising signs of an emerging Mennonite feminist pneumatology that can be noted. One sign comes from historians studying early Anabaptist women prophets. These prophets claimed the Holy Spirit's inspiration to announce God's judgment against the oppression of the poor.[98] Another sign comes from feminist biblical scholars who identify the Spirit's empowerment of women "to come to the Bible and to the church institution with suspicion, confident that the Spirit has authorized their effort to detect oppressive ideology."[99] A third sign comes from the systematic theologian Nancy Bedford who, reflecting on both pneumatic early Anabaptist women and trinitarian hermeneutics, portrays the Spirit as enabling contextually appropriate discipleship to challenge "common sense about gender or race or unjust societal structures."[100]

Together these signs point to a picture of the Spirit sanctifying by giving life to confrontations with oppressive forces of death. Spirit-inspired disciples defend the sacredness of those who have been subjugated by church institutions and other social structures. The history of North American Mennonite women's movements however cautions against interpreting this picture as simply anti-institutional. In other words, the picture arose within a context defined, at least in part, by a contest over institutional power. Women organized within their denominational institutions, not simply to "fit in" to predetermined structures but rather to contribute their own creative agency to the remaking of those structures so that they might be more life-giving for women. In short, they reorganized the institutions to broaden those institutions' capacities to support solidarity and well-being for all members. The example of North

---

[98]Lois Y. Barrett, "Ursula Jost and Barbara Rebstock," in *Profiles of Anabaptist Women: Sixteenth-century Reforming Pioneers*, eds. C. Arnold Snyder and Linda A. Huebert Hecht (Waterloo, ON: Canadian Corporation for Studies in Religion, 1996), 277; Lois Y. Barrett, "Wreath of Glory: Ursula Jost's Prophetic Visions in the Context of Reformation and Revolt in Southwestern Germany, 1524–1530" (PhD dissertation, the Union Institute, 1992); Christina Moss, "An Examination of the Visions of Ursula Jost in the Context of Early Anabaptism and Late Medieval Christianity" (MA thesis, University of Waterloo, 2013); Christina Moss, " 'Your Sons and Daughters Shall Prophecy': Visions, Apocalypticism, and Gender in Strasbourg, 1522–1539" (PhD dissertation, University of Waterloo, 2019).
[99]Harder, *Obedience, Suspicion, and the Gospel of Mark*, 73.
[100]Nancy Bedford, "A Narrow Gate? Proceeding along the Way of Jesus by the Spirit," *Mennonite Quarterly Review* 92 (October 2018): 495.

American Mennonite women suggests that the Spirit who sanctifies by raising up critics of institutions can use their judgments, suspicions, and challenges to stir up institutional reform.

This picture both affirms and adds complexity to the picture drawn from Rogers's and Coakley's work.[101] On the one hand, it affirms the possibility of ecclesial reform as a sociological consequence of participation in Spirit sanctification. On the other hand, it more clearly exhibits church institutions as an object of reformation and is more transparent about the role of critique and contestation in bringing about reform. The picture that emerges from North American Mennonite women's history and pneumatology also pushes Coakley's sociological division between communities and institutions beyond "mixed-types" toward a more relational conception of organizations. In this conception, an organization such as an institution is not a set-apart, mostly static entity resisting disturbance from internal and external communities, but rather a dynamically structured field composed of relations between various organizational structures. The women discussed here did not simply start new communities within Mennonite institutions; they created new institutional structures that in some ways supported and in other ways conflicted with other institutional structures. The Mennonite Church denomination, when considered as an institution, was constituted by both patriarchal governance structures and women's organizations. The institution encompassed both kinds of structures and was defined by relations between those structures. Those relations were, to be sure, highly unequal, as evidenced by the ability of the MC mission board to shut down the WMS in the 1920s. But just because the latter was marginalized and eventually excluded does not mean it was not part of the institution. The WMS was created as a denominational organization. Its creation changed its denominational institution as did the conflicts surrounding it. Similar comments could be made about many other Mennonite women's organizations, such as the Committee on Women's Concerns that was formed within Mennonite Central Committee. These were reforming agencies within existing institutions, not extra-institutional challengers.

---

[101] As stated in Chapter 1, I regard the history discussed in this section as a normative source within my tradition. I am using the history both to flesh out the picture drawn from (other) theological sources and to modify that picture.

Although this point may seem trivial, it shifts the pneumatological-sociological picture of the sanctifying Spirit in important ways. Conceiving of institutions as organizational fields leads away from an overly rigid and isolated image of institutions, in which the latter can only be challenged from without or, as in Coakley's mixed-type, from purportedly noninstitutional communities nested within institutions. Reorganizing even some of the relations that constitute the field can have systemic effects, as did the creation of women's organizations within Mennonite denominational institutions. Institutional reform can be pursued from within. Reform may involve conflict that exacerbates an institution's internal tensions or contradictions. Conflict seems likely when reform is aimed at correcting historic injustices, such as the baseless exclusion of some from full participation in institutional leadership.

Acknowledging that reform involves conflict poses a theological problem—what does it mean to claim struggles for reform as potential means of participation in the Spirit? The previous chapter identified harmony, not conflict, as the hovering Spirit's goal for creation. Nevertheless, in conditions marked by sin some sort of conflict seems to be an inevitable corollary of the pursuit of harmony. If sin disorganizes creation, then sanctification requires a difficult reorganization. Coakley reminds us that mystics often speak of their sanctifying encounters with the Spirit in terms of "purgation." Perhaps engaging in processes of institutional reformation for the sake of life-giving solidarity requires a similar vocabulary. Participation in the sanctifying Spirit can spark the challenging work of changing institutions. This work may include the creation of new, sometimes unwelcome institutional structures as well as criticism of extant structures.

From Pessimism to Progress?

The pneumatological-sociological picture of Spirit sanctification derived from Rogers, Coakley, and North American Mennonite women's history and theology presumes the possibility of naming the Spirit in connection to concrete changes inside and outside of the church. The picture entails a "progressive" theology and practice in which participation in the sanctifying Spirit increasingly opens institutions to include those who were formerly excluded. As just discussed, this progress is likely to involve a difficult, conflictual process of institutional reorganization. Not all theologians have been satisfied with this progressive approach. Here I focus on two critics coming from quite different ideological perspectives, Linn Tonstad and Ephraim Radner.

Tonstad is a queer theologian who sees "inclusion" as complicit with the reproduction of the church and its inherent logic of exclusion. Reforming the church to include some previously excluded class of persons is always, she argues, predicated on the continuing exclusion of some other class of persons.[102] Successful reforms may, for example, allow cis-women to assume positions of leadership, but may still exclude transwomen from the same; or reforms may include same-sex couples in Christian marriage and ministry, yet see promiscuous queer persons as beyond the pale.[103] In brief, inclusion-oriented reforms preserve a normative order that, even when modified, continues to identify some as worthy of inclusion and some as worthy of exclusion. Tonstad accordingly challenges Coakley and others who see the Spirit as the divine agent fomenting change in the church by incorporating the excluded into Christ's body.[104] The logic of incorporation, according to Tonstad, is a "penetrative" heterosexual logic, in which the church is figured as a receptive female womb awaiting insemination. If the pneumatologically inseminated church gives birth to a body that is slightly different from that of previous generations, the "new" body carries the oppressive, norming DNA of the old. Instead of seeking more for the Spirit to do and include, Tonstad says we should ask less of the Spirit and thereby cease—or even "abort"—ecclesial reproduction.[105] In place of a reproductive, incorporative

---

[102]Linn Marie Tonstad, *God and Difference* (New York: Routledge, 2016), 254–86. The specific examples in this sentence are mine. Tonstad discusses the conflict between the campaign for gay marriage and "those indecent queers who seek neither reproduction nor integration" (256). Tonstad takes the language of "indecency" and "decency" from Marcella Althaus Reid, *Indecent Theology: Theological Perversions in Sex, Gender, and Politics* (New York: Routledge, 2000).

[103]Tonstad, *God and Difference*, 254–7.

[104]On Coakley, see Tonstad, *God and Difference*, 98–132. Tonstad also gives critical attention to Jürgen Moltmann, Wolfhart Pannenberg, Kathryn Tanner, and Graham Ward.

[105]Tonstad, *God and Difference*, 269.

pneumatology, Tonstad offers the image of the Spirit alongside different bodies, pleasuring them without trying to penetrate and insert them into Christ's body.[106] With reproduction foreclosed and no future on the horizon, the world deprived of Christ's body stands at an apocalyptic precipice.

Tonstad's theology presents an ecclesiological vision in which the church "aspire[s] to be a church that chooses abortion over reproduction. For the church signifies its own end: there is neither church nor temple in the new Jerusalem, and the Lamb's presence is its light."[107] In such a prefigurative church-to-be-aborted, the "banquet table" of eucharistic fellowship is opened to all, whose salvation is predicated on God's grace alone and not on their competitive conformity to a "decent" identity—even those identities newly categorized as decent by a reforming, reproductive church.[108] It is the Spirit, moreover, "who sets us free and gives us full access to the banquet that God has prepared for God's people."[109] This "nonreproductive" church demonstrates how "multiple bodies can occupy the same space noncompetitively" rather than being normed by reproductive ecclesial institutions.[110] The Spirit-formed church, on this account, is a motley crew of persons with wildly different identities. Neither the Spirit nor the church exercises pressure on those gathered at God's banquet to cohere in any way.

Although Tonstad does not use the language of "institutions" in *God and Difference*, the assembly of different bodies she envisions as church is difficult to render in terms of formal organization. Even the Spirit is limited to action that takes place horizontally alongside humans in Tonstad's picture, so there can be no sense in which the Spirit inspires the organization of complex institutions at multiple scales for the purpose of building creaturely solidarities. Tonstad positions the church as a negation of the status quo rather than its transformation. She therefore writes that she hopes to "recenter Christianity around a spectral vision of redemption that denies neither fragmentation nor futility, while recognizing the surprising

---

[106]Tonstad, *God and Difference*, 276.
[107]Tonstad, *God and Difference*, 269.
[108]Tonstad, *God and Difference*, 158, 191, 238–42.
[109]Tonstad, *God and Difference*, 235.
[110]Tonstad, *God and Difference*, 240, 257.

goods of existence amid fragility and loss."[111] This vision eschews not only reform but also revolution, issuing in a kind of quietism awaiting apocalyptic intervention.

Similar themes have been voiced by postliberal theologian Ephraim Radner. Radner takes the enduring lack of Christian unity since the Reformation as a sign of the Spirit's absence from the church. Accepting this absence entails giving up on the quixotic quest for ecumenical convergence, and instead pursuing penitential, "antiprogrammatic" Christian practice as an irretrievably fragmented church.[112] What the Spirit does for us, he suggests, is point us to Christ's broken body, thereby disciplining our impulses to change the church and the world. Radner rejects the modern fantasy of "pneumatology" as perpetuated by theologians such as Rogers, Coakley, and Mennonite feminists.[113] By bringing us back to Christ crucified, the Spirit reminds us that faithful witness results in suffering, and not its escape through ameliorative reform—reform that wrongly assumes we know what measures would genuinely promote well-being and lessen suffering. Life in the Spirit is wandering and uncertain, and best takes the form of a "normal" life of discipleship centered on church and heterosexual family.

Radner and Tonstad clearly differ in their sexual politics and assessment of "the normal,"[114] but they share to a significant extent a pessimism about the church as an institutional reality whose unity, however partial, enables it to progressively address injustice. Both employ what Albert Hirschman has termed a "rhetoric of reaction," in which progressive change is opposed because of the ultimate futility of reform.[115] For Tonstad, reform just sets up a new normative order that excludes someone besides those who

---

[111]Tonstad, *God and Difference*, 263.
[112]Ephraim Radner, *The End of the Church: A Pneumatology of Christian Division in the West* (Grand Rapids, MI: Eerdmans, 1998), 352–3. I discuss Radner's project in greater detail in Chapter 1.
[113]Ephraim Radner, *A Profound Ignorance: Modern Pneumatology and Its Anti-Modern Redemption* (Waco, TX: Baylor University Press, 2019).
[114]This difference is registered theologically in Tonstad's focus on the absence of Christ's body after the resurrection and Radner's focus on the presence of Christ's crucified body in and as the church.
[115]Albert O. Hirschman, *The Rhetoric of Reaction: Perversity, Futility, Jeopardy* (Cambridge: Harvard University Press, 1991), 43–80.

have now been included.[116] For Radner, reform purports to know something we Christians cannot know, how to better the world before Christ's return. Better, then, to take refuge in a community that prefigures what we cannot have generally but only hope for eschatologically—the eucharistic body of Christ in which diverse multitudes gather without changing their identities (Tonstad) or, rather, in which a normal, decent identity is accepted (Radner) and the suffering consequences endured. A minimalistic pneumatology underwrites this pessimism, given that the Spirit at most assembles individuals without forming them into a transformative political force (Tonstad) or reminds them of Christ's broken body as a sign of the futility of seeking political change (Radner).

A pneumatological interpretation of the story of North American Mennonite women challenges this pessimism. At the end of the previous section I suggested that a picture of the sanctifying Spirit can plausibly be connected to the efforts of North American Mennonite women to reform their denominational institutions to include them as leaders, address their areas of concern, and promote their well-being. Without downplaying either the practical complexity or the unfinished nature of the reformation, it is not too much to say that North American Mennonite women's reform efforts have been *successful*. Women now serve MC Canada and MC USA as pastors of congregations and executive leaders of regional and national denominational agencies. Women preach and teach openly, including in denominational seminaries. Their preaching and teaching have, to an important extent, shifted core Mennonite doctrinal views on Jesus, discipleship, biblical interpretation, the church, and peace. They have successfully reformed the church and have done so as participants in the Spirit's sanctification of the church. Again, to call this reform "successful" does not signify that it is complete. There are doubtless ways that these denominations

---

[116]Tonstad may object that she is not rejecting reform or an institutional response to heterosexism, but only "a fantasy of the church as a site of access to the truth of one's identity in its positive, achieved form in Christ, an identity that provides a stable site for action and recognition and can decisively be distinguished from other, non-Christian identities" (*God and Difference*, 267). If that is the case, then the language of the church's abortion and the organizationally vague "banquet" image do not do justice to her argument. I join Tonstad in rejecting the fantasy of an exclusive and stable "Christian identity" in Chapter 4, while still portraying ecclesial institutions as relatively stable sites for actions aimed at justice.

continue to require reform to more fully empower women and respond to their concerns. To call this reform "successful" is also not to say that it offers a clear paradigm that can be replicated easily in other institutional settings or by other reforming movements, for instance the movement for queer inclusion in the church. But to deny its success would be to deny the history of progressive transformation of Mennonite institutions by women for their own inclusion and empowerment. That would also be a denial of the possibility that these women's pursuit of institutional change was a means of participation in the Spirit.

Would affirming the picture of North American Mennonite women's participation in the sanctifying Spirit negate the concerns raised by Tonstad and Radner? Not necessarily. Tonstad is right to worry about the viciously reproductive character of (church) institutions. According to Bourdieu, fields—including organizational fields—tend toward reproduction.[117] Habitus formed within a field typically misrecognizes the capital pursued within the field and the field's structure as legitimate and unalterable, rather than as the contingent result of ongoing struggles over power. In other words, the individuals and groups with the most power within a field are likely to see their status as "natural" or beneficent and seek to reproduce conditions conducive to maintaining it. They may not do this intentionally, they may even work to redistribute power, but their best efforts may be hampered by their habitual practices and ways of conceptualizing the field that result from their formation. The same goes for agents occupying other field positions—the general trend of their practices, taken together, is to reproduce the field's structure.

This interpretation suggests that all participants in a field have some responsibility for the field's reproduction. Bourdieu somewhat controversially argues that many attempts to transform fields end up contributing to reproduction since, in many cases, the people

---

[117]Pierre Bourdieu, "Stratégies de reproduction et modes de domination," *Actes de la Recherche en Sciences Sociales* 105 (1994): 3–12; Pierre Bourdieu and Jean-Claude Passeron, *Reproduction in Education, Society and Culture*, 2d ed., trans., Richard Nice (London: Sage, 1990); Pierre Bourdieu and Loïc J. D. Wacquant, *An Invitation to Reflexive Sociology* (Chicago: University of Chicago Press, 1992), 139–40.

seeking change were formed within the same fields.[118] Even the move to reject reproduction for a "futile" gathering of different bodies may help reproduce the normative order recognized as pernicious. Strategic withdrawal from reproductive institutions may, "perversely," perpetuate them.[119] While we should not dismiss strategic withdrawal out of hand—more on this topic below— nor should we assume it avoids the moral, political, and spiritual complications of strategic participation. Both strategies are *social*, both operate within logics shaped by the fields they contest. Yet the possibility of strategic participation indicates that the contest for capital (social, cultural, material, symbolic)—including for its nature and meaning, for *what* capital a field will aim at—and for the structure of a field remains open to us. North American Mennonite women struggled for capital within Mennonite institutions, winning material capital (salaried jobs, budgets for women's organizations, the right to raise funds), cultural capital (the right to pursue theological education and publishing), social capital (networking among women and with male leaders), and symbolic capital (the meaning of the denominations' core theological commitments). In doing so they transformed their organizational fields, giving rise to new organizations, new forms of gathering, new ways of leadership, and new possibilities for participation for many members. They did not, as Tonstad and queer Mennonites would point out, fully challenge the logic of exclusion that structures Mennonite institutions. But they did make progress, progress that some queer Mennonites are building on in their own ongoing struggles. Struggle, not futile quiescence, is an option.

Radner's concern that we do not know what changes would ameliorate suffering deserves to be taken seriously even if it is a case of reactionary *docta ignorantia*.[120] Social life is not mechanistic and

---

[118]For example, Bourdieu argues in *Masculine Domination*, trans. Richard Nice (Polity: Cambridge, 2001), that some feminist strategies have perpetuated rule by men, e.g., by assuming (even in defiance) symbolic definitions of the human promulgated by men (62–3).

[119]Cf. Hirschman's discussion of the rhetoric of "perversity" (claims that you should not try to change things because your attempt will just make things worse) in *The Rhetoric of Reaction*, 11–42.

[120]The doctrine of ignorance has been at the heart of neoliberal rhetoric opposing social planning. See Philip Mirowski, *Never Let a Serious Crisis Go to Waste: How Neoliberalism Survived the Financial Meltdown* (New York: Verso, 2013), 68–83.

resists simplistic solutions to its ills. The complexity and dynamism of social life require equally complex and dynamic responses. Acknowledging these facts, however, should not end in a counsel of futility. Difficulty is not impossibility. As the case of North American Mennonite women shows, positive transformation is possible and is not negated for being partial and contingent. What lessons the case has for those engaging in other struggles have to be debated by those active in the relevant struggles. Yet close attention to the case, alive to potential patterns of struggle that might emerge from it, considered especially in comparison to other cases of progressive struggle—such as the other cases discussed in this book—may provide crucial guidance in the present for a better future, for a more *holy* future in which even our institutions bear witness to the sacredness of women and gender and sexual minorities by promoting their flourishing.

With regard to the need to remain open to multiple institutional possibilities, consider further Wittgenstein's claim that rules are not like "rails invisibly laid to infinity."[121] Even learning to count is not a mechanistic process such that, once a pupil has mastered a basic sequence or pattern they can go on forever without error. Knowing "how to go on" requires ongoing training, not just to learn additional rules but also to determine how a rule must be put to work—even, perhaps, changed—to fit a given context. This insight aligns with Wittgenstein's central belief that attempts to homogenize cases or rules into a "theory" of how all things work (or even ontologically "are") are frequently misguided—"I'll teach you differences," as he famously said.[122] Learning differences is the process of carefully comparing inherited rules with present context to determine a possible fit. This is the nub of Wittgenstein and his inheritors' "ordinary language" analysis—learning from studies of ordinary language the variety of ways different bits of language can

---

[121] Ludwig Wittgenstein, *Philosophical Investigations*, rev. 4th ed., trans. G. E. M. Anscombe, P. M. S. Hacker, and Joachim Shulte (Oxford: Blackwell, 2009), §218.

[122] Wittgenstein told his friend Maurice O'Connor Drury that he was considering this line from King Lear (Act I, scene iv) as a motto for one of his books. In the conversation he said, "Hegel seems to me to be always wanting to say that things that look different are really the same. Whereas my interest is in showing that things which look the same are really different." See Ray Monk, *Wittgenstein: The Duty of Genius* (New York: Free Press, 1990), 536–7.

be put to use in different contexts in order to loosen the grip of the illusion that such bits of language must "mean" one (and only one) thing and fit in one (and only one) way.

Given Bourdieu's affinity for Wittgenstein,[123] his work can be seen as an extension of this approach to sociology, to "ordinary" social realities and the many things that can be done with them. This point is worth dwelling on because the criticisms of institutions, institutional change, and institutions' role in broader social change that we have reviewed in this and earlier chapters can be seen as resting, in part, on the theoretical illusion that institutions are and can only do one thing. With Tonstad in mind, that means that although institutions *do* strongly reproduce pernicious normative orders, that does not mean that that is their only function—institutions do not run on rails. They are susceptible to contest, such as the contests waged by women and queer persons in church institutions to expand the scope of their inclusivity. With Radner in mind, that means that although church members and institutions have no roadmap to solve "the problem of suffering," they do have the capacity to study and learn from past cases, to carefully assess present context—and try their best. Each struggle, moreover, will be different, will have a different context and the inherited institutions will "mean" something different in that context. In some cases, the struggle may look like strategic withdrawal, either into an acceptable "normal" or into a new, unruly mass. In some cases, the struggle might look like strategic participation, whether participation aimed at abolishing some set of institutions and establishing others, or participation aimed at reforming existing institutions. The Spirit blows where she will. And the Spirit organizes and sanctifies.

Conclusion

Rogers and Coakley envision the Spirit as sanctifying the church and its members by expanding the former to more fully include women and same-sex couples, and increasing virtue in the latter

---

[123]Bruno Ambroise, "Wittgenstein et Bourdieu: Contributions à une critique de la vision scolastique," *Europe* 906 (2004): 258–71; Mariano Croce, "The *Habitus* and the Critique of the Present: A Wittgensteinian Reading of Bourdieu's Social Theory," *Sociological Theory* 33, no. 4 (December 2015): 327–46.

through participation in the church and its practices. The case of North American Mennonite women brings clarity to the question of how the church might change in the process of its expansion toward greater inclusion, and so clarity as to how reforming movements within ecclesial institutions might seek to join the work of the sanctifying Spirit. In brief, ecclesial change may, at least in some circumstances, involve contest over institutions that takes the form of organizing new institutional structures and reorganizing older ones. In response to anxieties that investing in such movements reproduces exclusionary violence or pretends to know how such violence could be ended, I brought out and defended the "progressive" character of the pneumatological picture drawn from Rogers, Coakley, and Mennonite feminists. Advocating for progress, however, entails neither an uncritical devotion to institutional reformation—some institutions should be abolished, and withdrawal is sometimes appropriate—nor a mechanistic or rationalistic view of social betterment. We cannot end all vicious reproduction and we cannot know how to solve all the world's problems. But we can engage in struggles to better our conditions and promote general well-being, including by struggling to reform our institutions, and we can count the success of such struggles as progress—even, perhaps, as participating in the sanctifying Spirit.

4

Doubling Spirit

During the period that I have been writing this book, I have also been working with a colleague on an oral history project. The project involved interviews with seventeen African American elders with strong connections to the Benham West neighborhood of Elkhart, Indiana. For a fifty-year period between 1920 and 1970, Elkhart's white leaders—politicians, police, bankers, real estate agents—confined much of African American community life into a small triangle built around the southern edge of the city's rail yard. African Americans, however, developed their common life to the extent that many of our interviewees described Benham West as a "village" full of fruit trees, mutual aid, and thriving Black-owned businesses and Black-run community organizations. In the 1970s, the neighborhood was cleared in the name of "urban renewal." Although the federal urban renewal process required the creation of a board of residents to determine the shape of redevelopment plans, the board's creative plan—which emphasized urban forests and parkland—was scuppered by white city leaders. Residents' homes and businesses were torn down, with most of the latter never to reopen. Almost forty-five years later Benham West is still largely empty. Initial screenings of our project's documentary film in the summer of 2023, however, encouraged the city mayor and Chamber of Commerce director, both African Americans with family ties to the neighborhood, to hasten redevelopment planning.[1]

---

[1] Oliver Pettis, dir., *What Happened at Benham West: African American Stories of Community, Displacement, and Hope* (Black Lion Cinematography, 2023); Nekeisha Alayna Alexis and Jamie Pitts, *What Happened at Benham West: African American Stories of Community, Displacement, and Hope* (South Bend, IN: Wolfson, 2024).

I mention the Benham West project to reflect on two dynamics. First, community organizations were, as just stated, a significant part of the life of Benham West. These organizations included churches and a community center, as well as political organizations. A study of Benham West rightfully attends to these organizations' local leadership and activities, striving to understand how they helped shape their community. At the same time, it should be noted that the churches were part of national denominations (African Methodist Episcopal, Church of God in Christ) and international traditions (Baptist, Methodist, Pentecostal). The community center was originally founded by another national organization, the Women's Christian Temperance Union, and was later funded by the United Way. Benham West's main political organizations were branches of the National Association for the Advancement of Colored People and the Urban League. There is no sense that the local organizations that served the neighborhood were *merely* local. That much should not be surprising after the previous chapters.

The range of organizations active in Benham West points to a second dynamic, which concerns the relationship between ecclesial and other institutions. This dynamic has been present in previous chapters without receiving detailed treatment. Although the focus of Chapter 3 was on church institutions, I acknowledged that some have been excluded from those institutions and have gone on to do important organizing work elsewhere. Can "organizing institutions elsewhere" be thought of as somehow participating in the work of the organizing Spirit if it tends toward life, solidarity, and inclusivity? How might we think about extra-ecclesial environmental institutions, or the institutional organizing work of those who leave the church, in connection to the hovering, sanctifying Spirit? How might we think about the long decades of struggle in and for a neighborhood like Benham West—a struggle that has certainly involved church-going Christians, but by no means has been limited to them and has been waged via numerous

---

For a report on the effect of the documentary on city redevelopment planning, see Deborah Domine, "Elkhart Reconciliation Will Benefit All of Elkhart County," Goshen News, September 5, 2023, https://www.goshennews.com/opinion/elkhart-reconciliation-will-benefit-all-of-elkhart-county/article_12a0a130-4b59-11ee-bd10-4702069fb122.html.

institutions (and other organizations) beyond the church? These questions occupy the present chapter.

Introducing these questions with Benham West's story raises a subsidiary issue. What happened to the African American residents of Benham West is rightly described as racism. Residents were racialized as Black and, on that basis, subordinated within the city's white-dominated racial order. Christian institutions might seek solidarity with Benham West's African Americans by making racial identity their raison d'être, aiming for instance to improve the city's "race relations" to ensure that Black people are involved in banks' decisions about home loans, the local government's redevelopment plans, and oversight of police conduct and the real estate industry. Or Christian institutions might propose local congregations as sites of interracial community and justice, in which a unified identity in Christ trumps race-based divisions. I do not wish to slander either impulse, which would respectively be coded as "liberationist" and "postliberal" in contemporary theology. But in this chapter, I want to press harder on the matters of "identity" and "identity politics" as part of the exploration of the organizing Spirit and extra-ecclesial institutions. Can organizing—and, more specifically, organizing *institutions*—in the name of oppressed identities be thought of as participating in the Spirit? How would such institutions relate to institutions rooted in "Christian identity," and to that other contested center of organizing activities, the betterment of material conditions?

In order to respond to these questions, I move in the chapter's first section to another story. This story concerns Vincent Harding, an African American man who spent several years as a Mennonite pastor and peace worker before leaving Mennonite circles to pursue radical Black nationalist scholarship and organizing. After providing an outline of Harding's story, narrating the development of his life and work, I trace his persistent tendency to use theological terms, including divine "Spirit" and "spirit," to describe the Black freedom struggle. Reading this tendency in light of scholarship on African American religion suggests that Harding was engaged in a project of "conjuration," in which strategic "doubling" of the language of Black struggle with theological words and imagery was meant to bring about Black liberation. If we take Harding as our guide to the work of the Spirit, then we are left with a picture of the Spirit doubling—enlivening and empowering—the spirit of Black struggle.² This picture is resonant with themes in Black liberation theology, but Harding's view of the centrality of "freedom institutions" to Black struggle allows for a supplement to this literature,³ and to our broader understanding of the organizing Spirit. In short, part of how the Spirit doubles movements is to inspire the organization of institutions that seek to make freedom—and the solidarities formed in the quest for freedom—enduring, that seek to prolong liberation moments into liberated forms of life. Harding's example, and the history he writes about, suggests that the Spirit does this work broadly, and not just within the church. Harding's example also confirms other aspects of the picture of the organizing Spirit, namely, that institutional participation in the Spirit is frail, can go wrong, and takes time.

Consideration of Harding's trajectory from Mennonite to Black nationalist organizing, which he described as a journey "deep into blackness,"⁴ also facilitates investigation of questions related to identity politics. Although Harding certainly put identity at the heart of his Black nationalist period, the institutional politics he pursued in the name of "blackness" took as its horizon anti-colonial internationalism. In view of concerns in theology and other

---

²As noted in Chapter 1, I am reading Harding's life and work as a source especially relevant to, and to some degree from or within, my Mennonite theological tradition. As discussed below, Harding rejected the idea that he had "shifted" away from the Mennonite tradition and he continued to claim Anabaptist identity throughout his life. Like the Mennonite women discussed in the previous chapter, Harding both exemplifies the pneumatological-sociological picture I am developing and provides normative criteria for the further elaboration of that picture.

³It could, for example, be read as affirming and developing J. Deotis Roberts's claim that "the church as a creation of the Spirit is both an institution and a community. Institutions belong to the world of structures. Communities belong to the world of persons. In the church, institution and community, institute and event, are interrelated." Roberts further suggests that the "black church tradition illustrates the relationship between the church as event and the church as institute," and that "Martin Luther King Jr. moved from the church as event to the church as institute." Roberts, *Black Theology in Dialogue* (Philadelphia: Westminster, 1987), 62–3. For an overview of Black pneumatology, see James H. Evans, "The Holy Spirit in African American Theology," in *The Oxford Handbook of African American Theology*, eds. Katie G. Cannon and Anthony B. Pinn (New York: Oxford University Press, 2014), 164–73.

⁴Joanna Shenk, *The Movement Makes Us Human: An Interview with Dr. Vincent Harding on Mennonites, Vietnam, and MLK* (Eugene, OR: Wipf & Stock, 2018), 48.

disciplines that identity politics leads only to the fragmentation of solidarities, Harding, at least in his Black nationalist years, reminds us of another possibility—the possibility that an institutional politics centered on particular identities can powerfully double institutional politics waged in the name of the universal. This doubling, too, can be taken as a sign of the Spirit.

Vincent Harding: Life and Work

In this section I first describe Harding's life, focusing especially on his work initiating and building institutions, and then examine the place of institutions in his historiography of Black struggle.[5]

Harding's Life

Vincent Harding was born in Harlem in 1931.[6] Although he was reared in a Black, nonresistant Seventh Day Christian church,[7] he aspired to a career in military intelligence and joined the Army after college. Increasingly convinced that following Jesus was incompatible with military service, he left the Army after two years for graduate studies and a Seventh Day pastorate in Chicago. In

---

[5]This section and the following section originally appeared in Jamie Pitts, "Vincent Harding, the Black Freedom Struggle, and Just Institutions," in *On a Pilgrimage of Justice and Peace: Global Mennonite Perspectives on Peacebuilding*, eds. Fernando Enns, Nina Schroeder, and Andrés Pacheco Lozano (Eugene, OR: Wipf & Stock, 2023), 376–84. Used by permission of Wipf and Stock Publishers, www.wipfandstock.com.

[6]I have gathered Harding's biography from the following sources: Rosemarie Freeney Harding with Rachel E. Harding, *Remnants: A Memoir of Spirit, Activism, and Mothering* (Durham, NC: Duke University Press, 2015); Vincent Harding and Daisuke Ikeda, *America Will Be! Conversations on Hope, Freedom, and Democracy* (Cambridge, MA: Dialogue Path, 2013); Tobin Miller Shearer, "A Prophet Pushed Out: Vincent Harding and the Mennonites," *Mennonite Life* 69 (2015), https://ml.bethelks.edu/issue/vol-69/article/a-prophet-pushed-out-vincent-harding-and-the-menno/; Shearer, "Vincent Harding's Dual Demonstration," in *Daily Demonstrators: The Civil Rights Movement in Mennonite Homes and Sanctuaries* (Baltimore: Johns Hopkins University Press, 2010), 98–129; Shenk, *The Movement Makes Us Human*.

[7]The Seventh Day Christian church is a Black offshoot of the Seventh Day Adventists.

Chicago he met Mennonites who shared his understanding of Jesus and who were experimenting with interracial community. In 1957 they invited him to co-pastor a congregation on the South Side of Chicago. Harding and his wife, Rosemarie Freeney Harding, moved to Atlanta in 1961 with Mennonite Central Committee and founded Mennonite House, an interracial guest house and movement center. They ran Mennonite House until 1964. After finishing his dissertation in Chicago, Harding became the chair of Spelman College's history department in 1965. He continued to address Mennonite audiences over the next few years, but his attention largely moved to teaching and activism in Atlanta and throughout the South.

Harding's advocacy of global nonviolent revolution never won universal acclaim in what was then an almost entirely white Mennonite denomination dedicated to a theology of nonresistance, in which following Jesus meant not participating in or interfering with the government. Harding's message was too much for many white Mennonites to bear, especially after his arrest in 1962 during a prayer demonstration in Albany, Georgia. Harding became, in Mennonite historian Tobin Miller Shearer's words, "a prophet pushed out."[8]

Reflecting on this period late in life, Harding described it in terms of a spiritual journey with God "deep into blackness."[9] In doing so he identified his growing alignment with a broader transformation in Black struggle toward Black power and Black nationalism, in other words, toward Black organizational, financial, and cultural autonomy.[10] Harding changed his employment from white-controlled Mennonite Central Committee to historically Black Spelman College, and his organizational activity from

---

[8]Shearer, "A Prophet Pushed Out." Harding continued to work with MCC until 1965, when he resigned after admitting he had committed "sexual undiscipline and a lack of honesty." Shearer, "Vincent Harding's Dual Demonstration," 126.
[9]Shenk, *The Movement Makes Us Human*, 48.
[10]On Harding's Black nationalism, see Shenk, *The Movement Makes Us Human*, 47–52; Derrick E. White, *The Challenge of Blackness: The Institute of the Black World and Political Activism in the 1970s* (Gainesville, FL: University Press of Florida, 2011), 8–9. For a brief definition of Black nationalism, see Fabio Rojas, *From Black Power to Black Studies: How a Radical Social Movement Became an Academic Discipline* (Baltimore: Johns Hopkins University Press, 2007), xvii.

Mennonite House to closer collaboration with Martin Luther King Jr., the Southern Christian Leadership Conference, and the Student Nonviolent Coordinating Committee. During this period, Harding wrote King's famous speech, "Beyond Vietnam: A Time to Break Silence," in which King came out on a national stage against the Vietnam War.[11]

After King's assassination in 1968, Harding was asked by his widow, Coretta Scott King, to be the founding director of the King Center in Atlanta. Harding was expected to offer general administrative oversight, collect King's papers, and develop an oral history project, though he also hoped the King Center would house an initiative he was considering with colleagues at Spelman and the other historically Black colleges of the Atlanta University Center (AUC). This initiative, initially named the W. E. B. Du Bois Institute for Advanced Black Studies, was intended to convert the AUC into a regional Black Studies hub.[12]

The King Center accepted the Du Bois Institute, and Harding accepted the directorship of the King Center. But the relationship quickly soured after two members of the Institute's planning committee were involved with protests demanding Black Studies programming at the AUC. They were fired from the AUC, and Harding only salvaged the Institute's connection to the King Center by agreeing to their removal from the planning committee. Harding and his colleagues now thought their Institute, soon renamed the Institute of the Black World (IBW), had sufficient autonomy to pursue their vision for Black Studies. They quickly became known for promoting the "Black University," in which a Black university's entire curriculum was to be oriented to the needs and flourishing of the Black community.[13] This approach contrasted, in Harding's and

---

[11] Martin Luther King, "Beyond Vietnam" (1967), https://www.americanrhetoric.com/speeches/mlkatimetobreaksilence.htm.

[12] White, *The Challenge of Blackness*, 35–44. During the 1960s, Black student protestors at universities across the United States demanded that universities offer courses on Black history and thought, create academic departments to house such courses and their faculty, and develop programs for local Black communities. The collective demands came to be known as "Black Studies." See Rojas, *From Black Power to Black Studies*.

[13] White, *The Challenge of Blackness*, 19–58. This model has recently been celebrated by Andrew J. Douglas and Jared Loggins in their essay "The Lost Promise of Black Study," *Boston Review*, September 28, 2021, https://www.bostonreview.net/articles/the-lost-promise-of-black-study/.

his colleagues' eyes, with the typical mission of Black universities, which they saw as preparing elite Black students for success in the white world.

Harding and the IBW, moreover, were convinced that the movement for Black Studies in the United States should connect to global Black struggle. Harding and other IBW associates published books that referenced Caribbean theorist and freedom fighter Frantz Fanon,[14] hosted a lecture by Black Power icon Stokely Carmichael, and forged enduring connections to the Trinidadian Marxist historian C. L. R. James. In response, the King Center board attempted to restrict Harding's research activities to King's life and writing, and to impose a "loyalty oath" to nonviolence on IBW staff.[15] Harding felt that the board was trying to position itself as King's official interpreter on the basis of a narrow reading of his life and legacy—a reading friendly to white liberals.[16] By mid-1970 the IBW and the King Center had formally parted ways.

The IBW occupied much of Harding's time over the next decade, though the Institute's financial struggles soon required him and other leaders to seek full-time employment elsewhere. After the break with the King Center, the IBW reimagined itself as an activist think tank dedicated to what historian Derrick E. White describes as "pragmatic nationalism and synthetic analyses fostered by collective scholarship."[17] The "pragmatic" and "synthetic" character of the Harding-led IBW was its openness to a variety of theoretical and practical approaches to Black freedom. It was this openness that had led to friction with the King Center, but now the IBW pursued its vision through publications, research seminars, and concrete involvement in politics.[18]

In 1974, the Hardings left Atlanta for Philadelphia, where Vincent taught at local universities before moving to the nearby Pendle Hill

---

[14]E.g., Harding, *Beyond Chaos: Black History and the Search for a New Land* (Atlanta: Institute of the Black World, 1970).
[15]White, *The Challenge of Blackness*, 76.
[16]White, *The Challenge of Blackness*, 60–1.
[17]White, *The Challenge of Blackness*, 87.
[18]In 1972, the IBW helped Maynard Jackson become the first Black mayor of Atlanta, and crafted the political agenda for the Gary Convention, a national gathering of Black politicians and activists in Gary, Indiana. White, *The Challenge of Blackness*, 113–34.

Quaker study center in 1980. At Pendle Hill, Harding wrote and, with Rosemarie, led intergenerational spiritual retreats drawing on the history of the Black freedom struggle.[19] Harding remained involved in the IBW throughout the 1970s and early 1980s, though ongoing financial problems, staff issues—caused in part by Harding and his male colleagues' failure to recognize and promote women leaders[20]—and a series of break-ins (possibly instigated by the FBI or CIA)[21] led to its decline. Before the IBW shuttered in 1983, it published Harding's *The Other American Revolution*, an accessible introduction to Black struggle from the shores of Africa to the late 1960s.[22] Harding soon published a more academic version of this history, ending after the American Civil War, as *There Is a River*.[23]

In 1981 the Hardings moved to Denver for Vincent to take up a permanent faculty position at Iliff School of Theology. He remained at Iliff until his retirement in 2004—which was also the year of Rosemarie's death—and in Denver until his death in 2014. He remained active as a scholar over the last decades of his life, publishing a textbook for young people on African American history from the Second World War through the Civil Rights movement;[24] a book aimed at teachers on the transformational uses of stories from the Black freedom struggles of the 1950s, 1960s, and 1970s;[25] a collection of essays on Martin Luther King's "inconveniently" radical legacy;[26] a lengthy "letter" to young American radical

---

[19]Shenk, *The Movement Makes Us Human*, 88–9.
[20]White, *The Challenge of Blackness*, 92–100.
[21]White, *The Challenge of Blackness*, 166–91.
[22]Vincent Harding, *The Other American Revolution* (Los Angeles: Center for African American Studies, University of California Los Angeles; Atlanta: Institute of the Black World, 1980).
[23]Vincent Harding, *There Is a River: The Black Struggle for Freedom in America* (New York: Harcourt Brace Jovanovich, 1981).
[24]Vincent Harding, Robin D. G. Kelly, and Earl Lewis, *We Changed the World: African Americans, 1945–1970* (New York: Oxford University Press, 1997).
[25]Vincent Harding, *Hope and History: Why We Must Share the Story of the Movement* (Maryknoll, NY: Orbis, 1990).
[26]Vincent Harding, *Martin Luther King: The Inconvenient Hero*, rev. ed. (Maryknoll, NY: Orbis, 2008).

democracy activists;[27] and a reflective interview on his life and spiritual-political vision with Buddhist leader Daisaku Ikeda.[28]

Meanwhile, Harding continued to develop institutions aimed at sustaining the insights of past democratic movements and connecting those insights with emerging leaders. In 1997, Vincent and Rosemarie founded the Veterans of Hope Project, dedicated to sharing stories from past movement leaders and, through the Ambassadors of Hope initiative, put veteran and young activists in conversation. Vincent Harding was also a founding member of another, similar organization, the National Council of Elders, which began in 2011. Harding clearly viewed institutions as a key component to achieving movement goals of a more just, democratic society.

Institutions in Harding's Historiography of Black Struggle

Harding's writings indeed offer a history and theology of what he describes as institutions of freedom and hope.[29] Reflecting his own experience with the IBW as well as his own Black nationalist commitments, Harding's historiography of Black struggle repeatedly returns to the value of autonomous institutions as both achievements of Black freedom and bases for further freedom organizing. In *The Other American Revolution*, for example, Harding assessed the weakness of the influential abolitionist organization, the American Anti-Slavery Society, as its lack of Black control. Black-led organizations following the Society's split in 1840 tended to be far more radical in their commitment to Black freedom.[30] *There Is a River* further draws attention to the formation of Black churches, schools, and community-service organizations before, during, and after to the Civil War.[31] Harding gives close attention to the

---

[27]Vincent Harding, *Is America Possible? To My Young Companions on the Journey of Hope* (Kalamazoo, MI: Fetzer Institute, 2007).
[28]Harding and Ikeda, *America Will Be!*
[29]Harding, *There Is a River*, xii, 260, 264.
[30]Harding, *The Other American Revolution*, 48–50.
[31]Harding, *There Is a River*, 43–4, 111, 259, 265, 278, 296, 310.

importance of these institutions in the birth and nurturance of the freedom movements during the 1950s and 1960s.[32]

The critical dimension of Harding's conception of freedom institutions surfaces in his discussion of dominant white institutions. In *There Is a River*, Harding identifies the slave ships—"prisons and kennels," "mini-states with their own polity, their own laws and government"—as the earliest white institutional form encountered by enslaved Africans.[33] During the eighteenth century, "those institutions [were] transferred to the plantations, the counties, and the colonies themselves."[34] White churches fit well in this context: "like every other institution in the North American colonies, [they] had been used to defend white supremacy and justify Black slavery," including by attempting to erase all memory of and loyalty to African traditions among the enslaved.[35] The creation of Black churches, newspapers, schools, and other institutions before and after American independence was, in Harding's eyes, a crucial form of resistance, an essential contribution to the Black "struggle for self-definition, for identity, ultimately for a certain degree of autonomy."[36] Writing of the "clear responsibilities" emerging in the American North prior to the Civil War, Harding likewise says that "it was absolutely necessary to build Black institutions …, partly as a base for ongoing fights against injustice, but largely as repositories for the visions and hopes of the future." Black institutions of freedom, in other words, were counter institutions, institutions that opposed the dominant, death-dealing white institutions, enabling Black survival, facilitating resistance, and sparking dreams of a liberated future. The possibility born of this inter-institutional conflict came to a head at the end of the Civil War:

> The old institution of slavery was surely dying, but what would be the shape of the institution of freedom? … For just as slavery had been an institution with economic, political, religious, and psychological manifestations and meanings, so it became

---

[32] Harding, *Hope and History*, 75–90; Harding, Kelley, and Lewis, *We Changed the World*, 52, 56.
[33] Harding, *There Is a River*, 10–11.
[34] Harding, *There Is a River*, 36.
[35] Harding, *There Is a River*, 43–4.
[36] Harding, *There Is a River*, 111.

increasingly clear to many black persons that freedom must also become a full-blown institution, affecting the totality of their lives and the lives of others, eventually requiring the entire nation to become "the land of the free."[37]

Freedom Institutions and Pneumatological Doubling

From Harding's perspective, the most radical forms of resistance to white domination, the most radical "streams" or currents in the river of Black struggle, were those that "raised the most profound questions about the nature of white society and the legitimacy of its power to control and define black people."[38] More "mainstream" protest, by contrast, took up the rhetoric of the American revolutionary state, particularly its Constitution, in setting out the terms of Black freedom.[39] Harding finds in Black revolutionary movements and in the Civil War confirmation of the radical view that the spilling of blood would be a necessary component of Black freedom.[40] The long experience of suffering mixed with political realism and a cross-centered, providentialist theology to produce a radical vision of liberation through blood. Black radicalism could include hope for the renewal of America, for America to live up to and expand its Constitutional promise, but it recognized and rebuked the deep-seated commitment of white America to racial supremacy. Such a response to white hegemony would, without a doubt, incur a violent reaction.

Harding accordingly concludes *There Is a River* with a lyrical evocation of the blood spilt during the struggle and, in the final words of the book, describes Black celebration of the passage of the 13th Amendment, which outlawed slavery, in the following terms:

---

[37] Harding, *There Is a River*, 260.
[38] Harding, *There Is a River*, 29.
[39] Harding, *There Is a River*, 42.
[40] Harding, *There Is a River*, 149, 331–2.

They sang and prayed and cried into the night, the night when slavery was officially ended in the United States, black people were celebrating themselves, honoring their forebears, holding up their children to the midnight sun, praising the mysterious, delivering God who had made it possible for them, and all who lived before them, to come so far and stand so firm in the deep red flooding of Jordan.[41]

The river of struggle is a river of blood, a river of divine liberation and, at the same time, of self-deliverance. These words contain the lineaments of Harding's theology of freedom struggle, the theology he employs to assess institutions.

Harding's theology can be surveyed by attending to clusters of terms he employs repeatedly to describe and commend freedom struggle. Among these terms are providence and God; freedom and movement, including references to the exodus narrative; Jesus, the cross, and salvation; the Word and human words; the Spirit and the spirit of movements; and new creation and new humanity. After describing these clusters, I consider them in light of research on African American religion in order to suggest that Harding was engaged in a conjuring practice of "doubling" the power of human efforts, including his own writing, with divine power. This perspective facilitates the analogical development of a pneumatology in which the Spirit's doubling of human liberation movements includes the inspiration of freedom institutions.

Theological Doubles

Harding deploys the language of "Spirit" and "spirit" as part of a larger lexicon in which human liberation efforts are doubled by divine action. The lexicon serves as a kind of systematic theology in miniature, insofar as it treats several interconnected loci. In order to get the pneumatological point of Harding's doubling, we need to see it in its "systematic" context, where pneumatology is related to doctrines of providence, salvation, Christology, and redemption. This review, moreover, clarifies our picture of Harding's

---

[41]Harding, *There Is a River*, 332.

critical theology of institutions, in which institutional life is assessed according to its congruence with the liberating work of God, Word, and Spirit.

Harding's emphasis on providence is most clear in the narrative of Black struggle in *There Is a River*. In Harding's judgment, abolitionist and newspaper editor Frederick Douglass's deep faith in "the nineteenth-century understanding of Providence, [in] the rational, loving, guiding hand of God" both fortified him and distracted him from the real character of the struggle.[42] Black people generally, according to Harding, welcomed the Civil War as a "vindication of their trust in Providence,"[43] and after the war trusted Providence to "usher in a new kingdom," "a new society where true freedom would reign."[44] Belief in providence, however, was not a call to quietism; rather, as articulated in an "Address to the White Inhabitants of the State of South Carolina" from the Colored People's Convention in 1865, providence manifested as Black self-liberation in America and around the world.[45]

This "synergistic" conception of divine action, in which humans participate in God's work of ordering and saving, is visible throughout Harding's theological descriptions and recommendations.[46] A study of references to "God" in Harding's book on Martin Luther King confirms this judgment. "King," Harding says, "placed the evolving black struggle that he was even then re-dreaming and re-visioning into the context of God's larger world,"[47] and he was motivated in large part by his conviction of his own identity as a

---

[42] Harding, *There Is a River*, 148.
[43] Harding, *There Is a River*, 219.
[44] Harding, *There Is a River*, 243.
[45] Harding, *There Is a River*, 325–6.
[46] Historians and theologians have argued that such a synergistic soteriology is central to Anabaptist theology. See Thomas N. Finger, *Contemporary Anabaptist Theology: Biblical, Historical, Constructive* (Downers Grove, IL: Intervarsity, 2004), 357–60; C. Arnold Snyder, *Anabaptist History and Theology: An Introduction* (Kitchener, ON: Pandora, 1995), 88.
[47] Harding, *Martin Luther King*, 20.

child of God—and so of his freedom to act in and for unity with all of humanity.[48] For Harding, inheriting and developing King's legacy require a similar "dancing, embracing, wrestling with our God, by whatever name—or silence—that God is known in our heart,"[49] and so an openness to the surprise of divine creativity in the nonviolent pursuit of justice.[50]

The prevalent riparian imagery of *There Is a River* sets the movement for Black freedom in the context of the biblical exodus narrative. As mentioned above, *There Is a River* concludes with a vision of the "deep red flooding of Jordan," the river the ancient Israelites had to cross to inhabit the land they had been promised prior to leaving Egypt. Although Harding takes up the frequent descriptions by slaves of the North as "Canaan,"[51] he perhaps surprisingly depicts the Black community after slavery praising God for their ability to "stand firm" in the bloody, flooded Jordan.[52] Harding locates divine freedom in the river, in learning to find one's footing in it and learning to move with it. This perspective issues in a rich theology of "movement" that Harding offers in a meditation on what it means to "keep going" after King.[53] According to Harding, keeping going today does not entail imitating King, but rather being captivated by his "voice, vision, and way"[54] and creatively exploring personal, vocational, institutional, and political possibilities for integrating peace and justice.[55] Harding expresses this view thematically: "to keep moving is to become willing, among and beyond ourselves, which draws us into the company of the committed, helping us to become voluntary companions, fellow travelers with our brother Martin."[56] Taken together, and put in

---

[48]Harding, *Martin Luther King*, 54, 69, 105, 114, 115, 117, 119. Vincent Lloyd has described the "early" King's reliance on a tradition of "black natural law," or trust in the ultimate victory of God's liberating justice. Lloyd, *Black Natural Law* (New York: Oxford University Press, 2016), 88–117. Harding's work suggests that the "later" King also drew on such a theology of providence.

[49]Harding, *Martin Luther King*, 108.

[50]Harding, *Martin Luther King*, 147–50.

[51]Harding, *There Is a River*, 116.

[52]Harding, *There Is a River*, 332.

[53]Harding, *Martin Luther King*, 78–110.

[54]Harding, *Martin Luther King*, 88–9.

[55]Harding, *Martin Luther King*, 106–10.

[56]Harding, *Martin Luther King*, 108.

light of King and Harding's trust in God, the images of the river and movement again evoke a conception of divine liberation that invites, and indeed requires, the active participation of those being liberated.

On Harding's telling, many participants in historic Black struggle have been sustained by their conviction that the salvation wrought by Jesus came through much suffering—through the cross. Reading their own sufferings in light of Jesus allowed them to equate political freedom with freedom in Christ. Noting that Black church elders in the 1960s were happy for younger activists to change the lyrics of "Woke up with my mind stayed on Jesus" to "stayed on freedom," Harding editorializes: "Jesus, Freedom ... Didn't it all mean the same thing?"[57] King, in Harding's view, had a particularly developed Christological conception of his own contribution to the freedom struggle. Alongside King's theology of providence was a theology of the power of Jesus's nonviolent, suffering love. King declared himself and his ministry as under the authority of this Jesus.[58] As Harding summarizes, King "believed that the only true revolution is a revolution that manifests the spirit of Jesus of Nazareth—nonviolent, loving, determined, defiant, and compassionate."[59]

In calling our attention to King's guiding Christology, Harding points us to see how King was another Christ, one whose "second coming" we await by "beginning again," by finding King in all the troubling conflicts of our own day.[60] Harding further explores the incarnational character of Black struggle through reflections on the confluence of divine Word and human words in the history of Black freedom movements. Enslaved Black communities in early-nineteenth-century America received "word" of white debate over slavery's legitimacy and "word" of successful Black revolution in Haiti and elsewhere; and "beyond and above" these words they heard "the word from the Lord, the word from the Word" promising freedom.[61] Harding, moreover, claims that "the word of black radicalism had been made flesh" in revolutionary leader Nat Turner

---

[57]Harding, *The Other American Revolution*, 168.
[58]Harding, *Martin Luther King*, 13, 32, 41, 54, 62, 69, 114.
[59]Harding, *Martin Luther King*, 120.
[60]Harding, *Martin Luther King*, vi–viii.
[61]Harding, *There Is a River*, 74.

and abolitionist journalist David Walker.[62] Visionary preacher Turner "transformed the Word and words into a roaring passion" of armed struggle. Walker's newspaper illuminated the role of words throughout the history of Black struggle to strengthen the faltering, protest domination, and organize for freedom, and to display the power of "words spoken honestly from the Bible, the Word, telling men and women of a humanity no one could deny them, reminding a people that God opposed injustice and the oppression of the weak, encouraging believers to seek for messianic signs in the heavens, for blood on the leaves [as Turner had]."[63] From Harding's vantage, Black struggle could be wrongly "confined to the word," yet the word could also stretch the struggle's ideology to new heights.[64] Human words, like God's Word, had to become flesh in order to save.[65]

The incarnation of the liberating Word is, for Harding, made possible by the Spirit of God, who is made effective and tangible in the "spirit" of the freedom movements. Harding may have seen Turner and Walker as enfleshing the deepest impulses of Black struggle, but he reports that they both saw themselves as responding to the divine Spirit.[66] Harding also describes Richard Allen, who at the end of the 1700s broke away from white Methodism to begin the African Methodist Episcopal Church, as rejecting white Christian definitions of the "place" of Black people, "definitions which had nothing to do with the spirit of a living and just God."[67] But that "spirit" was alive in the Black churches, and Harding tells of their "spirit-filled movement toward a righteous community" in

---

[62]Harding, *There Is a River*, 101.
[63]Harding, *There Is a River*, 82.
[64]Harding, *There Is a River*, 187.
[65]Cf. the early Anabaptist leader Pilgram Marpeck's Christology. Marpeck argues that in the incarnation the divine-human Christ savingly "communicates" to spiritual-material humans. Salvation thus necessarily takes a spiritual and material form, the latter taking shape in the church. See Marpeck, "Concerning the Humanity of Christ; Concerning the Son of Man," in *Jörg Maler's Kunstbuch: Writings of the Pilgram Marpeck Circle*, ed. John D. Rempel (Kitchener, ON: Pandora, 2010), 359–60; Walter Klaassen, ed., *Anabaptism in Outline: Selected Primary Sources* (Walden, NY: Plough, 2019), 1.7–1.9.
[66]Harding, *There Is a River*, 74, 78, 85.
[67]Harding, *There Is a River*, 44.

the 1950s and 1960s.[68] In those days "the spirit persisted" among white Christian and Jewish communities, leading to "the process of internal struggle and renewal of institutions" that took shape as transformative participation in the struggles for Black freedom, gender equality, and the antiwar movement.[69] Writing to Christian communities of color at the end of the 1980s, Harding challenged them to recover the possibility that "'advanced ideas' concerning democracy and advanced life in the spirit of God go together."[70] Harding himself offered personal testimony to spirit-leading throughout his career.[71]

The aim of providence and the shape of freedom, the purpose of Jesus and the point of the Word, the outcome of the Spirit's movement—all are encapsulated for Harding in the revolutionary biblical images of a renewed humanity, people, land, and entire creation. These phrases occur again and again in his *oeuvre* and are notably present in his early IBW publication on Black Studies, *Beyond Chaos: Black History and the Search for a New Land*. Drawing implicitly on the Bible (2 Cor. 5:17; Rev. 21–22) and explicitly on Frantz Fanon, Harding casts a vision for Black Studies as "part of the search for the new land, the new society, the new being,"[72] which results when Black people control their own institutions and can tell their own stories.[73] In his later reflection on the "fallen" state of Black Studies at the end of the 1970s, Harding similarly calls Black Studies scholars into renewed spiritual-religious inquiry in order to "expand and deepen the capacities of our own vision of the cosmos" and "participate fully in the creation of a fundamentally new reality."[74]

In this theological vision, as consistent with the other dimensions of Harding's theology, the new creation is both gift ("grace") and goal of struggle. Struggle includes institutionalization, and the birth and nurture of institutions can be seen as forms of participation in God's liberating providence, in the tandem work of Christ

---

[68] Harding, *Hope and History*, 81.
[69] Harding, *Hope and History*, 116.
[70] Harding, *Hope and History*, 215.
[71] Harding, *There Is a River*, 334, 338; Harding, *Martin Luther King*, 146.
[72] Harding, *Beyond Chaos*, 26.
[73] Harding, *Beyond Chaos*, 27.
[74] Harding, *The Other American Revolution*, 227–9.

and Spirit, and in the advent of new creation. Harding's theology precludes the formulation of a theory of institutions that would defend "institutions as such." Rather, Harding places institutions under the normative sign of the love of God, the grace of Christ, and the fellowship of the Spirit (2 Cor. 13:14). When, and only when, institutions contribute to the spread of this liberating love, grace, and fellowship can they be viewed as institutions of freedom and hope.

Doubling Spirit, Movement Institutions, and the Church

With these clusters of terms Harding consistently intertwines or overlays theological, and especially biblical, language with the language of Black struggle to describe a world in which the latter is critically shaped and strengthened by divine action.[75] Black theologian Theophus Smith has described this methodological practice of "doubling" as a typical strategy of African American folk religion. Smith names the strategy "conjure," locating its roots in African magical practice, in which objects representing powerful spirits and intended effects are used in mimetic rituals for various "pharmacological" ends—for ends of healing and liberation. In North America, following Smith, the Bible becomes the preeminent "conjure book" for African Americans, who render their world in terms of the biblical world, with the latter "reconfigured" as a "pharmacopeic cosmos" or "'pharmacosm,' which designates a world capable of hosting myriad performances of healing and harming, in accordance with an ideal world as envisioned by ancestral sources."[76] This reconfiguration involves African Americans calling upon biblical "figures" or patterns—people,

---

[75] This and the following paragraph contain material I presented at a session of the Afro-American Religious History Unit at the 2019 American Academy of Religion Annual Meeting in San Diego, as "Black Studies as Black Religion: Vincent Harding, the Institute of the Black World, and the Movement 'Deep into Blackness.'" I am grateful to the organizers, respondents, and audience for their feedback.
[76] Theophus Smith, *Conjuring Culture: Biblical Formations of Black America* (New York: Oxford University Press, 1994), 44.

places, imagery—to powerfully name and, therefore, transform their world. The doubling of biblical narrative and ongoing Black struggle unleashes spiritual force that enables, for example, slaves to escape North, President Lincoln to proclaim emancipation, and former slaves and their descendants to resist Jim Crow.[77]

Viewed against its background in Black religion, Harding's doubling practice can be seen not just as a historiographic method but also as transformative conjuration. Harding writes to conjure a new world. He does so, on his own account, as motivated and guided by God's Spirit for the purpose of incarnating God's liberating Word, to participate in the coming new creation. Given what Harding says about the contribution of institutions to liberation movements, it is also possible to comprehend his own work as an institution builder under a similar rubric of Spirit inspiration. Harding organized institutions that would double the Spirit's healing and liberation movement.

If Harding sought to conjure freedom, in part, by organizing institutions, then those institutions are subject to the same critical standards he outlined in his historical writings. The protest by IBW women staff members of their subordination and mistreatment by Harding and other male leaders stands out as a sign of judgment against the shortcomings of Harding's organizing. Although the protest could be taken to confirm the "pessimistic" stance toward institutions described in the last chapter, it could also be interpreted as a form of participation in the sanctification of institutions that in some significant respects successfully doubled the work of God's Spirit. Success, as we also saw previously, does not equate with complete or perfect transformation. The institutions that arise from and are sanctified by human participation in the doubling Spirit will be fallible and subject to development over time.

---

[77] Doubling is evident in prominent examples of Black liberation and womanist theology. Delores Williams, for example, doubles contemporary Black women's struggles with Hagar's story, while James Cone doubles the cross and the lynching tree, Christ's execution and the executions of African Americans. In each case, Black life is overlaid with biblical narrative to conjure survival and liberation. Delores S. Williams, *Sisters in the Wilderness: The Challenge of Womanist God-Talk* (Maryknoll, NY: Orbis, 1993); James H. Cone, *The Cross and the Lynching Tree* (Maryknoll, NY: Orbis, 2011).

These considerations also clarify our understanding of why the organizing Spirit might inspire the institutionalization of movements. From Harding's perspective, the good of institutions is their contribution to movements that enact God's liberation of creation from bondage. With his life and writings in mind, we can see that such institutions provide a power base for movements and a shared center for organizing; for deepening understanding through collective study; and for sustaining hope and imagining an alternative future. Harding also frequently discusses the role of counter-institutions that embody freedom through their autonomy and difference from oppressive modes of social organization. On this account, institutionalization does not equate with movements' ethical stultification and political compromise. Institutionalization can rather be a means of movement flourishing. If in Chapter 3 we saw the advantage of thinking of institutions as dynamic organizational fields, here we might think of movements in similar terms.[78] Movements can be organizationally complex and include institutions; those institutions can, at least at times, facilitate the achievement of movement goals. Institutionalization may conjure freedom by doubling the material and symbolic resources of a liberation movement in the form of relatively stable organizations that provide a platform for solidarity building. This doubling may, at its best, participate in the Spirit. The Spirit doubles by calling forth organizing to sustain and strengthen freedom struggles, and this organizing can result in the development and leadership of institutions.

Harding may convince us that institutions in general are a potential arena for participation in the Spirit's work of bringing about the new humanity in Christ—but what of the church and its institutions? Although Harding's historical writings demonstrate the entwinement of Black Christianity in the Black freedom struggle, he left Mennonite church institutions not for Black church institutions but rather to generate autonomous Black nationalist organizations. Although this move is intelligible from the perspective of Black

---

[78]For field studies of social movements, see Joseph Ibrahim, "The Struggle for Symbolic Dominance in the British 'Anti-Capitalist Movement Field,'" *Social Movement Studies* 12, no. 1 (2013): 63–80; David Landy, "Bringing the Outside In: Field Interaction and Transformation from Below in Political Struggles," *Social Movement Studies* 14, no. 3 (2015): 255–69.

and other liberation theologies[79]—and could be celebrated as a "realistic" appraisal of the church and its institutions—some theologians are liable to judge it as an abandonment of the locus of the divine economy, and even as a betrayal of the Spirit whose work preeminently organizes the church. These theologians have tended to highlight the church—as a community of those explicitly committed to following Jesus in the power of the Spirit—as the primary context in which racism and other forms of oppression are overcome.[80] Christian identity, moreover, is often thought to supersede other forms of identity, so exchanging ecclesial organizing for organizing in the name of "blackness" might be seen from this perspective as a form of idolatry or at least as a confusion between the church and the "world" (defined here as the fallen cosmos—not as "creation" as such).

As an initial response to this argument, consider that the church and the world are both parts of God's good creation. If they are distinct, the distinction is contextual and relational.[81] The distinction is *contextual* because the shape of the world at a given time and place impinges upon how it is similar or different to the church. In one context, the world's militaristic devotion to death may set it apart from a church participating in the Spirit's organization of life.

---

[79]For example, Cone describes the Black Power movement as empowered by the Spirit to do God's will "even though [the movement is] not consciously seeking to be Christian." He offers the example of God's use of Persian King Cyrus (Isa. 45) and the criteria of treatment of "the least of these" (Matt. 25). James H. Cone, *Black Theology and Black Power* (Maryknoll, NY: Orbis, 1997), 59–60.

[80]A strong version of this argument is found in Jonathan Tran, *Asian Americans and the Spirit of Racial Capitalism* (New York: Oxford University Press, 2021). J. Kameron Carter, *Race: A Theological Account* (New York: Oxford University Press, 2008) is somewhat less driven by ecclesiology, but puts forward the view that "to enter into Christ's flesh through the Holy Spirit's pentecostal overshadowing is to exit the gendered economy and protocols of modern racial reasoning" (340). Entering Christ's flesh by the Spirit, moreover, "transfigures social space": "the Spirit of Christ is the architect of a new mode of life together, that of the *ecclesia*, the church of Christ" (338).

[81]I have developed similar arguments in response to Anabaptist and postliberal theologies of ecclesial witness in Pitts, *Principalities and Powers: Revising John Howard Yoder's Sociological Theology* (Eugene, OR: Pickwick, 2013), esp. 146–8, 157–8, 188–91; Pitts, "Baptism, Postliberal and Anabaptist Theologies, and the Ambiguity of Christian Practice," *Mennonite Quarterly Review* 90 (July 2016): 323–44.

In another context, the world's opposition to sexism, homophobia, and racism may align with an inclusive, justice-oriented church.

How the church and the world differ is a contextual matter. It is also a *relational* matter insofar as the church exists in and for the world, and the church and the world are defined in relation to one another. The fact that the church is "in the world" (Jn 17:11) suggests that from one vantage the world is the encompassing reality within which the church exists. For that reason, it is no surprise that the church shares much of its language, practices, and organizational patterns with the world. One basic way the church is related to the world, therefore, is that it partakes in much of the world's way of life. Part of what it means to "be the church" is to engage in an ongoing process to discern the extent to which this way of life participates in life in the Spirit. This discernment, again, should be contextual and attentive to the enduring relationship between the church and the world. At times, Christian discernment affirms certain aspects of the world's way of life and is even open to learning from the world about the church's own vocation. This positive relation of the church to the world is possible because, however fallen the world is, it remains part of God's good creation and is accordingly drawn to the same end as the church—and all of creation.[82] Yet at other times the church modifies or rejects aspects of the world's way of life as marked by sin and so as

---

[82] The question of whether that end is reached exclusively in and through the church—as, perhaps, the church's universal expansion—has to wrestle with matters such as Paul's complex portrait of the eschatological relationship between Jews and Christians in Romans 1–11. I am, however, claiming that all of creation is *drawn toward* (and not just called to) saving union with God on the basis of the New Testament's many passages describing the reconciliation and redemption of "all things" (1 Cor. 15:27–8; Col. 1:20; Eph. 1:10; Rev. 21:5; cf. Rom. 8:22–3). For related discussion, see David Bentley Hart, *That All Shall Be Saved: Hell, Heaven, and Universal Salvation* (New Haven: Yale University Press, 2019). Hart focuses on the universal salvation of individual humans, while I am also interested in the organizational "things" undergoing redemption. As I argue throughout *Principalities and Powers*, the social character of human beings entails that no sharp boundary can be drawn between human individuals and the structures that relate them to one another. If that is the case, then organizations figure in some way in eschatological consummation.

tending away from life in the Spirit.[83] There cannot be an absolute dualism between the church and the world because both are part of creation, both are dynamic structures—albeit with somewhat different orientations and shapes—within creation's relational field that is sustained by and subject to the divine economy.

The world, therefore, is prone to influence from the Spirit insofar as the Spirit hovers over all of creation. Since the hovering Spirit organizes creation's dynamic structures and elicits a human organizational response, Christians should expect to find signs of the hovering Spirit—signs of "anonymous participation in the Spirit"[84]—in "worldly" organizing and organizations, including in worldly institutions. If the church is defined theologically as the more or less organized ensemble of persons explicitly and practically committed to pursuing life in the Spirit,[85] this ensemble may identify resemblances between its goal and that of some organizational efforts in the world.[86] On the basis of such resemblances we can

---

[83]This formulation takes account of Kathryn Tanner's relational conception of the church–world relation and her associated argument that the church should primarily see its role as one of tweaking or making minor adjustments to what it shares with the world, though those adjustments may have significant consequences. See especially Tanner, *Theories of Culture* (Minneapolis: Augsburg Fortress, 1997), 91–117. Contra Tanner, we should construe the church's posture toward the world in more contextual and flexible terms—sometimes a more hostile, "abolitionist" posture is warranted.

[84]This phrase of course plays on Karl Rahner's concept of the "anonymous Christian," someone who does not believe in Christ yet whose "devotion to his material duties and the demands made upon him by those under his care" suggest that he has responded affirmatively to the revelation of divine grace that lies at the heart of his (and every human) being. Karl Rahner, "Anonymous Christians," in *Theological Investigations, vol. 6: Concerning Vatican Council II*, trans. Karl-H. Kruger and Boniface Kruger (New York: Crossroad, 1982), 390–8. The quotation is from page 394.

[85]This definition reflects the Anabaptist theology of the "visible church," in which a committed group of disciples is taken to be the basic form of the church.

[86]Rahner's language of "degrees" of church membership is instructive here. He argues that we should speak of not only an "ascending order" of membership from baptism through full eucharistic participation in the life of the church, but also a "descending order from the explicitness of baptism into a non-official and anonymous Christianity which can and should yet be called Christianity in a meaningful sense, even though it itself cannot and would not describe itself as such." Rahner, "Anonymous Christians," 391. Whether or not we agree with Rahner that extra-ecclesial movements should be called "Christian"—especially against the will of movement participants—we can affirm the concept of degrees of participation in God's one Spirit, degrees that include explicit commitment to discipleship community as well as those that do not.

speak of the Spirit's doubled work in the church and the world, and hope for alliances across the church–world boundary that advance the Spirit's organizing aims. Some of these alliances may be interinstitutional, doubling the solidarities enabled by institutions in and out of the church. At the same time, the church's commitment wavers and the quality of its discernment and discipleship varies widely. This situation, combined with the world's status as an arena of Spirit action, may lead to multiple outcomes. Organizers in the world may claim inspiration from the church's message yet refrain from participating in Christian institutions and other organizations.[87] Others may reject Christianity (message and organization) and yet still be regarded, by some Christians at least, as embodying aspects of life in the Spirit. Christians may also discern that "worldly" organizing apart from the church is compatible with the broad aims of the church and seek alliances on that basis. Discerning Christians may also take stock of the church's sorry state and conclude that a worldly organization or organizing movement is the Spirit's sign of judgment on the church.[88]

Harding, at least, identified continuity between his Mennonite church and Black activist organizing, claiming that he had not "shifted" from one to the other, but that "the same God who had led me deep into faith [also took] me deep into blackness and [did] not leave me."[89] Historian Tobin Miller Shearer has accordingly written of Harding's "dual demonstration" in the church and society.[90] Of course, that language raises the question of why Harding could not go deep into blackness within or confine his demonstration to the church. His story as told above indicates that his largely white Mennonite church was resistant to his journey, to where God was leading him. In that case, his departure from the church and turn to organizing outside of it can be understood precisely as a judgment on it. Participation in the Spirit can lead one out of existing church institutions to form alternative institutions "in the world" that seek to double the Spirit's gifts of life and creaturely

---

[87] A famous line often attributed to Gandhi sums up this stance: "I like your Christ, I do not like your Christians. Your Christians are so unlike your Christ."
[88] So Rowan Williams, "The Judgment of the World," in *On Christian Theology* (Oxford: Blackwell, 2000), 39: "the Church judges the world; but it also hears God's judgment on itself in the judgment passed upon it by the world."
[89] Shenk, *The Movement Makes Us Human*, 48.
[90] Shearer, "Vincent Harding's Dual Demonstration."

solidarity.[91] A figure such as Harding can be seen as a conjurer whose double institutional organizing in the church and the world has the potential to transform both—and in doing so to participate in the coming of the new creation.

Identity, Theology, and Politics

The status of extra-ecclesial institutions in the divine economy bears on the question of extra-Christian identities, such as those purportedly defined by race, gender, sexuality, other religions, and so on. Each of these identity categories could have quotation marks around them, given the large body of critical work that has appeared in recent decades highlighting their historically and socially "constructed" nature.[92] Should these politics be judged as insufficiently Christian, insofar as Paul declares to the church at Galatia that categories such as gender, ethnicity, and status as free or enslaved have been superseded by a common identity in Christ (Gal. 3:28)? Doesn't Christ's razing of the "dividing wall" between Jews and Gentiles (Eph. 2:14) portend the abolition of all identities save one—Christian? And, the crucial question for this book, shouldn't Spirit-oriented institutions seek to overcome identity politics if these tend to sunder solidarities?

An initial response to these questions might simply extend the argument about extra-ecclesial institutions to extra-ecclesial identities. But this extension is problematized by the great extent

---

[91]These institutions might also overlap church institutions and other organizations in a variety of ways, by receiving funding from church sources, copying structural and process models from the church, hiring church members, using theological language or narratives, and so on. Although the preceding paragraphs have, for the sake of argument, assumed a relatively clear distinction between the church and the world, these possibilities of overlap points to a more ambiguous reality. I develop a more relational conception of the "church and world" below, with reference to the question of identities.

[92]Classic studies of identity include Homi K. Bhabha, *The Location of Culture* (New York: Routledge, 1994); Judith Butler, *Gender Trouble: Feminism and the Subversion of Identity* (New York: Routledge, 1990); Paul Gilroy, *The Black Atlantic: Modernity and Double Consciousness* (Cambridge, MA: Harvard University Press, 1993).

to which identities cross ecclesial borders. This border crossing, of course, is not a modern phenomenon and is at issue in the Pauline texts cited above. Those texts can perhaps be cited in favor of a supersession or abolition of any identity that is not merely Christian, but a wider reading of the New Testament offers a more nuanced view. Recent scholarship on the gospels emphasize Jesus's Jewishness vis-à-vis his Roman, Samaritan, and other Gentile interlocutors.[93] The gospel writers depicted Jesus's gathering of the Gentiles as the fulfillment of distinctly Jewish messianic hopes, and not as the supersession of Jewish identity. Relatedly, in Acts 6 the Hellenists' complaint is not overruled in the name of a single baptismal identity that relativizes Hellenist and Hebrew identities. Rather, the apostles instructed the Hellenists to organize their own committee to ensure that their widows received a due allotment of food. Even in the Pauline literature the status of identity is notoriously complex, since "abolitionist" passages rub up against the "household codes" that seem to insist on maintaining traditional gender, parent–child, and slave–free roles (e.g., Eph. 5:22–6:8; Col. 3:18–4:1). However these passages are to be interpreted—a matter that is itself notoriously complex—they clearly indicate the persistence of multiple identities within the church.[94] Similarly, Paul's argument in Romans 1–11 about the persistence of the Jews in God's plan of salvation is difficult to square with a simplistic account of Christian identity replacing Jewish (and by extension other) identities. That being the case, there can be no suggestion that what the Spirit does in the church through the formation of an exclusively "Christian" identity is or can be doubled through

---

[93]Daniel Boyarin, *The Jewish Gospels: The Story of the Jewish Christ* (New York: New Press, 2012); Amy-Jill Levine, *The Misunderstood Jew: The Church and the Scandal of the Jewish Jesus* (New York: HarperCollins, 2006); Matthew Thiessen, *Jesus and the Forces of Death: The Gospels' Portrayal of Ritual Impurity within First-century Judaism* (Grand Rapids, MI: Baker Academic, 2020).

[94]Modern Anabaptist scholarship on the Household Codes includes David Schroeder, "The New Testament Haustafeln: Egalitarian or Status Quo?" and Mary Schertz, "'Likewise You Wives ... ': Another Look at 1 Peter 2:11–5:11," both in *Perspectives on Feminist Hermeneutics*, eds., Gayle Gerber Koontz and Willard Swartley (Elkhart, IN: Institute of Mennonite Studies, 1987). For more recent discussion, see James P. Hering, *The Colossian and Ephesian* Haustafeln *in Theological Context: An Analysis of Their Origins, Relationship, and Message* (New York: Peter Lang, 2007).

the formation of (some) other identities outside of the church—identities are not discretely separable in this way.

This scenario is to be expected if identities are formed within relational fields. Mustafa Emirbayer and Matthew Desmond, for example, argue that a racialized society—a society in which members are identified as belonging to one or more "races"—is composed in part by a racial field in which different races compete for cultural legitimacy and material success.[95] Each race, in turn, is itself a space of capital-defined social positions. To be racialized as Black, white, Latino, or Asian in such a society is to undergo a social process of identity formation. "Racial identity" is a relational property, an effect of the dynamics of the racial field. That being the case, organizations within a racialized society are unlikely to be able to escape fully the logic of racialization. They may attempt to overcome racialization—one type of identity transformation—but in the meantime organizational members' identities will remain defined to some extent by their society's racial order. In a society where racialization has a long history and the racial order is central to the overall social order, this work will be slow and difficult. The prolonged character of the work may offer opportunities for members to reflect not only on the debilitating or limiting dimensions of racialization, but also on certain goods they may associate with their racial identities.[96] In this way, identities may overlap, and this overlapping may come to be seen as not merely an obstacle to overcome but also a question to explore.

A relational conception of identity developed along these lines challenges the idea that "the church" names an organization or institution whose members all possess a singular and exclusive Christian identity. Church members' Christian identities overlap with other identities. Depending on the context, these identities may be related to gender, sexuality, race, nationality, work, etc. The plural character of "Christian identity" itself is at least partially a

---

[95] Mustafa Emirbayer and Matthew Desmond, *The Racial Order* (Chicago: University of Chicago Press, 2015).

[96] This of course has been a major feature of minoritized racial movements for justice—consider the place of the "Black is beautiful" slogan and Afrocentrism in African American struggle. But Harding also instructs white people to reflect on how their whiteness could be a "gift in the struggle to overcome white dominance." Shenk, *The Movement Makes Us Human*, 72.

factor of the contextual nature of the relations among Christian and other identities. Christian identity is relationally constituted, it is always formed in relation to a dynamic set of other possible identities. Those relations may be negative or critical, as Christians seek to distinguish themselves from others; in other cases, those relations may be more ambiguous or positive. Just as the phrase "church and world" names a constellation of relational possibilities, so the potential relations among Christian and other identities are contextually determined and require ongoing discernment.

It is at this point where we might speak of the Spirit's doubling. Spirit-inspired incorporation of new members into the church doubles their other identities with a Christian identity. This doubling may be liberating in cases where aspects of those other identities are confining and oppressive. The process of doubling need not always cancel or abolish the other identities, but rather could renewingly transform them by freeing them from the violence of domination. The Irenaean doctrine of salvation as recapitulation fits here, as it depicts Christ's incarnation as a lived identification with the entire human experience.[97] If this experience is taken to include human identity and processes of identification, then we could by extension speak of the doubling of divine and human identities in Christ, which doubling liberates the latter from bondage to sin. This approach would be one way to make sense of the claim by liberation theologians that God-in-Christ is Black, a woman, a Black woman, Latin American, or queer. Christ identifies with particular identities for their salvation. Since identities are by definition particular, it is fitting to claim Christ's liberating identification with and as particular identities.[98]

---

[97]Kathryn Tanner deploys Irenaeus's doctrine of recapitulation to respond to womanist and feminist challenges to atonement theology. See Tanner, "Incarnation, Cross, and Sacrifice: A Feminist-inspired Reappraisal," *Anglican Theological Review* 86, no. 1 (2004): 35–56.

[98]Of course, liberation theologians make the claim that God-in-Christ identifies as Black, etc. because of God's preferential option for the poor and oppressed. That argument is compatible with the wider one I am making here. Cone, for example, defends his identification of Christ as Black on the grounds that "there is no universalism that is not particular." The universality of God's liberation of the oppressed runs through Christ's identification with particular oppressed communities. James H. Cone, *God of the Oppressed*, 2d ed. (Maryknoll, NY: Orbis, 1997), 126.

This insight can be further developed by reference to womanist theologian Eboni Marshall Turman's interpretation of Chalcedonian Christology. Turman sees the Chalcedonian Definition as affirming that what happened to Christ's body (*kata sarka*: "according to the flesh") is savingly transformed by its assumption in the incarnation (*en sarki*: "in the flesh"). Chalcedon affirms the reality of Jesus's historical experience of fragmenting violence, while at the same time proclaiming that he is not finally determined by that experience. "There is something that occurs in the flesh of Jesus," namely, the incarnation, "that functions as an essential given of Jesus' identity."[99] Jesus's identity includes his historical experience, includes his humanity, yet is not finally described by it. For Turman, the fully human and fully divine Jesus offers hope to Black women that their own experiences of fragmenting violence do not have the last word. From the perspective of a recapitulative soteriology, it is precisely insofar as Christ is a Black woman—recapitulates and so identifies with the experiences of Black women—that he savingly assumes their flesh.[100] To put the same point in the pneumatological terms of this chapter, Black women are saved when the Spirit doubles their identities in and as Christ. This logic applies of course to all identities, to all creatures. Conceptualizing the body of Christ, the church, as an organization of those whose identities have been doubled in this way defies any simplistic account of Christian identity as necessarily subsuming other identities. Ecclesial institutions can reject any agenda dedicated to the replacement of diverse identities with a single Christian identity.

Nevertheless, an account of liberation as the result of the Spirit's doubling of identities in and as Christ runs into two problems. Institutions seeking to participate in Spirit doubling need to reckon with these issues. The first problem concerns the endurance

---

[99]Eboni Marshall Turman, *Toward a Womanist Ethic of Incarnation: Black Bodies, the Black Church, and the Council of Chalcedon* (New York: Palgrave Macmillan, 2013), 43. Turman is developing arguments from Christopher Morse, *Not Every Spirit: A Dogmatics of Christian Disbelief* (Valley Forge, PA: Trinity, 1994), who in turn is developing language from 2 Cor. 5:16–19. Turman's main argument in this section is that Christ holds together or "mediates" fragmentation in his body, which provides an ethical template for the Black church and, specifically, for Black women.
[100]Behind the wording of this sentence is McClendon's narrative theory of identity. See James Wm. McClendon, *Doctrine: Systematic Theology, Volume 2* (Nashville: Abingdon, 1994), 195–6, 248.

of liberated identities. Many identity categories, perhaps most obviously racial ones, are products of histories of exploitation and domination. Even if, as suggested above, members of subjugated racialized groups may associate certain goods with their racial identities, there may be a good case for seeking to abolish or, to the best of our limited ability, "undo" such oppressive, imposed identities.[101] Something similar could be said about dominant identities ("whiteness") or identities rooted in conditions that, while not originating in moral or political perfidy, might be judged as less than ideal. One response to this issue comes from Pentecostal theologian Amos Yong's writings on Down Syndrome. Yong proposes a "dynamic eschatology" in which the Spirit's work of "creatively enable[ing] and empower[ing] our full humanity in relationship to ourselves, others, and God, even in the most ambiguous situations" is carried on in the new creation.[102] The Spirit continues to "sanctify and beautify" bodies of all abilities,[103] resulting in both the eschatological preservation and transformation of difference. "Disability will be transformed even if its particular scars and marks will be redeemed, not eliminated. In this view, the body itself finds its rest in the unending process of being transformed by the glory of God in ways that overturn the binary dichotomies not only of male/female but also of disabled/nondisabled."[104] By drawing a parallel between gender- and ability-based identities, Yong licenses the extension of his argument to wider questions of identity. His work points to a model in which identities endure in a meaningful way outside of "binary dichotomies" rooted in

---

[101] For an argument for abolishing racial categories, see Karen E. Fields and Barbara J. Fields, *Racecraft: The Soul of Inequality in American Life* (London: Verso, 2014). Tran, *Asian Americans and the Spirit of Racial Capitalism*, builds on the Fields and others to argue for the church as a community oriented beyond racial identity. The language of "undoing" comes from Judith Butler's *Undoing Gender* (New York: Routledge, 2004). Butler maintains that although hegemonic gender/sex identities cannot be simply eliminated, they can be partially undone through performative queering.

[102] Amos Yong, *Theology and Down Syndrome: Reimagining Disability in Late Modernity* (Waco: Baylor University Press, 2007), 180–1, 278.

[103] "The resurrection body is hence both continuous with and yet transformed—sanctified and even beautified …—by the life-giving Spirit of God." Yong, *Theology and Down Syndrome*, 279.

[104] Yong, *Theology and Down Syndrome*, 281.

"hierarchical relationships of oppression,"[105] but to that extent they are changed into something "now inconceivable to us."[106] This model can guide our understanding of how the Spirit's doubling of identities in and as Christ saves them—not by freezing them exactly as they are nor by abolishing them, but by liberating them from oppression into an unknown, but surely good, future. Ecclesial institutions can participate in this aspect of Spirit doubling by offering opportunities for the affirmation and transformation of identities in the context of diverse solidarities. Complex institutional structures lend themselves to patterns of gathering and separation that may facilitate such opportunities. The time necessary for this work may be another important gift that institutions can offer those seeking the liberation of their identities through life in the Spirit.

This solution to the problem of identities' endurance may seem to exacerbate a second problem with my account of the Spirit's doubling. For assigning identities some eschatological purchase would seem to heighten the stakes of "identity politics"—this politics now takes on an eschatological, even apocalyptic cast. Many critics charge identity politics with sundering wider solidarities that might be formed, for instance, by emphasizing common "material conditions" such as the ownership of the means of production, the division of labor, the class structure, and so on.[107] If identities are "eternal" in some sense, then Christians might have a very good reason to focus all of their efforts on the transformation of identities rather than the transformation of material conditions. This fear is only vindicated if identities somehow float free of material conditions. Turman and Yong at least point toward a different way of thinking about identity. Turman locates her work within a womanist trajectory of theological ethics in which race and gender are treated alongside socioeconomic class.[108] This trajectory, in turn, can be comprehended in relation to a larger tradition of Black feminism that takes racism, sexism, and economic oppression

---

[105] Yong, *Theology and Down Syndrome*, 281.
[106] Yong, *Theology and Down Syndrome*, 285.
[107] As mentioned, Tran, *Asian Americans and the Spirit of Capitalism*, cites and develops the work of many such critics. Tran argues that the church embodies an alternative political economy to the economy of racial capitalism, and in doing so loosens the grip of racialization on its members.
[108] Turman, *Toward a Womanist Ethic of the Incarnation*, 57.

as intertwined.[109] For his part, Yong understands disability to be an economic, political, and social experience; his eschatological hope rests on the Spirit's ongoing formation of a "body politic" that corrects for every form of injustice.[110] Yong is here reflecting the "social model" of disability that is widely shared among disability scholars and activists.[111] The queer theologians discussed in the previous chapter similarly contend that sexual identities are part of an order of decency rooted in colonial economic exploitation and political domination.[112]

The idea that identity is intrinsically related to material conditions is arguably at the base of identity politics. The phrase "identity politics" was first used by a small group of Boston-based Black feminists in the 1970s called the Combahee River Collective (CRC). According to historian Keeanga-Yamahtta Taylor, the CRC used the phrase to signal, first, that their experiences as poor Black women had led to their political radicalization and, second, that they were committed to a revolutionary politics of overthrowing all of the structures—racist, sexist, and capitalist—that had shaped their oppressive experiences.[113] CRC members had participated in New Left organizations, male-dominated Black power organizations, and white-run feminist organizations.[114] All of these organizations sought their allegiance, but only at the cost of neglecting some aspect of their lived experience and political commitments. On this basis, the CRC sought in identity politics a mode of action that would effectively confront all the forces that bedeviled their existence. Taylor forthrightly acknowledges that identity politics became a slogan for political movements that neglected material conditions

---

[109]Keeanga-Yamahtta Taylor, ed., *How We Get Free: Black Feminism and the Combahee River Collective* (Chicago: Haymarket, 2017).
[110]Yong, *Theology and Down Syndrome*, 285–6. This work is ongoing because it is already underway in the church.
[111]For an account of this model, see Daniel Rempel, "The Witness of Disability in a Medicalized World," *Anabaptist Witness* 9, no. 2 (October 2022): 49–50.
[112]Marcella Althaus-Reid, *Indecent Theology* (New York: Routledge, 2000); Linn Marie Tonstad, *Queer Theology: Beyond Apologetics* (Eugene, OR: Wipf & Stock, 2018).
[113]See Taylor's introduction to *How We Get Free*.
[114]See the CRC statement and the interviews with CRC members included in Taylor, ed., *How We Get Free*.

and their relation to identity-based modes of domination.[115] As a Black feminist socialist, however, she seeks to renew identity politics in the spirit of the CRC.

Vincent Harding's journey "deep into blackness" can be seen as recommending an analogous form of identity politics. As the founding director of the Institute of the Black World, Harding organized and studied with a diverse group of Black nationalists involved in pan-Africanist anti-colonial politics. As part of this work, he wrote the foreword to Walter Rodney's Marxist classic, *How Europe Underdeveloped Africa*.[116] He collaborated with other pan-Africanists such as the Marxist scholar C. L. R. James and Stokely Carmichael, the former Black Panther who moved to Guinea and dedicated his life to organizing the All-African People's Revolutionary Party. None of these figures can be accused of promoting a form of politics that centered identity to the detriment of attention to material conditions, even if all of them took Blackness or African-descent as a key for political analysis and action.[117] These figures were, furthermore, involved in a wider anti-colonial struggle that actively sought diverse coalition partners in order to reshape the international economic and political order.[118]

These examples enable a rendering of identity politics as doubling movements for economic liberation with movements that seek to end identity-based oppression. When this doubling is successful, it can unleash powerful forces for justice as seen in the CRC as well as in Harding and his colleagues. The power of politics that double identity and economics could be viewed as rooted in the bifurcated structure of social fields. As discussed in Chapter 1, Bourdieu depicts fields as divided between "cultural" and "material" polls. This division reflects the different forms of capital pursued within a given field and reminds us that capital always has material in

---

[115]In addition to her remarks in *How We Get Free*, see her book *From #BlackLivesMatter to Black Liberation* (Chicago: Haymarket, 2016).

[116]Walter Rodney, *How Europe Underdeveloped Africa* (New York: Verso, 2018).

[117]For recent work that names and develops this tradition, see Charisse Burden-Stelly, "Modern US Racial Capitalism: Some Theoretical Insights," *Monthly Review*, July 1, 2020, https://monthlyreview.org/2020/07/01/modern-u-s-racial-capitalism/.

[118]See Adom Getachew, *Worldmaking after Empire: The Rise and Fall of Self-determination* (Princeton: Princeton University Press, 2019). Keeanga-Yamahtta Taylor also emphasizes the coalitional character of Black socialist politics in the United States in *From #BlackLivesMatter to Black Liberation*.

addition to cultural and symbolic dimensions. If a field is a space of ordered relations among positions defined by their differential possession of capital, and some of those positions dominate others, then freedom from domination is unlikely to occur by politics that one-sidedly emphasize either identity (understood as a cultural-symbolic formation) or material conditions. Rather, a politics that doubles identity and economics is needed.

Although this perspective on identity politics may resonate on historical and social theoretical grounds, it remains to be seen how it might connect to the doubling Spirit. In Chapter 2, we saw that the Spirit hovers over creation to organize chaos into life-giving, dynamically structured cosmos. Creatures within this cosmos participate in Spirit hovering by employing their God-given agency to generate new dynamic structures oriented to life and creaturely solidarity. The collaborative and interactive quality of creaturely creativity warrants its general description as "social." Human activities aimed at participation in the Spirit are social activities that involve organizing and organization. Organizations of various types and levels of complexity are thus potential outcomes of participation in the organizing Spirit. Here we may add that insofar as the relational web of creation is physical and social, creation's structures are simultaneously material and symbolic—they are laden with symbolic meanings via their constitutive relation to God and through the symbolic production of humans and perhaps other species.[119] Creation has permanent significance, it is always meaningful, since it is God's creation. Humans and other symbol-generating creatures organize and reorganize creation's symbolic structures in the process typically referred to as "culture."[120] In brief, creation itself has material and symbolic dimensions as a result of its organization by the Spirit. An account of effective

---

[119] Accounts of humans as uniquely symbolic (or unique in the complexity of our symbolic development) include Ernst Cassirer, *An Essay on Man: An Introduction to a Philosophy of Human Culture* (New Haven: Yale University Press, 2021 [1944]); and Terrence W. Deacon, *The Symbolic Species: The Co-evolution of Language and the Brain* (New York: W. W. Norton, 1997).

[120] Cassirer equates the development of symbolic meaning with culture, and Bourdieu's synthesizes this approach with Marxist and Weberian emphases on domination and a conception of "misrecognition" rooted in the habitus. See Pierre Bourdieu, "Sur le pouvoir symbolique," *Annales* 32, no. 3 (1977): 405–11.

political action as seeking to double these dimensions can therefore be seen as ultimately rooted in creation's nature.[121] When identity politics are oriented to this doubling, then they may be means of participating in the doubling Spirit.

Just as ecclesial institutions may facilitate the transformational doubling of identities by the Spirit, so might they contribute to the doubling of material and identity politics. The organization and sustenance of institutions requires the ongoing formation of a material base at the same time as some more or less clearly defined institutional mission. In other words, institutions themselves partake in the double character of creation as material and symbolic. When institutions aim to participate in Spirit doubling, they bring together material and symbolic resources to advance the Spirit's purposes of life and solidarity, healing and freedom. They, therefore, offer a unique context for the doubling of politics focused on material conditions and those focused on identity-based liberation.

Conclusion

One of the more challenging statements made during our oral history interviews about urban renewal in Elkhart's Benham West neighborhood concerns integration as a solution to racism and racial injustice. The interviewee, historian of the region's underground railroad Sandra Mose Ursery, said:

> This may sound controversial but, you know, segregation—I think I like segregation. And I think that might be one of our biggest downfalls, trying to get what somebody else had instead of taking what we had and just working with it and going on

---

[121] Anabaptist readers will again be reminded of Marpeck's Christology, noted above, in which the dual spiritual-material constitution of humans required a spiritual-material savior. Also relevant is the general Anabaptist insistence that spiritual conviction must take material shape within a visible community of disciples. Mutual aid or the sharing of material goods is to be a hallmark of that community, the tangible realization of the love of disciples for one another. I discuss this tradition in Jamie Pitts, "Communitarian Proto-Socialism in Christian History," in *Cambridge Companion to Christian Socialism*, eds. Christophe Chalamet and Daniel Smith-Christopher (Cambridge: Cambridge University Press, forthcoming).

to live. Integration was just "poof" [shudders]. We had all we needed. We didn't need what they had. We needed to keep our children wherever they were. We needed to raise them the way we wanted them to be raised, and not the way somebody else felt was a better life. Like I said, the grass is not greener on the other side all the time.[122]

This statement can be understood in at least two ways. First, Ursery is rejecting the politics of integration as that unfolded through urban renewal and the forced displacement of African Americans. In Elkhart, the clearance of Benham West resulted in the elimination of Black-owned businesses and the dispersal of the "village" community. Ursery draws special attention to the deleterious effect of these events on African American children, who, she says, continue to be put "at the back of the wagon" in schools and now lack an environing community to assist and guide them. Other interviewees also noted the harm done to displaced elderly residents, who were put in a position of taking out new mortgages after they had already paid off their homes and retired.[123] The loss of community, then, was felt acutely at both ends of life. Ursery acknowledges that questioning integration is controversial but provides evidence that the history of integration has been far from beneficent.[124]

A second way to understand Ursery's words is to view them as highlighting the power of Black community as it formed under conditions of segregation. As we have seen with reference both to Benham West and to African American history more generally, communal autonomy has been a significant component of Black resistance to white supremacism. Harding notes the central role of "freedom institutions" in embodying and promoting such autonomy, and this point finds confirmation when considered in relation to the churches, community center, political organizations, and businesses

---

[122]Alexis and Pitts, *What Happened at Benham West*.
[123]Alexis and Pitts, *What Happened at Benham West*.
[124]See also Keeanga-Yamahtta Taylor, *Race for Profit: How Banks and the Real Estate Industry Undermined Black Homeownership* (Chapel Hill, NC: University of North Carolina Press, 2019). Taylor argues that African Americans suffered "predatory inclusion" in the housing market in the post-segregation period. In other words, the terms of integration for African Americans were ongoing economic dispossession.

of Benham West, many of which were themselves members of larger national and international institutional bodies and movements. As Harding's historiography demonstrates, African Americans have not, since the barracoons, been privileged to choose the conditions of their autonomy. But given persistent conditions of unfreedom, they have nevertheless courageously fought for and won some measure of autonomy throughout modernity's long centuries. Ursery does not have to be taken as a segregationist—as someone who endorses the conditions that led to and maintained segregation—to appreciate the logic of her criticism of integration and her affinity for the autonomous Black community that developed under the condition of segregation.

Further reflection on the category of "autonomy" helps us tie together the threads of this chapter. One of Harding's criteria for assessing the liberating status of institutions was their contribution to the autonomy of Black freedom struggle. This autonomy can be understood contextually, as autonomy from domination by white supremacist institutions and autonomy for the promotion of flourishing of an oppressed group. Nevertheless, the language of "autonomy" has come under attack especially from postliberal theologians who see it as a relic of liberal ideology that atomizes community on the basis of the illusion that we can simply remake our lives at will, without the ongoing mediation of the resources of a "tradition." Perhaps, then, we should assess Harding as Stanley Hauerwas assessed Gustavo Gutiérrez's liberation theology—as a faux-radical, typically liberal attempt to escape the bonds of community in the name of a vague conception of freedom.[125]

This chapter provides resources for responding to this concern. The autonomy pursued by Black freedom institutions need not be pictured as eluding tradition, community, or some kind of tie to history and divine action that might offer it coherence. To an important degree those institutions, and the movements in which they participate, can be viewed instead as attempts to face historical

---

[125]Stanley Hauerwas, *After Christendom: How the Church Is to Behave if Freedom, Justice, and a Christian Nation Are Bad Ideas* (Nashville, TN: Abingdon, 1991), 50–8.

reality, to find ways to keep going after the violence of colonization that draw from but are not nostalgically limited to precolonial models. "Autonomy" here refers just to this effort to seek radical renewal unbounded by regnant liberal political models, as exampled by Harding's writings and organizing activities. With reference to his writings, Harding narrates a tradition of Black struggle whose character is expressed in part through its generation of counter-institutions and counter-ideologies to dominant white liberal ones. The autonomy of these movements is not envisioned as an end in itself, but rather as a means of foreclosing further oppression and advancing a more egalitarian alternative.[126] At the same time, Harding critically engages American liberalism's core idiom, doubling it through phrases such as "the other American revolution." This doubling, as with Harding's larger project of conjuration, acknowledges the historical situatedness of the American front in the global Black struggle even as it seeks to transform the fundamental situation beyond a standard liberal horizon.[127] This dynamic is also visible within Harding's organizing activities, which sought to build radical coalitions for Black study and political change. Harding's own freedom institutions doubled the freedom movements in which he participated, movements dedicated to broad social transformation through, not in spite of,

---

[126] In keeping with the general argument of this book, the autonomy sought by Harding could be described as a "relational autonomy," as differentiation within community.

[127] As noted above, Harding sees this move as intelligible within African American history. Cf. Corey D. B. Walker, "Social Theory and African American Theology," in *The Oxford Handbook of African American Theology*, eds. Katie G. Cannon and Anthony B. Pinn (New York: Oxford University Press, 2014), 379: "those people not included within the [US Constitution's] circle of 'the people' developed critical strategies to expand the scope and meaning of the political principles in an effort to reestablish the grounds of political community on a logic of explicit inclusion rather than a logic of implicit exclusion. In so doing, new political actors fashioned political languages that did not adhere to the neat and clean divides between the theological and the political that statesmen like Jefferson sought to maintain. Instead, they would tarry on the boundaries of the theological and the political in advancing their claims and commitments for political inclusion in the service of expanding the framework of the political and redefining such key principles as freedom, liberty, and citizenship."

their autonomy.[128] Moreover, on Harding's account the construction of institutions was ingredient—not incidental—to the achievement of liberating autonomy.

This autonomy also should not be pictured as somehow in opposition to the church's witness. Here it suffices to rehearse the arguments developed earlier in the chapter. The organizing Spirit can double church-based liberation organizations, including institutions, in the world. When the church fails to live up to its vocation, the Spirit can also inspire "worldly" institutions to call the church to faithfulness. If this form of doubling can be viewed as a judgment on the church, then it is precisely the worldly institution's autonomy from the church that allows for the necessary distance from the church to enact the judgment. Although there are good reasons to be wary of political movements launched in the name of identities, these movements and accompanying institutions can be vehicles of liberation given their potential to be formed through experiences of oppression and political struggles that are clear-eyed about relations between identities and material conditions. Indeed, if identities—even identities formed in less-than-ideal conditions—endure in some respects eschatologically, then Christians ought to be concerned about identity politics. But just to the extent that such politics is sometimes the Spirit's sign of judgment on the church, Christians can in some circumstances support the autonomy of identity political movements as a good aligned with the doubling Spirit.

For Harding, such movements are served by institutions that strengthen movement power, offer practical resources for political organizing and understanding, and sustain hope for future transformation. Institutions, furthermore, offer organizational contexts through which solidaristic alliances can be formed across the church-world boundary and in which identities can be transformed and identity politics connected to material politics. Christians can assess the extent to which specific institutions participate in the work of the doubling Spirit according to

---

[128] Getachew, *Worldmaking after Empire*, 157, 159, 170, observes that mid-twentieth-century postcolonial movements sought a combination of national political independence and international economic interdependence. This goal represented a break from the status quo ante of colonial political subjugation and/or national economic dependence.

Harding's robust, even systematic set of theological and political criteria, which encompass doctrines of providence, Christology, salvation and redemption, and pneumatology. Among the political criteria is the institutions' contribution to movement autonomy, understood in a global or "world" context of common struggles against domination. Harding's global vision takes in not only identity-based movements, but also institutions aimed at a mode of liberation that is material—and shared.

5

Organizing Spirit

Picturing Organizing Spirit

Contemporary theologians advance a pneumatological-sociological picture that foregrounds the Spirit's formation of communities and movements, typically at a local level and with the potential for effecting "bottom-up" social change. Even when theologians such as Sarah Coakley complicate the picture by writing of "mixed-type" individuals and communities that witness to the Spirit within institutions, "institutions" are still figured as in some way inherently antithetical or resistant to the transforming winds of Spirit change. This book has offered an alternative picture through which participation in the work of institutions might be viewed as a means of participation in the Spirit. In this concluding chapter, I provide a final view of the picture and then go on to explore some of its practical implications for the church's present witness.

Imagining the Spirit as primarily or exclusively concerned with local and bottom-up action neglects creation's relational constitution. As a work of the divine economy, creation exists only in relation to God. God calls creation into being and graciously sustains it, acting decisively in Israel, Christ, and the church to redeem it from sin. Taking the divine economy as a guide, we rightly conceive of creation's transformation as a bottom-up process initiated, for instance, in the interpersonal character of sin, the election of a particular people, and the incarnation of Jesus Christ. Yet we should not miss the "top-down" dynamics that define creation and its changes, such as creation's universal source and destiny in God, the universal distribution of wisdom, or the cosmic power of sin. We might also attend to the role of mid-level influences (such as regional "names" or authority figures) in moving from a dualistic top-bottom imaginary toward a more relational conception of creation as a web of interlocking and overlapping forces. Viewing creation under the aspect of the divine economy, in other words, results in a picture of creation as constituted through its "external" relation to God and its diverse "internal" relations. The divine act of creation can therefore be understood as a founding organization of creation's relations (relations that otherwise would not exist), while God's redemptive action reorganizes those relations in response to sin's disorganization of them.

The internal or immanent dimensions of this picture are broadly consonant with the approach of Pierre Bourdieu's relational sociology, which renders the social as a dynamic set of "fields." The individuals, groups, and organizations that make up a social field are formed insofar as they pursue the specific types of capital that are valued within the field. Field positions are defined by the quantity and type of capital they possess relative to other positions, indicating that the nature or identity of a given position (individual, group, organization) is an inherently relational phenomenon. From this perspective, specific organizational forms such as local communities, social movements, and institutions (formal organizations) do not possess singular essences derived from their formal properties, but rather occur within the dynamic socio-logic of historically instantiated fields. Normative critique of organizations accordingly must attend to their positions and trajectories within their constitutive social fields, rather than relying solely on formal analysis. The tendency to ignore or denigrate institutions within contemporary pneumatology is mistaken to the extent that it handles "institutions" as a general or formal category and on that basis prescinds from an engagement with existing institutions as relational phenomena within determinate social contexts.

The error, however, is not merely sociological. If a theological rendering of creation as a relational web is valid, then attempts to limit the scope of divine action to creation's local, small-scale, or bottom-up dimensions miss out on the organizational breadth of the divine economy. Attempts to limit the organizational scope of human participation in the divine are similarly misguided. This point does not diminish organizational activities that primarily occur within specific localities, that are small in scale and relatively simple in structure, or that operate from the underside of a social hierarchy. Instead, it locates the integrity of such activity within a wider relational setting. The work of a local congregation, for instance, has theological integrity not because it is local, small, or socially marginal, but because it is a promised site of indwelling by Christ's Spirit (Matt. 18:20) and to the extent that it joins that Spirit's work. A congregation's existence and local effects are highly significant on these grounds. Yet we should not isolate congregational existence to "the local." The same Spirit who is present to even the smallest gatherings in Christ's name is also the universal Lord and giver of life and, on a practical level, congregations frequently draw on and contribute to regional, national, and international organizational bodies in their work. If the integrity of local organizing and organizations should not be impugned on formal or theological grounds, neither should organizational efforts that seek to be translocal, large, structurally complex, or socially inclusive (encompassing members from various social positions). In brief, institutions are a potential organizational venue for participation in the Spirit.

This argument is deepened by a focus on the Spirit's activity in creation. The hovering Spirit partners with God's Word to organize creation's complex and dynamic relations. The Spirit brings harmonious, dancing structure out of chaos, not just "in the beginning" but characteristically and continuously. The hovering Creator Spirit providentially tends creation, turning entropy to life-sustaining order. The Spirit's gift of life signals, again, creation's dependence on God as well as God's purpose in creation. This purpose is specially seen in the electing work of God's Spirit to liberate and form a people whose life together embodies peace with God and all creatures. Election's horizon, however, is not the well-being of an isolated community but rather universal well-being. Election in this way testifies to the relational differentiation that the Spirit grants creation. Just as the Spirit separates day from night and water from dry land, so the Spirit separates elect and non-elect—not for the exaltation of one and the denigration of the other, but for all of creation's blessing. In election the Spirit organizes human sociality so that parts of it—discrete organized social groupings—would, in the face of persistent forces of chaos, permanently (though falteringly) bear witness to the Spirit's universally available gifts of life and solidarity. Human organizational activities participate in the hovering Spirit insofar as they partake in this witness. The scale and structure of those activities are subordinate to their participatory purpose. If election's particularity points to an affinity for the small and local, then its universal horizon—a corollary of the universal sweep of the hovering Spirit—opens the entire creation to varieties of translocal organizing and organizations, including what are commonly known as institutions.

This vision of the hovering Spirit has consequences for debates in environmental ethics about the location of ecological politics. In contrast to those theological ethicists who delimit ecological politics to a church's watershed or other local context, the hovering Spirit connects localities and invites translocal organizing. The example of the Elkhart River Watershed exhibits the Spirit-given relationality at the heart of every locality, a relationality that is at once social and ecological. Working for a locality's flourishing entails working at the relations that constitute it. It entails, for instance, working at the wider ecological, political, and economic forces operating in a watershed. Although local organizing is vital for that work, there are no general theological or practical reasons to confine such organizing to the local. At the practical level, many local organizations rely in some way on resources from regional, national, and international institutions in their work. The problems besetting localities, moreover, are rarely isolable. To the contrary, they are as interconnected as watersheds and wind patterns and call for a coordinated response, as is most evident today with climate change. The organizational capacity of institutions positions them well to lead or at least be a major part of that response. Picturing every locality as lovingly inhabited—and lovingly connected—by the hovering Spirit removes barriers to initiating or joining translocal institutions devoted to an ecological politics of life and creaturely solidarity.

In this picture, Christian congregations have a special role as local participants in the work of the hovering Spirit, but not an exclusive role. Many congregations are members of denominational and other institutions, institutions that may provide important resources for both the local and translocal dimensions of shared struggles for justice. Yet those institutions can also hinder that work, such as when they exclude participants because of their gender and sexuality. Some theologians have depicted processes aimed at widening participation to those formerly excluded on that basis (women, LGBTQ people) as part of the Spirit's work of sanctification. The Spirit sanctifies, they argue, by transforming the formerly excluded through practices such as prayer or same-sex marriage and by opening ecclesial communities to their full participation. Although there is some acknowledgment that this sanctifying "opening" involves church institutions, the institutional dimension of sanctification tends to be underspecified in contemporary pneumatology. Examining a case of women's organizing within denominational institutions provides a helpful image of how Spirit sanctification might lead to institutional reform. In this case, Mennonite women in North America successfully, though with much difficulty, challenged their denominations to accept their leadership. As they did so some of them claimed the inspiration of the Spirit, thereby offering additional support for a pneumatological-sociological picture in which the sanctifying Spirit fosters holiness not only in individuals and communities but also in institutions. Participating in the progressive reform of institutions can be a way of participating in the sanctifying Spirit.

This picture challenges more pessimistic theologies that foreclose the possibility of significant change within this life and, on that basis, diminish or ignore institutions' potential contributions to Christian ministry and mission. These accounts raise valid concerns about institutions' tendencies to reproduce oppressive structures and about the fantasy of infallible knowledge that can lie behind institution-driven reform efforts. Nevertheless, affirming institutions as potential means of participating in the Spirit need not deny their capacity for harm nor their epistemological (and other) limits. Institutions do not run on rails to infinity (Wittgenstein) and, again, must be analyzed within their specific historical and social contexts, i.e., as organizational fields, as to their suitability for promoting life and an inclusive solidarity among creatures. This formulation signifies that the incorporation of institutions into the pneumatological-sociological picture is a critical and not just an affirmative process. Claiming that institutions may be sanctified by the Spirit suggests that institutions may be *sanctioned* by the Spirit, in both the positive and negative senses of that word.

A skeptic of institutions as such might take solace in Vincent Harding's departure from Mennonite church circles in the late 1960s. Surely his choice of radical Black nationalist movements over Mennonite institutions reflects the bankruptcy of institutions, and of ecclesial institutions in particular? That is not how Harding saw it, however, as he narrated his journey with God into both Mennonite institutions and Black nationalism. Harding's post-Mennonite itinerary defies dualisms that would pit social movements against institutions, and ecclesial against non-ecclesial ("worldly") institutions. He not only started a series of institutions but also theorized the role of "freedom institutions" in fostering the Black freedom movement. His life and writings, replete with theological and especially biblical allusions, point to a Spirit who doubles the spirit of movements, in part by inspiring the formation of institutions to promote movement aims. Conceptualizing movements as social fields helps clarify how institutions and institutionalization processes might occur within movements without replacing or undermining but rather amplifying and sustaining their power. Institutions may further movement ends by gathering and developing the movement's material and symbolic resources. Institutionalization is risky, of course, but so is refusing it. Harding, at least, saw the potential for institutionalization to enhance movements' power.

Harding also offered a variety of criteria for discerning the extent to which institutions participate in the Spirit's doubling of movements—and so of what movements the Spirit seeks to double with institutions. Movements and institutions that are dedicated to the freedom and healing of the oppressed, especially to those oppressed by colonialism throughout the world, witness to God's providential care for creation, the gracious liberation of the crucified Christ, and the solidaristic fellowship of the Holy Spirit. For Harding, these theological terms and social movements and institutions are mutually intelligible in light of each other— they double each other. We come to understand how the Spirit organizes by attending to liberation movements and institutions, and our theological view of the organizing Spirit critically shapes our interpretation of those movements and institutions. Similarly, movement institutions operating outside of the church should not be regarded as ineligible for participation in the Spirit. The contextual and relational character of the church and its connections to "the world" caution against any simplistic church–world dualism that would rule extra-ecclesial institutions out of bounds in this way. The Spirit may indeed raise up such autonomous institutions as signs of judgment on ecclesial failures—and perhaps this is one way to understand Harding's Black nationalist institutions. On the other hand, prohibiting ecclesial institutions from freedom movements ignores the history that Harding so ably covers and therefore neglects possibilities that may arise from the Spirit's doubling of ecclesial and extra-ecclesial institutions.

The work of institutions today at times seems to be undermined by competing claims for justice based on different personal and group identities. Some activists and scholars, including theologians, have accordingly called for the surpassing of identity politics by a solidaristic politics focused on material conditions. A particular theological worry that arises in this regard has to do with the Spirit's formation of the church as a community with a shared identity in Christ. If the Spirit cancels other identities and integrates believers into a single identity, then surely identity politics is a dead end. But the New Testament is more ambiguous about the relationship between identity in Christ and other identities, insisting, for instance, on Christ's Jewish identity and on the church as made up of members with multiple identities. The avoidance of Christian supersessionism further militates against a uniformly negative posture toward "non-Christian" identities, as do sociological considerations about identities' relational character—identities are in practice not easily separable from one another. The picture of the doubling Spirit assists here, too, as it lends itself to an imagination of the Spirit doubling diverse identities with and in Christ. The Spirit saves us by applying to us Christ's recapitulation of our entire human experience, including our experience of group and personal identification. This approach avoids the specter of an eschatological preservation of the harmful or sinful aspects of identities, such as their deformation by social hierarchies, as it promises that the Spirit will transform all identities at the eschaton. Identities' eschatological future may be shrouded in mystery, but that future surely avoids both supersessionism and the perpetuation of identity-based oppression.

Rather than reject identity politics, institutions might consider what they have to offer toward a better version of identity politics that aligns more with the doubling Spirit. For instance, institutions' organizational complexity and extended temporal horizons may facilitate a more nuanced and open-ended exploration of identities consonant with Spirit doubling. Institutions can also downplay the frequently exclusive and apocalyptic character of identity politics by mooring it to struggles for material conditions. Recognizing that identities exist within relational social fields constituted by both cultural and material capital facilitates this effort to connect both kinds of struggles. Institutions are well positioned to merge or double these struggles insofar as their work already involves the gathering of significant cultural and material resources. A possible agenda for institutions is to consider how the material capital they raise can support the inclusive liberation of all those oppressed on the basis of their identity, and in turn how the cultural capital they amass might be directed toward broad-based material solidarity and flourishing. In taking up this agenda, institutions may participate in the Spirit who doubles the symbolic and the material while organizing creation's eco-social fields.

The hovering, sanctifying, and doubling Spirit is the one organizing Spirit of God. It is the divine organizing Spirit who turns creational chaos into cosmos, sanctifies for collective flourishing, and heals and liberates the oppressed. Although the Spirit does not directly organize or reorganize institutions (is not their secondary cause), the Spirit encourages or empowers them by eliciting a human organizational response. Describing this response as "participatory" clarifies institutions' normative horizon without confusing their fallible work with God's. Whether or not an institution can be judged as participating in the work of the organizing Spirit is a matter of discernment, a matter on which Christians are likely to disagree. Chapters 2, 3, and 4 each set forth criteria that can be used when discerning whether or not, or the extent to which, an institution participates in the Spirit. Among these criteria are the institution's dedication to life and creaturely solidarity (Chapter 2); to progressive inclusion of formerly excluded people and groups for the sake of collective flourishing (Chapter 3); and to global anti-colonial healing and justice in the way of Jesus (Chapter 4).

Imagining institutions as potential modes of participation in the Spirit does not warrant the identification of specific institutions much less the blanket approbation of institutions in general as favored or directed by the Spirit. Another criterion for discernment that appeared throughout the book was the acknowledgment that all institutions are fallible and liable to go wrong. The denial of this condition is a sure sign that an institution, and its members or leaders, have failed to understand the shape of pneumatological participation. Institutional participants in the Spirit may dare to organize—dare to plan, to gather resources for their work, to assign tasks, to design complex organizational structures—but not to claim a special dispensation from the Spirit that guarantees their moral purity or practical efficacy. Participants in institutions might, in the best cases, combine enthusiastic commitment to the work of their institutions with a posture of critical vigilance. They might, in other words, dedicate themselves to the continual reformation of their institutions as they organize toward life in the Spirit. In less ideal situations their organizing may lead them to switch their institutional affiliations or start new institutions. Whatever the case may be, to the extent that they seek to participate in the Spirit they will not abandon the organization of creation's complex eco-social relations—which would amount to the abandonment of creation as such.

Neoliberalism, Global Imagination, and Pneumatological Political Theology

By offering an alternative pneumatological-sociological picture to the dominant one in contemporary theology, this book seeks to intervene in discussions among Christian theologians about the social shape of the Spirit's work and human responses to the Spirit. My hope is that theologians will devote more time to the institutional dimensions of pneumatology and pneumatological ecclesiology and will consider further the role of pneumatic institutions in pursuing God's good. The goods of environmental, gender and sexual, and racial justice can and have been advanced by institutions. Theologians can help institutions continue to make progress in these areas by developing theologies of institutions that offer standards for institutional structure and conduct, standards that are at once aspirational and critical. Imagining institutions within the divine economy will help ensure that institutions refrain from prioritizing self-preservation over justice and develop policies, structures, and procedures that demonstrate love for their members and all those affected by their work. Taking up this theological task will remind institutional leaders that their work, and their institutions, are gifts of the organizing Spirit and as such contain opportunities for pneumatological participation—opportunities that carry the weighty and joyful responsibility to join the Spirit in fostering life and creaturely solidarity, inclusive collective flourishing, and healing and justice for all.

This book can also be read as offering a distinctive approach to political theology, insofar as it explores in various ways theological justifications for political institutions. Clarifying and extending the book's political theological argument elucidate the stakes of a theology of institutions in the present context.

The institutions I have described and recommended throughout the book are political in the basic sense that they are engaged in organizing power. They exist in relation to the ultimate source of power, God, and their activities involve the gathering, distribution, and exercise of power. Many theologians think that institutions are illegitimate means of organizing power, or at least that their legitimacy is so weak—especially in comparison to organizational forms such as communities and movements—that they are barely worth mentioning. While acknowledging the force of some criticisms of institutions' claims to theological legitimacy, I have also advanced reasons for taking their legitimacy seriously at a formal level. That is, I have rejected any attempt to legitimize particular institutions and have instead described general features of institutions that might be said to legitimately participate in the Spirit. Whether a particular institution does or does not participate in the Spirit should be an open question for critical discernment and debate. As with matters of identity, the justification—the salvation—of institutions and other social realities has an ineradicably eschatological dimension that refuses premature declarations of the sanctity of such and such institution. The grammar of pneumatological participation is a grammar of critical hope and of hopeful criticism.

By taking up questions of legitimacy I am following Adam Kotsko's argument that political theology should broadly interrogate the social structures of legitimation rather than focus narrowly on the borrowing of theological concepts in political discourse and vice versa.[1] In agreement with Kotsko, I have sought to fund a critical perspective on the theological legitimation of political institutions by specifying a variety of criteria by which that legitimacy can be named and subjected to critique. Going beyond Kotsko, and in concert with numerous Christian political theologians, I also engage theology as a constructive resource for generating standards of legitimation toward which institutions might aspire.[2] Although I am aware of the risks that beset such a project, I remain convinced that refusing constructive political theology is far more dangerous.

Bringing the Spirit into political theology relieves the discipline of a tendency toward a uniformly critical posture without thereby vitiating its critical energies. The Spirit of God imbues creation with legitimacy. From the dynamic structures at creation's heart to the breath that fills the lungs of sundry beasts—all is declared legitimate, and legitimately good, as a gift of the Spirit. Creaturely action is likewise legitimate *qua* creaturely action, its existence and form divinely blessed. Yet creaturely actions can go wrong, can miss the mark in discerning the shape of life in the Spirit and in seeking to participate (or not to participate) in that life. The critique of the legitimacy of certain actions or, more broadly, social patterns such as institutions and other organizations relies in this account on a positive vision of creation's legitimacy as always already granted by God's Spirit at the most fundamental level.

The pneumatological vision of creation put forward in this book also suggests that creation is fundamentally relational. Relational ontologies are hardly unique to theology these days, and this book has benefited from sustained consideration of Bourdieu's relational sociology. But the combination of a relational social ontology with pneumatology opens further possibilities for a political theology that seeks to be constructive as well as critical. Namely, such a political theology will hesitate before pronouncing some social or political phenomenon as irretrievably illegitimate and will

---

[1] Adam Kotsko, *Neoliberalism's Demons: On the Political Theology of Late Capital* (Stanford: Stanford University Press, 2018), 127–44. Kotsko specifically commends genealogical critique to political theologians. I will not discuss genealogy here, but I do argue that political theology should be constructive as well as critical.
[2] See, e.g., Peter Scott and William T. Cavanaugh, eds., *The Blackwell Companion to Political Theology* (Malden, MA: Blackwell, 2004).

insist on studying that phenomenon within its relational context.³ This context includes the presence of the Spirit who sustains it and beckons it to life, healing, solidarity, and justice. Attempting to discern the Spirit's work directs our attention not only to human failure (including inevitable failures of discernment) but also to the potential for human participation in that work. Creation's internal or immanent relationality also suggests that there may be latent participatory potential within even the direst of settings—it is unlikely that all the relations constituting an institution are evil. Getting clear about the shape of this potential is pneumatological political theology's contribution to critical political transformation.

The need for such a textured critical practice becomes evident in view of Kotsko's primary object of critique, neoliberalism. Although definitions of neoliberalism vary widely, here we can draw attention to two commonly named yet contrasting features that make countering it difficult yet necessary. Neoliberalism is strongly associated with both globalization, the systematic integration of the world's capitalist markets, and a resurgent political and cultural "tribalism," in which localized (though often globally distributed) identities have new and often explosive salience.⁴ If facing up to

---

³This is to say that political theologians should perform scholarly due diligence when offering political critique *as political theologians*. This is not to say that political theologians cannot offer harsh critiques, and it is not a statement directed to individuals speaking "prophetically" as citizens, activists, or politicians. Although the boundaries between scholarship and ordinary speech are often ambiguous, I follow Bourdieu in supposing that the public legitimacy of scholars' voices, such as it is, depends to a large degree on the legitimacy of our voices within our scholarly communities. In other words, scholars are best able to contribute to public political discourse *as scholars* when we have obtained significant credibility (significant cultural capital) within our scholarly fields. Bourdieu's view follows his understanding of the "circuits of legitimation" among fields. Pierre Bourdieu, "The Specificity of the Scientific Field and the Social Conditions of the Progress of Reason," trans. Richard Nice *Social Science Information* 14, no. 6 (1975): 19–46; Pierre Bourdieu, *Pascalian Meditations*, trans. Richard Nice (Cambridge: Polity, 2000), 93–127.

⁴Classic accounts of neoliberalism such as David Harvey, *A Brief History of Neoliberalism* (Oxford: Oxford University Press, 2005) focus on economic globalization but also bemoan the rise of identity politics (31, 41, 62, 198). For a more thorough repudiation of identity politics, seen as a major fruit of neoliberalism, see Walter Benn Michaels and Adolph Reed, *No Politics but Class Politics*, eds. Anton Jäger and Daniel Zamora (London: ERIS, 2022).

globalization would seem to call for a reinvigoration of localities, then resistance to tribalism would seem to point in an opposite, universalist direction.

This fissure can perhaps be explained by accounts of neoliberalism focused on efforts to "encase" the global economy in institutions subject to little or no democratic accountability.[5] These institutions include the International Monetary Fund (IMF), the World Bank, the World Trade Organization (WTO), the New York Federal Reserve, and the European Union (EU), as well as various regional multilateral trade associations. Many of these organizations were created or newly empowered to direct international economic policy in the wake of the Second World War.[6] In theory they were part of a larger international system that included the United Nations (UN), where representatives of most of the world's countries could debate policy matters and thus provide some sort of democratic legitimation and direction. As the process of decolonization in Africa and Asia advanced in the 1950s and 1960s, the newly independent nations joined the UN and together advocated for a fair global economy that would give them the

---

[5]Quinn Slobodian, *Globalists: The End of Empire and the Birth of Neoliberalism* (Cambridge: Harvard University Press, 2018). Slobodian, Philip Mirowski, and other scholars have pushed back against a description of neoliberalism as strictly antagonistic to government regulation. In Mirowski's words, "in practice, [neoliberal] 'deregulation' always cashes out as 'reregulation,' only under a different set of ukases." Mirowski, *Never Let a Serious Crisis Go to Waste: How Neoliberalism Survived the Financial Meltdown* (New York: Verso, 2013), 57. Keeanga-Yamahtta Taylor, *Race for Profit: How Banks and the Real Estate Industry Undermined Black Homeownership* (Chapel Hill, NC: University of North Carolina Press, 2019), 230–7, stresses how in the United States neoliberalism emerged as a racist reaction to the welfare state, a reaction that worked in part through new regulations that integrated private real estate brokers into federal housing policy.

[6]The World Trade Organization (WTO) was formed in 1995 as the successor of the General Agreement on Tariffs and Trade (GATT) that had been put into place in 1948. These organizations promoted multilateral trade agreements, especially in the 1990s heyday of neoliberalism. Many free trade associations were created in that decade such as the Association of Southeast Asian Nations (ASEAN) Free Trade Area (AFTA 1992), the Greater Arab Free Trade Area (GAFTA 1997), the North American Free Trade Agreement (NAFTA 1994, renegotiated in 2020 as the US-Mexico-Canada Agreement or USMCA), and the Central American Integration System (SICA 1993). The European Union was founded in 1993 but has roots in earlier regional economic agreements.

opportunity to develop the industries and welfare states enjoyed by European and North America countries. But the latter countries were largely hostile to such advocacy—nominally because of their fears of communism—leading to the disempowerment of the UN and the further erosion of democratic checks on capitalist expansion directed by the United States and its allies.[7] Neoliberalism, on this view, is the political project of subordinating the world to capitalist exploitation after the failure of direct imperialism. The fall of the Soviet Union in 1991 and the inclusion of China in the WTO a decade later opened onto a seemingly limitless and unchallengeable neoliberal future.

The antidemocratic institutional encasement of the global political economy had two effects relevant to the present discussion. First, national politics were increasingly subject to the influence of unaccountable global institutions. In the aftermath of the Second World War, West German "ordoliberals" pushed for strong state power to create a legal framework fostering and safeguarding economic competition from the labor movement.[8] According to historian Quinn Slobodian, Austrian neoliberals such as Friedrich Hayek and Ludwig von Mises expanded ordoliberal principles from the nation-state to the world.[9] In 1973, the democratically elected president of Chile, Salvador Allende, was overthrown by a coup and replaced by a dictator, Augusto Pinochet, who handed the country's economic policy to a group of neoliberal economists. These economists, known as the "Chicago Boys" due to their

---

[7] Adom Getachew, *Worldmaking after Empire: The Rise and Fall of Self Determination* (Princeton: Princeton University Press, 2019).
[8] Dieter Plehwe, "The Economic State and the Ordoliberal Critique of Keynesianism: Anti-Economic State or Just a Different Type of Economic State?," in *The Oxford Handbook of Ordoliberalism*, eds. Thomas Biebricher, Werner Bonefeld, and Peter Nedergaard (Oxford: Oxford University Press, 2022), 278–90. Ordoliberals are in theory also concerned with the threat of business monopolies to competition, but this concern has been moderated by its commitments to limit state intervention in the market and to prioritize the rights of property owners (287–8). Opposition to business monopolies is absent from Anglophone neoliberalism.
[9] Slobodian, *Globalists*, 7. Mirowski, *Never Let a Serious Crisis Go to Waste*, 42, argues that ordoliberalism is one of the main strands of the "neoliberal thought collective." For wider background on the centrality of West Germany and its economy to the Cold War, see Tony Judt, *Postwar: A History of Europe since 1945* (New York: Penguin, 2005), 100–128, 145–53.

training under the famed neoliberal economist Milton Friedman at the University of Chicago, dismantled Chile's social safety net.[10] Economically struggling countries from around the world, from Britain to Argentina to Thailand, accepted IMF loans on the condition of slashed social spending and tightened budgets.

At the same time as "austerity" became a watchword in national politics, an ethics of personal responsibility proliferated a promise of wealth. Global institutions had captured the global economy, and nations were largely powerless to do anything about it, but *you* could still get ahead if you worked hard enough—and if you didn't, you had only yourself to blame.[11] To manage this newly individualized social precarity, neoliberal politicians appealed to the heterosexual family as the site where dedicated workers would be formed and as a refuge of last resort.[12] Yet families also became key sites of conflict over gender, sexual, racial, and religious identities. Struggles waged over the rights and responsibilities of often fissiparous identity groupings came to dominate the neoliberal culture wars. This second, cultural effect of neoliberalism emerged in the space that democratic politics had vacated and has helped to justify unrestrained, winner-take-all economic competition and the resulting inequalities.

Neoliberalism organizes much of the world's political economy and culture. The possibility of global organizing and organizations follows from the Earth's creaturely status and relational constitution. All the Earth has been created by God and so is subject to the influence of the divine economy. The Spirit's dynamic structuration of the Earth entails that the Earth can be regarded both as a global whole and as an ensemble of differentiated-yet-related structures. Organizing across the Earth's structures, its many eco-social fields, can participate in the global character of the Spirit's creative

---

[10] Harvey, *A Brief History of Neoliberalism*, 7–9. A fascinating account of this history focused on technology is Evgeny Morozov's podcast *The Santiago Boys* (Chora Media, 2023), https://the-santiago-boys.com/.
[11] Limning the political theological features of this legitimating ethic is Kotsko's project in *Neoliberalism's Demons*. See also Kathryn Tanner, *Christianity and the New Spirit of Capitalism* (New Haven: Yale, 2019).
[12] Melinda Cooper, *Family Values: Between Neoliberalism and the New Social Conservatism* (New York: Zone, 2017).

hovering. Any institutions that result from such participative organizing are also subject to the sanctifying and doubling Spirit.

Imagining the world as indwelled by the organizing Spirit provides normative criteria with which to assess global organizing forces such as neoliberalism. In consideration of the picture of the organizing Spirit developed in this book, neoliberalism can be judged as a rival to global organizing and organizations aligned with the Spirit. Neoliberalism disempowers the majority of the world's inhabitants, perpetuates massive material inequalities, and undermines solidarity among oppressed groups. The neoliberal organization of the world is, in many respects, illegitimate. Global anti-neoliberal organizing, by contrast, is legitimate to the degree that it allies with the organizing Spirit. Global anti-neoliberal organizing that adopts many of the Spirit's goals yet rejects the range of organizational possibilities offered by the Spirit suffer from weak or moderate legitimacy. For example, such organizing could gain legitimacy through symbolic challenges to neoliberal dominance yet struggle to win the legitimacy that would obtain through an organizational strategy that is more successful in gathering and distributing material capital and its means of production. However, the legitimacy of global anti-neoliberal organizing that takes up a broader range of organizational possibilities without adopting the Spirit's goals is likewise questionable—see the discussion of "post-neoliberalism" below.

Pneumatological political theologians question neoliberalism's legitimacy while also recognizing it as a relational phenomenon occurring within a global context created and sustained by the Spirit. They thus avoid demonizing neoliberalism even while naming its shortcomings forthrightly. In one sense, neoliberalism is legitimate as a fruit of human activity and form of human sociality. It depends on and extends creaturely capacities for agency and social connection. If we rightly judge that "extension" to be harmful rather than healing and unjust rather than just—as illegitimate— we can still recognize neoliberalism's entanglement with and in the dynamic, complex structures that constitute creation as intended by the Spirit. Analyzing this entanglement may lead us to identify obscured potential in neoliberalism for a better or different mode of global organization.

A theological critique of neoliberalism attentive to the dual nature of its legitimacy might begin by acknowledging the theologian's own constitutive relations to neoliberalism. A reflexive starting point can remind us that we are intertwined with neoliberalism, as our thought-patterns, practices, and organizations are deeply shaped by it. As much as we might want to rid the world of neoliberalism, we hopefully do not want to rid the world of ourselves—that is, if we can accept ourselves as beloved gifts of the Spirit. Reflexivity in this way can fuel both critical transformation of aspects of oneself and context and acceptance, and even celebration, of other aspects.[13] It can dispose us toward what I earlier labeled a textured mode of moral and political criticism.[14] Such a criticism does not shy away from straightforward condemnation when that is called for, but also remains open to ambiguities arising from creation's ontological relation to God. By encompassing multiple modes of response to neoliberalism, a textured reflexive critique might better prepare us to move beyond neoliberalism than has critical discourse that is one-dimensionally negative.

A reflexive and textured theological criticism of neoliberalism will recognize that several aspects of contemporary theology's outlook—such as that encapsulated in the standard pneumatological-sociological picture described in Chapter 1—are complementary to neoliberalism. The fixation among theologians in recent decades on themes such as the local, the everyday, communities, identities, and largely spontaneous and minimally organized social movements validates the primary modes of politics that are allowed by neoliberalism's governing institutions.[15] In other words, these politics operate within the space evacuated of power by those institutions and do not fundamentally threaten to break the casing

---

[13]Contra Bourdieu, for whom reflexivity is only a means of critique, the radicalization of "radical doubt." Bourdieu, *Pascalian Meditations*, 28–32.

[14]Cf. Rita Felski, *The Limits of Critique* (Chicago: University of Chicago Press, 2015). I take Felski not to deny the importance of critique but rather to suggest that critique has a place within a critic's wide range of possible responses to an object of inquiry.

[15]Two studies connect Anabaptist articulations of similar themes to neoliberalism: Lucia Hulsether, *Capitalist Humanitarianism* (Durham, NC: Duke University Press, 2023), 25–48; Kevin Stewart Rose, "'The World Food Crisis Is Not a Fad': The *More-with-Less* Cookbook and Protestant Environmental Spirituality," *Religion and American Culture* 29, no. 2 (2019): 216–54.

that protects the global economy from democratic contestation. Furthermore, prominent members of contemporary theological movements such as neo-evangelicalism, postliberalism, and Radical Orthodoxy have had ties to neoliberal regimes and policies.[16] Even many purportedly radical theologies could be seen as unwittingly promulgating neoliberal culture. Ivan Petrella, for instance, has charged his fellow liberation theologians with exchanging the pursuit of grand "historic projects" meant to bring about justice with the theoretical elaboration of endlessly multiplying identity-based theologies.[17]

Theologians are certainly not alone in this regard—remembering this can help us avoid the sense that theology has somehow been uniquely corrupted by neoliberalism. A spate of recent criticism in fact locates similar themes to those valued by contemporary theologians broadly within neoliberal politics and culture.[18] Activists, scholars, and journalists worry that such themes have debilitated protest movements over the past thirty years.[19] Protest leaders have promoted spontaneity; relatively "horizontal" or leaderless structures; struggles waged in the name of particular identities (or a vague and undifferentiated "people"); and the "prefiguration" of desired political outcomes in a communal setting. Participants in such movements tend, in strategist Maurice Mitchell's words, to

---

[16] Joseph Forde, *Before and Beyond the "Big Society": John Milbank and the Church of England's Approach to Social Welfare* (Cambridge: James Clarke, 2022); Damon Linker, *The Theocons: Secular America under Siege* (New York: Anchor, 2006).

[17] Ivan Petrella, *Beyond Liberation Theology: A Polemic* (London: SCM, 2013); Ivan Petrella, *The Future of Liberation Theology: An Argument and Manifesto* (New York: Routledge, 2004). Ironically, Petrella's own attempt to foment "historic projects" has included a stint in the neoliberal president of Argentina Mauricio Macri's administration.

[18] For example, Arthur Boriello and Anton Jäger, *The Populist Moment* (New York: Verso, 2023); Stuart Jeffries, *Everything, All the Time, Everywhere: How We Became Postmodern* (London: Verso, 2021).

[19] Vincent Bevins, *If We Burn: The Mass Protest Decade and the Missing Revolution* (New York: PublicAffairs, 2023); Rodrigo Nunes, *Neither Horizontal nor Vertical: A Theory of Political Organization* (London: Verso, 2021); Jonathan Matthew Smucker, *Hegemony How-To: A Roadmap for Radicals* (Chico, CA: AK Press, 2017); Zeynep Tufekci, *Twitter and Tear Gas: The Power and Fragility of Networked Protest* (New Haven: Yale University Press, 2017).

"reflexively disdain ... institutions and organizations as inherently oppressive and antiquated."[20] For Mitchell and other concerned participants, effectively confronting neoliberalism will take a reinvestment in what is today frequently disdained—institutions.

Awareness of theology's saturation by neoliberalism's anti-institutional culture should encourage efforts to defy that culture and its companion political economy. Following Mitchell, one way theologians can partake in the struggle against neoliberalism is to articulate critical theological grounds for the legitimation of institutional organization and reform, grounds that specify how legitimate institutions contrast with neoliberalism. We must also ensure, however, that the contrast is sufficiently textured and that we are not missing the participatory potential within neoliberalism as a social and political formation constitutionally related to God's Spirit. For example, if a focus on particular identities characterizes neoliberal politics, that does not mean we should simply cast identity-talk overboard in the name of a reconstituted universalism.[21] If horizontal organizational structures have been celebrated in both neoliberal technology companies and social movements, that does not mean we should simply revert to authoritarian "verticality."[22] If "local" and "community" have become marketing slogans, that does not mean we should simply exchange communal prefiguration for impersonal bureaucracy.[23] And if spontaneity and quotidian practices have been prized over planning, that does not mean we should embrace "fixed," complex organizations for their own

---

[20] Maurice Mitchell, "Building Resilient Organizations: Toward Joy and Durable Power in a Time of Crisis," *NPQ*, November 29, 2022, https://nonprofitquarterly.org/building-resilient-organizations-toward-joy-and-durable-power-in-a-time-of-crisis/. I am grateful to Janna Hunter Bowman for sharing this article with me.

[21] Gary Gerstle has also made this point with reference to the "neoliberal order" in the United States—real freedoms were won under neoliberalism for people who have been marginalized on the basis of their identities, and these freedoms should not be compromised in whatever order comes next. Gary Gerstle, *The Rise and Fall of the Neoliberal Order* (Oxford: Oxford University Press, 2022), 183.

[22] See Nunes, *Neither Horizontal nor Vertical*.

[23] This is an especially pressing issue for Anabaptists, given the overriding emphasis in Anabaptist theology from the 1970s through the 2010s—years typically labeled as encompassing the neoliberal era—on communal prefiguration.

sake.²⁴ Theological struggle against neoliberalism benefits from a renewed, and relational, theological-sociological imagination in which the goods of institutions might be held alongside the goods of movements and communities that have come to the fore in the neoliberal era.

Our imagination should also be global, not only to match neoliberalism's global span but also, and more importantly, to match the global span of the organizing Spirit. Given that many theologians are part of denominations with global institutions and some collaborate with international ecumenical agencies such as the World Council of Churches or the Global Christian Forum, the lack of theological attention in recent years to the ecclesial status of such institutions is startling.²⁵ None of these institutions were mentioned in the contemporary pneumatological writings reviewed in Chapter 1.²⁶ Do we see them as merely instrumental, or do they have positive theological and political value? This book has tried to provide a basis for imagining the contribution of global ecclesial institutions to the church and its mission as a *theological contribution*—as a means of pneumatological participation. Similar comments could be made, following the discussion in Chapter 4,

---

²⁴In Chapter 1, I quoted Nancy Bedford's opposition between "fixed organizations" and just movements aligned with the Spirit. Bedford, "A Narrow Gate? Proceeding along the Way of Jesus by the Spirit," *Mennonite Quarterly Review* 92, no. 4 (October 2018): 495.

²⁵My hypothesis is that the global church institutions that were dominant in the mid-twentieth-century lost power for reasons similar to those that cast down the UN and other forums friendly to social democratic interests. Those institutions were designed by some of the same people who designed the other global institutions that were dethroned by neoliberalism. On this institutional legacy and its demise, see David Hollinger, *Protestants Abroad: How Missionaries Tried to Change the World but Changed America* (Princeton: Princeton University Press, 2017); Samuel Moyn, *Christian Human Rights* (Philadelphia: University of Pennsylvania Press, 2015); Gene Zubovich, *Before the Religious Right: Liberal Protestants, Human Rights, and the Polarization of the United States* (Philadelphia: University of Pennsylvania Press, 2022). My hope is not simply that we would repristinate these institutions. As an Anabaptist, I hope for robust global denominational and ecumenical institutions that are politically effective insofar as they are tied into larger democratic movements—that is, not based on the hegemony of a single religious group. I elaborate this vision in the next section.

²⁶I have also searched the databases of several ecumenical theology journals in vain for constructive theological treatments of ecclesial institutions, global or otherwise.

about extra-ecclesial global institutions such as the UN or the Global Social Forum.

Theologians who push back on the neoliberal character of our own discipline will therefore reconsider how institutions in general might serve the church's work and how global institutions in particular might provide resources for pursuing an alternative culture and political economy better aligned with the work of the organizing Spirit. We need, in short, a pneumatological political theology that legitimates global institutions on a formal level and provides robust ethical criteria and motivation for the critical work of forming, reforming, or abolishing particular global institutions.[27] Such a political theology will make use of older, pre-neoliberal theological-sociological models for legitimating, ethically assessing, and motivating participation in institutions. But it will also seek to protect the gains that have been made under neoliberal political economic and cultural conditions. Theologians must develop a progressive global imagination that contributes to a democratic institutional force to challenge neoliberal institutions.

Democratic Institutions and the Organizing Spirit

As of 2024 some observers identify signs of an emerging "post-neoliberal" consensus that is confronting the smooth functioning of encased global political economic institutions.[28] These signs include the US modest increases in infrastructure investment and

---

[27]When I say that political theology can legitimate global institutions "on a formal level," I mean only that it can suggest that such institutions are in general a valid organizational form. A Christian political theology will add that they are in general a valid ecclesiological form. Keeping legitimation formal keeps political theology from offering a blanket validation of particular institutions, though as noted it can also offer ethical criteria for assessing particular institutions. Political theology can contribute to the legitimation or de-legitimation of particular institutions in this indirect way.

[28]See, for example, the website *Post-Neoliberalism*, https://www.postneoliberalism.org/, and the symposium "Beyond Neoliberalism II," edited by Michael Tomasky, in *Democracy: A Journal of Ideas* 64 (Spring 2022), https://democracyjournal.org/category/magazine/64/.

the "onshoring" of previously globalized production processes and, relatedly, the imposition of trade tariffs against China—tariffs that especially target the crucial renewable energy sector. China's own rise as an alternative global political economic force to US-led neoliberal hegemony is also noteworthy in this respect. A concomitant signal of shifting cultural currents might be seen in the growing support for authoritarian nationalist politicians around the world—politicians who sometimes explicitly repudiate neoliberalism, whether or not they do anything about it when in office. These moves remind us that a post-neoliberal future is not necessarily a better future and could devolve into authoritarianism and global conflict.

Economist Daniela Gabor, moreover, describes the recent shifts in political economy as a further entrenchment of global finance in state structures and in global economic development. These shifts rely heavily on government promises to absorb the risks of private investment in development projects and public services by guaranteeing revenue through means such as tax breaks, grants, and friendly regulations.[29] In this strategy, states build capacity as "de-risking states" to attract institutional investors (e.g., pension funds and insurance companies) and asset managers (firms such as BlackRock or Vanguard Group) to lead the response to the global challenges of pandemic, poverty, geopolitical competition, and especially climate change. Gabor interprets this approach as "an attempt to re-orient the institutional mechanisms of the state towards protecting the political order of financial capitalism against climate justice movements and Green New Deal initiatives."[30] If post-neoliberalism centers the politics of de-risking, then it will share neoliberalism's commitment to encasing markets from democratic contestation.[31]

---

[29]Daniela Gabor, "The Wall Street Consensus," *Development and Change* 52, no. 3 (May 2021): 429–59. See also Daniela Gabor, "The (European) De-risking State," *Stato e mercato* 1, no. 127 (July 2023): 53–84.

[30]Gabor, "The Wall Street Consensus," 3.

[31]The genesis of the de-risking state could therefore be viewed as a classic case of social reproduction. As discussed in Chapter 3, Bourdieu sees social reproduction as a conflictual process in which dominant agents perpetuate their hegemony through constant change. Dominant agents, in this case powerful politicians and financial firms, possess the capital necessary to adapt to changing conditions and maintain the overall structure of the field of power.

Theologians opposed to neoliberalism's antidemocratic politics will therefore also be wary of the emerging forms of post-neoliberalism and push for global institutions that are avowedly democratic in character. These institutions will embrace various measures of accountability to ensure that they are genuinely representative and enjoy widespread legitimacy. Although the design of such institutions is beyond the scope of this book, some comments can be offered about why and how Christians should support them.

The Spirit organizes for life by eliciting creaturely creative agency that promotes solidarity and collective well-being. Although this description of the organizing Spirit's work does not simply amount to an endorsement of democracy, it does lead in the direction of a form of politics in which creatures' agency is respected as a constructive source in the pursuit of solidarity and well-being. Organizations formed to foment these goods in tune with the organizing Spirit will therefore be "democratic" in the sense that their work is grounded in, responsive to, and accountable to collective creaturely agency—and especially the agency of those whose well-being is most threatened.[32]

According to Peter Scott, "the way we acknowledge the importance of the negotiation of agency in our [human] political life is democracy."[33] For Scott, an ecological pneumatology orients humans toward a "fellowship in a common realm" with all creatures, a fellowship he refers to as a "democracy of the commons."[34] This democracy of the commons acknowledges that the diversity of creaturely agencies and their unity in fellowship are gifts of the Spirit. Maintaining the gift of difference-in-fellowship requires some means of peaceful negotiation, which is where democracy enters insofar as it "requires the redistribution of agency and the reconfiguration of power in negotiation."[35] Scott recognizes both that poverty is an obstacle to the achievement of human democracy—poverty circumscribes agency and so prevents full participation in fellowship—and that representation is necessary

---

[32]See Chapter 3 on sanctification and the "preferential option for the poor."
[33]Peter Scott, *A Political Theology of Nature* (Cambridge: Cambridge University Press, 2003), 226.
[34]Scott, *A Political Theology of Nature*, 225.
[35]Scott, *A Political Theology of Nature*, 228.

for the extension of democracy beyond the human.[36] It should be added that representation is also important for the extension of democracy to all humans, as variations in human cognitive ability defy rationalist conceptions of universal direct democracy.[37] Representation, however, depends on some sort of orderly and ordered process in which criteria for adequate representation can be discerned and the best representatives can be identified on that basis. These processes are embedded in what are typically called democratic institutions (in extant democracies these institutions include political parties, executive agencies, judiciaries, parliaments, etc.). In short, a functioning democracy of the commons will need to repudiate poverty-inducing political economies such as neoliberalism and embrace representative institutions that enable peaceful negotiations among different creaturely agencies.

The arguments developed in Chapter 4 with reference to the Spirit's extra-ecclesial doubling are relevant to consider here. They indicate that institutions do not have to be run by Christians or on explicitly Christian theological principles to garner support from Christians. Christians do, however, have the duty of discerning the moral and political shape of institutions and determining the extent to which participating in them can also be counted as participation in the work of the organizing Spirit. The way to Christian involvement in extra-ecclesial democratic institutions is open, albeit subject to ongoing discernment. Christians contribute in part to the democratic character of such institutions by articulating the particular, theologically informed reasons for their participation. If democracy involves the peaceful negotiation of difference, then hiding these reasons behind consistently "thin" and purportedly universal reasons undermines democratic possibilities. That is not to say that commonalities cannot be identified across differences, or that such commonalities cannot become the basis for a shared democratic vocabulary. But it does suppose that negotiating difference goes better when we do not minimize the differences

---

[36]Scott, *A Political Theology of Nature*, 229–30.
[37]See Alasdair MacIntyre, *Dependent Rational Animals: Why Human Beings Need the Virtues*, 2d ed. (Chicago: Open Court, 2001).

at issue.[38] These views are also consistent with the position taken in Chapter 4 on "identity politics"—we should neither minimize identity-based differences nor allow their acknowledgment to continue undermining efforts to form broad coalitions aimed at collective material well-being. What is needed is a renewed imagination for how particularist identity politics and universalist material politics might be doubled. Christians may have resources to offer this fundamental democratic challenge, insofar as they are able to affirm creation's irreducibly complex diversity as an aspect of its universal origin and destiny in the work of the organizing Spirit.

Naming democratic coalitions as a possible arena of Christian organizing signifies the limits of Christian power in the world. These limits have in recent decades often been either denied or circumscribed to local alliances forged by congregations.[39] The guiding convictions of this book prohibit the denial of any limits to Christian power. As an Anabaptist theologian, I am committed to my tradition's imperfect but substantive peace witness, and to the conviction shared by many fellow Anabaptists that peace and nonviolence are central to discipleship—and to life in the Spirit.[40] The commitment to nonviolence can be understood in part as a larger commitment to the refusal of domination—Christian politics should be guided by a love that "does not insist on its own way" (1 Cor. 13:5), as exemplified at the cross. Yet, for reasons developed throughout this book, I differ from some Anabaptist

---

[38] I have argued for this position on the basis of care ethics in Jamie Pitts, "Mother Eberly's Coin: Care Ethics, Democratic Politics, and North American Mennonite Women's Movements," in *Care Ethics, Religion, and Spiritual Traditions*, eds. Maurice Hamington and Maureen Sander-Staudt (Leuven: Peeters, 2020), 328–31. In brief, and contrary to the liberal universalism of most care ethicists, I suggest that caring for (marginalized) others entails paying close attention to their needs and desires without demanding that they first translate them into a dominant language.
[39] By referring to the denial of Christian limits to power I am somewhat polemically referring to movements such as Catholic integralism and certain strands of evangelicalism that seek the subordination of government to ecclesial authority. The reduction of Christian politics to the local was discussed in detail in Chapter 1.
[40] See my discussion of this tradition, with Luis Tapia Rubio, "Anabaptist Theology," in *St Andrews Encyclopaedia of Theology*, eds. Brendan N. Wolfe et al. (St Andrews: St Andrews University, 2022–), article published October 19, 2023, https://www.saet.ac.uk/Christianity/AnabaptistTheology.

theologians who contend that a nonviolent, anti-domination politics can only be embodied in local congregations or in evanescent social movements. Christians can also display their commitment to such politics by participating in the work of democratic institutions—including global ones—oriented to collective well-being.

This case does not depend on the denial of the church as the or a priority arena of Christian politics. Christians can work to ensure that our ecclesial institutions are internally democratic and committed to solidarity especially with those members whose well-being is marginal. Theologians and other Christian intellectuals should take our global ecclesial institutions much more seriously than we do, taking steps beyond this book to engage questions of institutional design. Scott's admonition that democracy is vitiated by poverty and lack of representation must also be taken to heart by institutional leaders. Authentic representation within global denominational and ecumenical bodies will only become possible when the vast economic inequalities dividing church members are addressed. Christians cannot overcome these divisions alone, which is one reason why we ought to participate in coalitional institutions. But we should also remember that the typical social response to the pouring out of the Spirit on all flesh, as described in Acts 2 and 4, is the sharing of all things within the Christian community. Can our institutions be means of participation in the Spirit in this way, too?

REFERENCES

Akram, Sadiya. *Bourdieu, Habitus, and Field: A Critical Realist Approach*. Cham: Palgrave Macmillan, 2023.
Alexis, Nekeisha Alayna and Jamie Pitts. *What Happened at Benham West: African American Stories of Community, Displacement, and Hope* South Bend, IN: Wolfson, 2024.
Althaus-Reid, Marcella. *Indecent Theology: Theological Perversions in Sex, Gender, and Politics*. New York: Routledge, 2000.
Althaus-Reid, Marcella. *The Queer God*. New York: Routledge, 2003.
Ambroise, Bruno. "Wittgenstein et Bourdieu: Contributions à une critique de la vision scolastique." *Europe* 906 (2004): 258–71.
Appadurai, Arjun. "The Production of Locality." In *Modernity at Large: Cultural Dimensions of Globalization*, 178–99. Minneapolis, MN: University of Minnesota Press, 1996.
Baker-Fletcher, Karen. *Dancing with God: The Trinity from a Womanist Perspective*. St. Louis: Chalice, 2006.
Baker-Fletcher, Karen. *Sisters of Dust, Sisters of Spirit: Womanist Wordings on God and Creation*. Minneapolis, MN: Fortress, 1998.
Barrett, Lois Y. "Ursula Jost and Barbara Rebstock." In *Profiles of Anabaptist Women: Sixteenth-century Reforming Pioneers*, edited by C. Arnold Snyder and Linda A. Huebert Hecht, 273–87. Waterloo, ON: Canadian Corporation for Studies in Religion, 1996.
Barrett, Lois Y. "Wreath of Glory: Ursula Jost's Prophetic Visions in the Context of Reformation and Revolt in Southwestern Germany, 1524–1530." PhD dissertation, the Union Institute, 1992.
Barrett, Lois Y. and Dorothy Nickel Friesen, eds. *Proclaiming the Good News: Mennonite Women's Voices, 1972–2006*. Elkhart, IN: Institute of Mennonite Studies, 2023.
Barth, Karl. *The Epistle to the Romans*. New York: Oxford University Press, 1933.
Basil of Caesarea. "Homily 2." *Hexaemeron*. Accessed August 23, 2024. https://www.newadvent.org/fathers/32012.htm.
Beck Kreider, Luke. "Stewardship, Settler Colonialism, and Solidarity." Paper presented at the Rooted and Grounded Conference on Land and Christian Discipleship, Anabaptist Mennonite Biblical Seminary, Elkhart, IN, October 15, 2021.

Beck Kreider, Luke. "Varieties of Anabaptist Environmentalism and Environmental Racism." *Mennonite Quarterly Review* 94, no. 1 (January 2020): 43–58.

Bedford, Nancy. "A Narrow Gate? Proceeding along the Way of Jesus by the Spirit." *Mennonite Quarterly Review* 92, no. 4 (October 2018): 485–97.

Bedford, Nancy. *La porfía de la resurrección: Ensayos desde el feminismo teológico latinoamericano*. Buenos Aires: Kairós, 2008.

Bell, Daniel M. *Liberation Theology after the End of History: The Refusal to Cease Suffering*. New York: Routledge, 2001.

Benn Michaels, Walter and Adolph Reed. *No Politics but Class Politics*, edited by Anton Jäger and Daniel Zamora. London: ERIS, 2022.

Benton Mennonite Church. "Creation Action." Accessed August 23, 2024. https://bentonchurch.org/creation-care/.

Bevins, Vincent. *If We Burn: The Mass Protest Decade and the Missing Revolution*. New York: PublicAffairs, 2023.

Bhabha, Homi. *The Location of Culture*. New York: Routledge, 1994.

Black Pine Animal Sanctuary. "Our Animals." Accessed August 23, 2024. https://www.bpsanctuary.org/about/animals/.

Black Pine Animal Sanctuary. "What Is the Big Cat Public Safety Act?" Accessed September 2, 2021. https://www.bpsanctuary.org/blog/what-is-the-big-cat-public-safety-act/.

Bock, Cherice. "Watershed Discipleship." In *An Ecotopian Lexicon*, edited by Matthew Schneider-Mayerson and Brent Ryan Bellamy, 305–16. Minneapolis, MN: University of Minnesota Press, 2019.

Boff, Leonard. *Ecclesiogenesis: The Base Communities Reinvent the Church*. Translated by Robert R. Barr. Maryknoll, NY: Orbis, 1986.

Bonhoeffer, Dietrich. *Discipleship*. Minneapolis, MN: Fortress, 2001.

Boriello, Arthur and Anton Jäger. *The Populist Moment*. New York: Verso, 2023.

Bourdieu, Pierre. "The Forms of Capital." In *Handbook of Theory and Research for the Sociology of Education*, edited by John G. Robinson, 241–58. Translated by Richard Nice. Westport, CT: Greenwood Press, 1986.

Bourdieu, Pierre. *Masculine Domination*. Translated by Richard Nice. Cambridge: Polity, 2001.

Bourdieu, Pierre. *Microcosmes: Théorie des champs*. Paris: Raison d'Agir, 2021.

Bourdieu, Pierre. *Pascalian Meditations*. Translated by Richard Nice. Cambridge: Polity, 2000.

Bourdieu, Pierre. "The Specificity of the Scientific Field and the Social Conditions of the Progress of Reason." Translated by Richard Nice. *Social Science Information* 14, no. 6 (1975): 19–46.

Bourdieu, Pierre. "Stratégies de reproduction et modes de domination." *Actes de la Recherche en Sciences Sociales* 105 (1994): 3–12.
Bourdieu, Pierre. "Sur le pouvoir symbolique." *Annales* 32, no. 3 (1977): 405–11.
Bourdieu, Pierre and Loïc J. D. Wacquant. *An Invitation to Reflexive Sociology.* Cambridge: Polity, 1992.
Bourdieu, Pierre and Jean-Claude Passeron. *Reproduction in Education, Society and Culture*, 2d ed. Translated by Richard Nice. London: Sage, 1990.
Boyarin, Daniel. *The Jewish Gospels: The Story of the Jewish Christ.* New York: New Press, 2012.
Brown, William P. *The Seven Pillars of Creation: The Bible, Science, and the Ecology of Wonder.* Oxford: Oxford University Press, 2010.
Burden-Stelly, Charisse. "Modern US Racial Capitalism: Some Theoretical Insights." *Monthly Review.* July 1, 2020, https://monthlyreview.org/2020/07/01/modern-u-s-racial-capitalism/.
Business Wire. "IFM Investors Completes Acquisition of Indiana Toll Road Concession Company." May 17, 2015. https://www.businesswire.com/news/home/20150527006535/en/IFM-Investors-completes-acquisition-of-Indiana-Toll-Road-Concession-Company.
Butler, Judith. *Gender Trouble: Feminism and the Subversion of Identity.* New York: Routledge, 1990.
Butler, Judith. *Undoing Gender.* New York: Routledge, 2004.
Bynum, John W. "Ye Will Know Them by Their Fruits: The Story of Herbert M. and Ruth Tolson and the Tolson Community Center and Youth Center." *The Village Note* 1, no. 1 (March 2015): 8–9.
Cai, Sophia and Michael Tobin. "RV Travel Was on Its Way Out. Then Came the Pandemic." *Fortune.* July 15, 2020. https://fortune.com/2020/07/15/coronavirus-summer-travel-rvs-road-trips/.
Carter, J. Kameron. *Race: A Theological Account.* New York: Oxford University Press, 2008.
Cassirer, Ernst. *An Essay on Man: An Introduction to a Philosophy of Human Culture.* New Haven, CT: Yale University Press, 2021 [1944].
Cavanaugh, William T. "The World in a Wafer: A Geography of the Eucharist as Resistance to Globalization." *Modern Theology* 15, no. 2 (April 1999): 181–96.
City of Elkhart. *2021–2025 Neighborhood Revitalization Strategy Area (NRSA) Plan (DRAFT).* March 28, 2021. https://elkhartindiana.org/wpfd_file/city-of-elkhart-draft-2021-2025-neighborhood-revitalization-strategy-area-nrsa-plan/.
City of Elkhart. "City of Elkhart Economic Diversification Study." *Elkhart 2040.* December 2017. https://elkhart2040.com/research-studies-and-reports.

City of Elkhart. "The St. Joseph River: It's Health from a Historical Perspective." *YouTube*. August 18, 2017. https://www.youtube.com/watch?v=ww5ZTdErCoM&ab_channel=CityOfElkhartIN.

CNN Business. "Norfolk Southern Corp." Accessed August 23, 2024. https://www.cnn.com/markets/stocks/NSC.

Coakley, Sarah. *Christ without Absolutes: A Study of the Christology of Ernst Troeltsch*. Oxford: Clarendon, 1988.

Coakley, Sarah. *God, Sexuality, and the Self: An Essay "On the Trinity."* Cambridge: Cambridge University Press, 2013.

Coakley, Sarah. *The New Asceticism: Sexuality, Gender, and the Quest for God*. London: Bloomsbury, 2015.

Coakley, Sarah. "Review of *After the Spirit: A Constructive Pneumatology from Resources outside the Modern West* by Eugene F. Rogers." *Journal of the American Academy of Religion* 75, no. 2 (2007): 429–32.

Comblin, José. *The Holy Spirit and Liberation*. Translated by Paul Burns. Maryknoll, NY: Orbis, 1989.

Cone, James H. *Black Theology and Black Power*. Maryknoll, NY: Orbis, 1997.

Cone, James H. *The Cross and the Lynching Tree*. Maryknoll, NY: Orbis, 2011.

Cone, James H. *God of the Oppressed*, 2d ed. Maryknoll, NY: Orbis, 1997.

Cooper, Melinda. *Family Values: Between Neoliberalism and the New Social Conservatism*. New York: Zone, 2017.

Crawley, Ashon T. *Blackpentecostal Breath: The Aesthetics of Possibility*. New York: Fordham University Press, 2016.

Croce, Mariano. "The *Habitus* and the Critique of the Present: A Wittgensteinian Reading of Bourdieu's Social Theory." *Sociological Theory* 33, no. 4 (December 2015): 327–46.

Davis, Ellen. "Land as Kin: Renewing the Imagination." In *Rooted and Grounded: Essays on Land and Christian Discipleship*, edited by Ryan D. Harker and Janeen Bertsche Johnson, 3–12. Eugene, OR: Pickwick, 2016.

Davis, Ellen. *Opening Israel's Scriptures*. Oxford: Oxford University Press, 2019.

Davison, Andrew. *Participation in God: A Study in Christian Doctrine and Metaphysics*. Cambridge: Cambridge University Press, 2019.

Deacon, Terrence W. *The Symbolic Species: The Co-evolution of Language and the Brain*. New York: W. W. Norton, 1997.

Domine, Deborah. "Elkhart Reconciliation Will Benefit All of Elkhart County." *Goshen News*, September 5, 2023. https://www.goshennews.com/opinion/elkhart-reconciliation-will-benefit-all-of-elkhart-county/article_12a0a130-4b59-11ee-bd10-4702069fb122.html.

Douglas, Andrew J. and Jared Loggins. "The Lost Promise of Black Study." *Boston Review*. September 28, 2021, https://www.bostonreview.net/articles/the-lost-promise-of-black-study/.

Dueck, J. Alicia. *Negotiating Sexual Identities: Lesbian, Gay, and Queer Perspectives on Being Mennonite*. Berlin: Lit, 2012.

Dula, Peter. "Anabaptist Environmental Ethics: A Review Essay." *Mennonite Quarterly Review* 94 (January 2020): 7–36.

Emirbayer, Mustafa and Matthew Desmond. *The Racial Order*. Chicago: University of Chicago Press, 2015.

Epp, Marlene. *Mennonite Women in Canada: A History*. Winnipeg: University of Manitoba Press, 2008.

Epp, Marlene. *Women without Men: Mennonite Refugees of the Second World War*. Toronto: University of Toronto Press, 2000.

Espejo, Paulina Ochoa. *On Borders: Territories, Legitimacy, and the Rights of Place*. Oxford: Oxford University Press, 2020.

Evans, James H. "The Holy Spirit in African American Theology." In *The Oxford Handbook of African American Theology*, edited by Katie G. Cannon and Anthony B. Pinn, 164–73. New York: Oxford University Press, 2014.

Felski, Rita. *The Limits of Critique*. Chicago, IL: University of Chicago Press, 2015.

Fields, Karen E. and Barbara J. Fields. *Racecraft: The Soul of Inequality in American Life*. London: Verso, 2014.

Finger, Thomas N. *A Contemporary Anabaptist Theology: Biblical, Historical, Constructive*. Downers Grove, IL: Intervarsity, 2004.

Food & Drink International. "Culver Duck Farms." Accessed October 16, 2021. https://www.fooddrink-magazine.com/sections/producers/1687-culver-duck-farms.

Forde, Joseph. *Before and beyond the "Big Society": John Milbank and the Church of England's Approach to Social Welfare*. Cambridge: James Clarke, 2022.

Foucault, Michel. *Discipline and Punish: The Birth of the Prison*. Translated by Alan Sheridan. New York: Vintage, 1995.

Foucault, Michel. *Madness and Civilization: A History of Insanity in the Age of Reason*. Translated by Richard Howard. New York: Routledge, 1989.

Freeney Harding, Rosemarie with Rachel E. Harding. *Remnants: A Memoir of Spirit, Activism, and Mothering*. Durham, NC: Duke University Press, 2015.

Friesen, Katerina. "The Great Commission: Watershed Conquest or Watershed Discipleship?" In *Watershed Discipleship: Reinhabiting Bioregional Faith and Practice*, edited by Ched Myers, 26–41. Eugene, OR: Cascade, 2016.

Gabor, Daniela. "The (European) Derisking State." *Stato e mercato* 1, no. 127 (July 2023): 53–84.
Gabor, Daniela. "The Wall Street Consensus." *Development and Change* 52, no. 3 (May 2021): 429–59.
Garcelon, Marc. "The Missing Key: Institutions, Networks, and the Project of Neoclassical Sociology." *Sociological Theory* 28, no. 3 (September 2010): 326–53.
Gerber Koontz, Gayle. "Seventy Times Seven: Abuse and the Frustratingly Extravagant Call to Forgive." *Mennonite Quarterly Review* 89, no. 1 (January 2015): 129–52.
Gerstle, Gary. *The Rise and Fall of the Neoliberal Order*. Oxford: Oxford University Press, 2022.
Getachew, Adom. *Worldmaking after Empire: The Rise and Fall of Self-determination*. Princeton, NJ: Princeton University Press, 2019.
Gilroy, Paul. *The Black Atlantic: Modernity and Double Consciousness*. Cambridge, MA: Harvard University Press, 1993.
Goering, Gladys. *Women in Search of Mission: A History of the General Conference Mennonite Women's Organizations*. Newton, KS: Faith and Life, 1980.
Good, Deirdre J., Willis J. Jenkins, Cynthia B. Kittredge, and Eugene F. Rogers. "A Theology of Marriage Including Same-Sex Couples: A View from the Liberals." *Anglican Theological Review* 93, no. 1 (Winter 2011): 51–88.
Goshen College. "Merry Lea Environmental Center of Goshen College." Accessed August 23, 2024. https://www.goshen.edu/merrylea/.
Guenther Loewen, Susanne. "Can the Cross Be 'Good News' for Women? Peace Theology and the Suffering of Women." *Anabaptist Witness* 3, no. 2 (December 2016): 109–21.
Gutiérrez, Gustavo. *We Drink from Our Own Wells: The Spiritual Journey of a People*. Translated by Matthew J. O'Connell. Maryknoll, NY: Orbis, 1985.
Hallet, Tim and Matthew Gougherty. "Bourdieu and Organizations: Hidden Traces, Macro Influence, and Micro Potential." In *The Oxford Handbook of Pierre Bourdieu*, edited by Jeffery Sallaz and Thomas Medvetz, 273–98. Oxford: Oxford University Press, 2018.
Harder, Lydia Neufeld. *The Challenge Is in the Naming: A Theological Journey*. Winnipeg: Canadian Mennonite University Press, 2018.
Harder, Lydia Neufeld. *Obedience, Suspicion, and the Gospel of Mark: A Mennonite-Feminist Exploration of Biblical Authority*. Waterloo, ON: Canadian Corporation for Studies of Religion, 1998.
Harding, Vincent. *Beyond Chaos: Black History and the Search for a New Land*. Atlanta, GA: Institute of the Black World, 1970.
Harding, Vincent. *Hope and History: Why We Must Share the Story of the Movement*. Maryknoll, NY: Orbis, 1990.

Harding, Vincent. *Is America Possible? To My Young Companions on the Journey of Hope*. Kalamazoo, MI: Fetzer Institute, 2007.
Harding, Vincent. *Martin Luther King: The Inconvenient Hero*, rev. ed. Maryknoll, NY: Orbis, 2008.
Harding, Vincent. *The Other American Revolution*. Los Angeles: Center for African American Studies, University of California Los Angeles; Atlanta, GA: Institute of the Black World, 1980.
Harding, Vincent. *There Is a River: The Black Struggle for Freedom in America*. New York: Harcourt Brace Jovanovich, 1981.
Harding, Vincent and Daisaku Ikeda. *America Will Be! Conversations on Hope, Freedom, and Democracy*. Cambridge, MA: Dialogue Path, 2013.
Harding, Vincent, Robin D. G. Kelley, and Earl Lewis. *We Changed the World: African Americans, 1945–1970*. New York: Oxford University Press, 1997.
Harnish, David. "Respectability and Reciprocity: How African Americans Formed a Community in Elkhart, Indiana," 2012. Mennonite Historical Library (Goshen College).
Hart, David Bentley. *That All Shall Be Saved: Hell, Heaven, and Universal Salvation*. New Haven, CT: Yale University Press, 2019.
Harvey, David. *A Brief History of Neoliberalism*. Oxford: Oxford University Press, 2005.
Hauerwas, Stanley. *After Christendom: How the Church Is to Behave If Freedom, Justice, and a Christian Nation Are Bad Ideas*. Nashville, TN: Abingdon, 1991.
Hering, James P. *The Colossian and Ephesian Haustafeln in Theological Context: An Analysis of Their Origins, Relationship, and Message*. New York: Peter Lang, 2007.
Hinojosa, Felipe. *Latino Mennonites: Civil Rights, Faith, and Evangelical Culture*. Baltimore, MD: Johns Hopkins University Press, 2014.
Hirschman, Albert O. *The Rhetoric of Reaction: Perversity, Futility, Jeopardy*. Cambridge, MA: Harvard University Press, 1991.
Hobbes, Thomas. *Leviathan*, edited by C. B. Macpherson. New York: Penguin, 1985 [1651].
Hollinger, David. *Protestants Abroad: How Missionaries Tried to Change the World but Changed America*. Princeton, NJ: Princeton University Press, 2017.
Horkheimer, Max and Theodore W. Adorno. "The Culture Industry: Enlightenment as Mass Deception." In *Dialectic of Enlightenment: Philosophical Fragments*, edited by Gunzelin Schmid Noerr, 94–136. Translated by Edmund Jephcott. Stanford, CA: Stanford University Press, 2002.
Horst Lehman, David. "Common Ground: Potawatomi and Europeans on the Elkhart Prairie." Unpublished paper, 2011, typescript.

Hulsether, Lucia. *Capitalist Humanitarianism.* Durham, NC: Duke University Press, 2023.
Humphrey, Matthew. "Lived Theology in the Little Campbell River Watershed: A Primer on Bioregional Discipleship." In *Rooted and Grounded: Essays on Land and Christian Discipleship*, edited by Ryan D. Harker and Janeen Bertsche Johnson, 112–23. Eugene, OR: Pickwick, 2016.
Ibrahim, Joseph. "The Struggle for Symbolic Dominance in the British 'Anti-Capitalist Movement Field.'" *Social Movement Studies* 12, no. 1 (2013): 63–80.
Indiana Department of Environmental Management. "Elkhart River WMP 6-177." Accessed August 23, 2024. https://www.in.gov/idem/nps/resources/watershed-management-plans/elkhart-river-wmp-6-177/.
Jackson, Marion T. "Perspective: The Indiana That Was." In *The Natural Heritage of Indiana*, edited by Marin T. Jackson, xvii–xxviii. Bloomington, IN: Indiana University Press, 1997.
Jasinski, Nicholas. "RV Sales Have Soared during the Pandemic. These Stocks Could See More Gains Ahead." *Barron's.* October 3, 2020. https://www.barrons.com/articles/recreational-vehicle-stocks-could-see-further-gains-51601671189.
Jeffries, Stuart. *Everything, All the Time, Everywhere: How We Became Postmodern.* London: Verso, 2021.
Jenkins, Willis. *The Future of Ethics: Sustainability, Social Justice, and Religious Creativity.* Washington, DC: Georgetown University Press, 2013.
Jennings, Willie James. *The Christian Imagination: Theology and the Origins of Race.* New Haven, CT: Yale University Press, 2010.
Johnson, Elizabeth A. *Ask the Beasts: Darwin and the God of Love.* London: T&T Clark, 2014.
Jones, Paul Daffyd. "On the 'Loving Mutations' of God, Sexuality, and the Self." *Syndicate.* November 11, 2015. https://syndicate.network/symposia/theology/sarah-coakley-god-sexuality-and-the-self/.
Josephson-Storm, Jason A. *The Myth of Disenchantment: Magic, Modernity, and the Birth of the Human Sciences.* Chicago, IL: University of Chicago Press, 2017.
Judt, Tony. *Postwar: A History of Europe since 1945.* New York: Penguin, 2005.
Kilby, Karen. "Perichoresis and Projection: Problems with Social Doctrines of the Trinity." *New Blackfriars* 81, no. 956 (October 2000): 432–45.
King, Martin Luther. "Beyond Vietnam: A Time to Break Silence." 1967. https://www.americanrhetoric.com/speeches/mlkatimetobreaksilence.htm.

Klaassen, Walter, ed. *Anabaptism in Outline: Selected Primary Sources.* Walden, NY: Plough, 2019.
Klinglesmith, Sharon. "Women in the Mennonite Church, 1900–1930." *Mennonite Quarterly Review* 54, no. 3 (1980): 163–207.
Kotsko, Adam. *Neoliberalism's Demons: On the Political Theology of Late Capital.* Stanford: Stanford University Press, 2018.
Krall, Ruth. *The Elephant in God's Living Room*, volume 3: *The Mennonite Church and John Howard Yoder, Collected Essays.* N.p.: Enduring Space, 2013. https://ruthkrall.com/books/the-elephants-in-gods-living-room-series/volume-three-the-mennonite-church-and-john-howard-yoder-collected-essays/.
Kretzer, Michelle. "Do You Believe Culver Duck Farms' Claims?" *PETA.* October 28, 2016. https://www.peta.org/blog/do-you-believe-culver-duck-farms-claims/.
Landy, David. "Bringing the Outside In: Field Interaction and Transformation from Below in Political Struggles." *Social Movement Studies* 14, no. 3 (2015): 255–69.
Lash, Nicholas. *Holiness, Speech and Silence: Reflections on the Question of God.* Burlington, VT: Ashgate, 2004.
Laughlin, Gerard. "Coming Alongside." *Syndicate.* May 17, 2017. https://syndicate.network/symposia/theology/god-and-difference/.
Levine, Amy-Jill. *The Misunderstood Jew: The Church and the Scandal of the Jewish Jesus.* New York: HarperCollins, 2006.
Linker, Damon. *The Theocons: Secular America under Siege.* New York: Anchor, 2006.
Lloyd, Vincent W. *Black Natural Law.* New York: Oxford University Press, 2016.
Loewen, Royden. "Privilege, Right, and Responsibility: Peace and the North American Mennonites." In *From Suffering to Solidarity: The Historical Seeds of Mennonite Interreligious, Interethnic, and International Peacebuilding*, edited by Andrew P. Klager, 58–70. Eugene, OR: Wipf and Stock, 2015.
Loewen, Royden and Steven M. Nolt. *Seeking Places of Peace: Global Mennonite History Series: North America.* Intercourse, PA: Good Books, 2012.
Longacre, Doris Janzen. *More-with-Less Cookbook*, 2d edition. Scottdale, PA: Herald, 2003.
Lord, Andy. *Network Church: A Pentecostal Ecclesiology Shaped by Mission.* Leiden: Brill, 2012.
Low, John N. "Pokégnek Bodéwadmik, the Pokagon Band of Potawatomi Indians, Keepers of the Fire: A History and Introduction to the Community through Text and Images." 2015. https://johnlowpokagon.files.wordpress.com/2015/11/keepers-of-the-fire.pdf.

MacIntyre, Alasdair. *After Virtue: A Study in Moral Theory*, 2d ed. Notre Dame, IN: University of Notre Dame Press, 1984.
MacIntyre, Alasdair. *Dependent Rational Animals: Why Human Beings Need the Virtues*, 2d ed. Chicago, IL: Open Court, 2001.
Madison, James H. *Hoosiers: A New History of Indiana*. Bloomington, IN: Indiana University Press, 2014.
Mair, Peter. *Ruling the Void: The Hollowing of Western Democracy*. New York: Verso, 2013.
Majewska, Ewa. *Feminist Antifacism: Counterpublics of the Common*. London: Verso, 2021.
Marpeck, Pilgram. "Concerning the Humanity of Christ; Concerning the Son of Man." In *Jörg Maler's Kunstbuch: Writings of the Pilgram Marpeck Circle*, edited by John D. Rempel, 355–66. Kitchener, ON: Pandora, 2010.
Martin, Vince. "5 RV Stocks Hoping for More Summer Travel: Pandemic Fears Have Stirred a Wave of RV Buying—and These 5 Stocks Could Benefit." *Investor Place*. July 7, 2020. https://investorplace.com/2020/07/5-rv-stocks-hoping-for-more-summer-travel/.
McClendon, James Wm. *Doctrine: Systematic Theology*, vol. 2. Nashville, TN: Abingdon, 1994.
Melhorn, Wilton T. "Indiana on Ice: The Late Tertiary and Ice Age History of Indiana Landscapes." In *The Natural Heritage of Indiana*, edited by Marion T. Jackson, 15–27. Bloomington, IN: Indiana University Press, 1997.
Mennonite Church USA. "John Howard Yoder Digest." Accessed August 23, 2024. https://www.mennoniteusa.org/resource-portal/resource/john-howard-yoder-digest/.
Meyer, Robinson. "A Major but Little-Known Supporter of Climate Denial: Freight Railroads." *The Atlantic*. December 13, 2019. https://www.theatlantic.com/science/archive/2019/12/freight-railroads-funded-climate-denial-decades/603559/.
Mirowski, Philip. *Never Let a Serious Crisis Go to Waste: How Neoliberalism Survived the Financial Meltdown*. New York: Verso, 2013.
Mitchell, Maurice. "Building Resilient Organizations: Toward Joy and Durable Power in a Time of Crisis." *NPQ*, November 29, 2022, https://nonprofitquarterly.org/building-resilient-organizations-toward-joy-and-durable-power-in-a-time-of-crisis/.
Moltmann, Jürgen. *The Church in the Power of the Spirit: A Contribution to Messianic Ecclesiology*. Minneapolis, MN: Fortress, 1993.
Moltmann, Jürgen. *The Spirit of Life: A Universal Affirmation*. Minneapolis, MN: Fortress, 1992.
Monk, Ray. *Wittgenstein: The Duty of Genius*. New York: Free Press, 1990.

Morozov, Evgeny. *The Santiago Boys*. Chora Media, 2023. https://the-santiago-boys.com/.

Morse, Christopher. *Not Every Spirit: A Dogmatics of Christian Disbelief*. Valley Forge, PA: Trinity, 1994.

Moss, Christina. "An Examination of the Visions of Ursula Jost in the Context of Early Anabaptism and Late Medieval Christianity." MA thesis, University of Waterloo, 2013.

Moss, Christina. "'Your Sons and Daughters Shall Prophecy': Visions, Apocalypticism, and Gender in Strasbourg, 1522–1539." PhD dissertation, University of Waterloo, 2019.

Mouw, Richard J. *Politics and the Biblical Drama*. Grand Rapids, MI: Eerdmans, 1976.

Moyn, Samuel. *Christian Human Rights*. Philadelphia, PA: University of Pennsylvania Press, 2015.

Myers, Ched. "From 'Creation Care' to 'Watershed Discipleship': Replacing Ecological Theology and Practice." *Conrad Grebel Review* 32, no. 3 (Fall 2014): 250–75.

Milbank, John. *The Suspended Middle: Henri de Lubac and the Debate Concerning the Supernatural*. Grand Rapids, MI: Eerdmans, 2005.

Miller, Ezra. *Changing Landscapes: Ambiguity, Imaginations, and Amish Settlers in Northern Indiana, 1825–1850*. PhD dissertation, Michigan State University, 2017.

Norges Bank Investment Management. "About the Fund." Accessed August 23, 2024. https://www.nbim.no/en/the-fund/about-the-fund/.

Nunes, Rodrigo. *Neither Vertical nor Horizontal: A Theory of Political Organization*. London: Verso, 2021.

Open Secrets. "PAC Profile: Sunrise PAC." Accessed August 23, 2024. https://www.opensecrets.org/political-action-committees-pacs/sunrise-pac/C00674697/summary/2020.

Peace Section Task Force on Women in Church and Society. "Current Developments." *Report* 1 (August 1973): 4–5.

Peace Section Task Force on Women in Church and Society. "Restoring Wholeness." *Report* 3 (December 1973): 1.

Pelikan, Jaroslav. *The Christian Tradition: A History of the Development of Doctrine*, vol. 1: *The Emergence of the Catholic Tradition (100–600)*. Chicago, IL: University of Chicago Press, 1971.

Penner, Carol. "Jesus and the Stories of Our Lives." In *Liberating the Politics of Jesus: Renewing Peace Theology through the Wisdom of Women*, edited by Elizabeth Soto Albrecht and Darryl W. Stephens, 38–47. London: T&T Clark, 2020.

Penner, Carol. "Mennonite Women Doing Theology: A Methodological Reflection on Twenty-Five Years of Conferences." In *Recovering from the Anabaptist Vision: New Essays in Anabaptist Identity and*

Theological Method, edited by Laura Schmidt Roberts, Paul Martens, and Myron Penner, 59–64. London: T&T Clark, 2020.

Perrow, Charles. "A Society of Organizations." *Theory and Society* 20, no. 6 (December 1991): 725–62.

Perrow, Charles. *Organizing America: Wealth, Power, and the Rise of Corporate Capitalism*. Princeton, NJ: Princeton University Press, 2002.

Petrella, Ivan. *Beyond Liberation Theology: A Polemic*. London: SCM, 2013.

Petrella, Ivan. *The Future of Liberation Theology: An Argument and Manifesto*. New York: Routledge, 2004.

Pettis, Oliver, dir. *What Happened at Benham West: African American Stories of Community, Displacement, and Hope* (Black Lion Cinematography, 2023), 78 min.

Pitts, Jamie. "Baptism, Postliberal and Anabaptist Theologies, and the Ambiguity of Christian Practice." *Mennonite Quarterly Review* 90, no. 3 (July 2016): 323–44.

Pitts, Jamie. "Black Studies as Black Religion: Vincent Harding, the Institute of the Black World, and the Movement 'Deep into Blackness.'" Paper presented at the Afro-American Religious History Unit, American Academy of Religion Annual Meeting, San Diego, November 24, 2019.

Pitts, Jamie. "Christian Ethics, the Bible, and the Powers of Reading." In *Scripture, Tradition, and Reason in Christian Ethics: Normative Dimensions*, edited by Bharat Ranganathan and Derek Woodard-Lehman, 17–43. New York: Palgrave Macmillan, 2019.

Pitts, Jamie. "Communitarian Proto-Socialism in Christian History." In *Cambridge Companion to Christian Socialism*, edited by Christophe Chalamet and Daniel Smith-Christopher. Cambridge: Cambridge University Press, forthcoming.

Pitts, Jamie. "The Hovering Spirit, the Elkhart River Watershed, and Political Institutions." *Mennonite Quarterly Review* 96, no. 1 (January 2022): 25–46.

Pitts, Jamie. *Love Seeking Integrity: An Introduction to Christian Theology in the Anabaptist Tradition*. Unpublished manuscript, 2023, typescript.

Pitts, Jamie. "Mother Eberly's Coin: Care Ethics, Democratic Politics, and North American Mennonite Women's Movements." In *Care Ethics, Religion, and Spiritual Traditions*, edited by Maurice Hamington and Maureen Sander-Staudt, 334–42. Leuven: Peeters, 2020.

Pitts, Jamie. "Pneumatology." In *T&T Clark Handbook of Anabaptism*, edited by Brian C. Brewer, 373–86. London: T&T Clark, 2021.

Pitts, Jamie. *Principalities and Powers: Revising John Howard Yoder's Sociological Theology*. Eugene, OR: Pickwick, 2013.
Pitts, Jamie. "Vincent Harding, the Black Freedom Struggle, and Just Institutions." In *On a Pilgrimage of Justice and Peace: Global Mennonite Perspectives on Peacebuilding*, edited by Fernando Enns, Nina Schroeder van 't Schip, and Andrés Pacheco Lozano, 376–84. Eugene, OR: Wipf & Stock, 2023.
Pitts, Jamie and Luis Tapia Rubio. "Anabaptist Theology." In *St Andrews Encyclopaedia of Theology*, edited by Brendan N. Wolfe et al. St Andrews: University of St Andrew, 2022–. Article published October 19, 2023. https://www.saet.ac.uk/Christianity/AnabaptistTheology.
Plehew, Dieter. "The Economic State and the Ordoliberal Critique of Keynesianism: Anti-Economic State or Just a Different Type of Economic State?" In *The Oxford Handbook of Ordoliberalism*, edited by Thomas Biebricher, Werner Bonefeld, and Peter Nedergaard, 278–90. Oxford: Oxford University Press, 2022.
Pochedley, Elan. "Restorative Cartography of the Theakiki Region: Mapping Potawatomi Presences in Indiana." *Open Rivers: Rethinking Water, Place & Community* 18 (Spring 2021): 7–49.
Pokégnek Bodéwadmik/Pokagon Band of Potawatomi. "Dowagiac River Re-meander Project." Accessed August 23, 2024. https://www.pokagonband-nsn.gov/departments/natural-resources/dowagiac-river-restoration-project/.
Polley, Sarah, dir. *Women Talking*. Universal Pictures, 2022. 104 minutes.
Puentes, Robert. "The Indiana Toll Road: How Did a Good Deal Go Bad?" *Forbes*. October 3, 2014. https://www.forbes.com/sites/realspin/2014/10/03/the-indiana-toll-road-how-did-a-good-deal-go-bad/?sh=68075bc82087.
Quiggle, Ben. "Dometic Announces New Location for HQ in Elkhart." *RVBusiness*. August 22, 2019. https://rvbusiness.com/dometic-announces-new-location-for-hq-in-elkhart/.
Radner, Ephraim. *A Profound Ignorance: Modern Pneumatology and Its Anti-modern Redemption*. Waco, TX: Baylor University Press, 2019.
Radner, Ephraim. *The End of the Church: A Pneumatology of Christian Division in the West*. Grand Rapids, MI: Eerdmans, 1998.
Radner, Ephraim. *Spirit and Nature: The Saint-Médard Miracles in 18th-Century Jansenism*. New York: Crossroad, 2002.
Rahner, Karl. "Anonymous Christians." In *Theological Investigations*, vol. 6: *Concerning Vatican Council II*, Translated by Karl-H. Kruger and Boniface Kruger, 390–8. New York: Crossroad, 1982.
Redekop, Gloria Neufeld. *The Work of Their Hands: Mennonite Women's Societies in Canada*. Waterloo, ON: Canadian Corporation for Studies in Religion, 1996.

Rempel, Daniel. "The Witness of Disability in a Medicalized World." *Anabaptist Witness* 9, no. 2 (October 2022): 43–61.

Rich, Elaine Sommers. *Mennonite Women: A Story of God's Faithfulness, 1683–1983*. Scottdale, PA: Herald, 1983.

Rieger, Joerg. "Sanctification." In *The Cambridge Dictionary of Theology*, edited by Ian A. McFarland, David A. S. Fergusson, Karen Kilby, and Iain R. Torrance, 459. Cambridge: Cambridge University Press, 2011.

Robert, Dana L. *American Women in Mission: A Social History of Their Thought and Practice*. Macon, GA: Mercer University Press, 1996.

Roberts, J. Deotis. *Black Theology in Dialogue*. Philadelphia, PA: Westminster, 1987.

Robertson, Roland. "Glocalization: Time-Space and Homogeneity-Heterogeneity." In *Global Modernities*, edited by Mike Featherstone, Scott M. Lash, and Roland Robertson, 35–53. London: Sage, 1995.

Rodney, Walter. *How Europe Underdeveloped Africa*. New York: Verso, 2018.

Rogers, Eugene F. *After the Spirit: A Constructive Pneumatology from Resources outside the Modern West*. Grand Rapids, MI: Eerdmans, 2005.

Rogers, Eugene F. *Sexuality and the Christian Body: Their Way into the Triune God*. Malden, MA: Blackwell, 1999.

Rojas, Fabio. *From Black Power to Black Studies: How a Radical Social Movement Became an Academic Discipline*. Baltimore, MD: Johns Hopkins University Press, 2007.

Rose, Kevin Stewart. "'The World Food Crisis Is Not a Fad': The *More-with-Less* Cookbook and Protestant Environmental Spirituality." *Religion and American Culture* 29, no. 2 (2019): 216–54.

Rothstein, Richard. *The Color of Law: A Forgotten History of How Our Government Segregated America*. New York: Liveright, 2017.

Roudometof, Victor. *Glocalization: A Critical Introduction*. New York: Routledge, 2016.

Schurr, Mark R., Terrance J. Martin, and W. Ben Secunda. "How the Pokagon Band Avoided Removal: Archaeological Evidence from the Faunal Assemblage of the Pokagon Village Site (20BE13)." *Midcontinental Journal of Archaeology* 31, no. 1 (Spring 2006): 143–63.

Scott, Peter. *A Political Theology of Nature*. Cambridge: Cambridge University Press, 2003.

Scott, Peter and William T. Cavanaugh, eds. *The Blackwell Companion to Political Theology*. Malden, MA: Blackwell, 2004.

Schertz, Mary. "'Likewise You Wives … ': Another Look at 1 Peter 2:11–5:11." In *Perspectives on Feminist Hermeneutics*, eds., Gayle Gerber Koontz and Willard Swartley, 29–39. Elkhart, IN: Institute of Mennonite Studies, 1987.

Schmidt, Kimberly, Diane Zimmerman Umble, and Steven D. Reschley, eds. *Strangers at Home: Amish and Mennonite Women in History*. Baltimore, MD: Johns Hopkins University Press, 2002.

Schroeder, David. "The New Testament Haustafeln: Egalitarian or Status Quo?" In *Perspectives on Feminist Hermeneutics*, eds., Gayle Gerber Koontz and Willard Swartley, 56–65. Elkhart, IN: Institute of Mennonite Studies, 1987.

Shearer, Tobin Miller. "A Prophet Pushed Out: Vincent Harding and the Mennonites." *Mennonite Life* 69 (2015), https://ml.bethelks.edu/issue/vol-69/article/a-prophet-pushed-out-vincent-harding-and-the-menno/.

Shearer, Tobin Miller. "Vincent Harding's Dual Demonstration." In *Daily Demonstrators: The Civil Rights Movement in Mennonite Homes and Sanctuaries*, 98–129. Baltimore, MD: Johns Hopkins University Press, 2010.

Shellenberg, Lovella et al. *Mennonite Girls Can Cook*. Harrisonburg, VA: Herald, 2011.

Shenk, Dan. "Portrait of a 'Sundown Town': Coming to Terms with Racism in a 'Mennonite' Community." *Mennonite World Review* 92, no. 2 (Jan. 14, 2014): 1, 12–13.

Shenk, Joanna. *The Movement Makes Us Human: An Interview with Dr. Vincent Harding on Mennonites, Vietnam, and MLK*. Eugene, OR: Wipf & Stock, 2018.

Sitwell, Brian. "Sunrise General Movement Update: September 2021." *Sunrise Movement*. September 17, 2021. https://www.sunrisemovement.org/movement-updates/sunrise-general-movement-update-september-2021/.

Slobodian, Quinn. *Globalists: The End of Empire and the Birth of Neoliberalism*. Cambridge, MA: Harvard University Press, 2018.

Smith, Theophus. *Conjuring Culture: Biblical Formations of Black America*. New York: Oxford University Press, 1994.

Smucker, Jonathan Matthew. *Hegemony How-To: A Roadmap for Radicals*. Chico, CA: AK Press, 2017.

Snyder, C. Arnold. *Anabaptist History and Theology: An Introduction*. Kitchener, ON: Pandora, 1995.

Snyder, C. Arnold and Linda A. Huebert Hecht, eds. *Profiles of Anabaptist Women: Sixteenth-Century Reforming Pioneers*. Waterloo, ON: Canadian Corporation for Studies in Religion, 1996.

Soto Albrecht, Elizabeth and Darryl W. Stephens, eds. *Liberating the Politics of Jesus: Renewing Peace Theology through the Wisdom of Women*. London: T&T Clark, 2020.

Sunrise Movement. "Our Principles: Who We Are." Accessed August 24, 2024, https://www.sunrisemovement.org/about/.

Sunrise Movement. "Sunrise's Principles." Accessed August 23, 2024. https://web.archive.org/web/20211009114812/https:/www.sunrisemovement.org/principles/?ms=Sunrise%27sPrinciples.

Susin, Luiz Carlos and Jon Sobrino, "Sage and Prophet: José Comblin (1923–2011)." In *Lord and Life Giver: Spirit Today* (*Concilium*), edited by Paul Murray, Diego Irarrázaval, and Maria Clara Bingemer, 148–53. London: SCM, 2011.

Tanner, Kathryn. *Christianity and the New Spirit of Capitalism*. New Haven, CA: Yale, 2019.

Tanner, Kathryn. "Incarnation, Cross, and Sacrifice: A Feminist-Inspired Reappraisal." *Anglican Theological Review* 86, no. 1 (2004): 35–56.

Tanner, Kathryn. *Theories of Culture*. Minneapolis, MN: Augsburg Fortress, 1997.

Taylor, Keeanga-Yamahtta. *From #BlackLivesMatter to Black Liberation*. Chicago: Haymarket, 2016.

Taylor, Keeanga-Yamahtta, ed. *How We Get Free: Black Feminism and the Combahee River Collective*. Chicago, IL: Haymarket, 2017.

Taylor, Keeanga-Yamahtta. *Race for Profit: How Banks and the Real Estate Industry Undermined Black Homeownership*. Chapel Hill, NC: University of North Carolina Press, 2019.

Thiessen, Matthew. *Jesus and the Forces of Death: The Gospels' Portrayal of Ritual Impurity within First-Century Judaism*. Grand Rapids, MI: Baker Academic, 2020.

Thompson, Sarah. "An Ecological Beloved Community: An Interview with Na'Taki Osborne Jelks of the West Atlanta Watershed Alliance." In *Watershed Discipleship: Reinhabiting Bioregional Faith and Practice*, edited by Ched Myers, 102–20. Eugene, OR: Cascade, 2016.

Toewes, Miriam. *Women Talking*. New York: Bloomsbury, 2018.

Tomasky, Michael, ed. "Beyond Neoliberalism II." *Democracy: A Journal of Ideas* 64 (Spring 2022), https://democracyjournal.org/category/magazine/64/.

Tönnies, Ferdinand. *Community and Civil Society*, edited by Jose Harris. Translated by Jose Harris and Margaret Hollis. Cambridge: Cambridge University Press, 2001 [1887].

Tonstad, Linn Marie. *God and Difference: The Trinity, Sexuality, and the Transformation of Finitude*. New York: Routledge, 2016.

Tran, Jonathan. *Asian Americans and the Spirit of Racial Capitalism*. New York: Oxford University Press, 2021.

Troeltsch, Ernst. *The Social Teaching of the Christian Churches*, 2 volumes, Translated by Olive Wyon. Louisville, KY: Westminster/John Knox, 1992.

Tufecki, Zeynep. *Twitter and Tear Gas: The Power and Fragility of Networked Protest*. New Haven, CT: Yale University Press, 2017.

Turman, Eboni Marshall. *Toward a Womanist Ethic of Incarnation: Black Bodies, the Black Church, and the Council of Chalcedon*. New York: Palgrave Macmillan, 2013.
Turner, Victor. *The Ritual Process: Structure and Anti-Structure*. London: Routledge and Keegan Paul, 1969.
United States Department of Agriculture, National Agricultural Statistics Service. "2017 Census of Agriculture, County Profile: Elkhart County, Indiana." 2017. https://www.nass.usda.gov/Publications/AgCensus/2017/Online_Resources/County_Profiles/Indiana/cp18039.pdf.
United States Environmental Protection Agency. "Summary of the Clean Water Act." *United States Environmental Protection Agency*. Accessed August 23, 2024. https://www.epa.gov/laws-regulations/summary-clean-water-act.
US Fish and Wildlife Service. "We Support the Pokagon in Restoring and Enhancing Their Land." April 6, 2016. https://www.fws.gov/midwest/news/PokagonRestoration.html.
V3 Companies. *Elkhart River Watershed Management Plan*. March 6, 2008. https://ecm.idem.in.gov/cs/idcplg?IdcService=GET_FILE&dID=83085669&dDocName=83085602&Rendition=web&allowInterrupt=1&noSaveAs=1.
Walker, Corey D. B. "Social Theory and African American Theology." In *The Oxford Handbook of African American Theology*, edited by Katie G. Cannon and Anthony B. Pinn, 377–89. New York: Oxford University Press, 2014.
Waltner Goossen, Rachel. "'Defanging the Beast': Mennonite Responses to John Howard Yoder's Sexual Abuse." *Mennonite Quarterly Review* 89, no. 1 (2015): 7–80.
Waltner Goossen, Rachel. "'Repent of the Sins of Homophobia': The Rise of Queer Mennonite Leaders." *Nova Religio* 24, no. 3 (2021): 68–95.
Waltner Goossen, Rachel. *Women against the Good War: Conscientious Objection and Gender on the American Home Front, 1941–1947*. Chapel Hill, NC: University of North Carolina Press, 1997.
Ward, Pete. *Liquid Church*. Eugene, OR: Wipf & Stock, 2013.
Waterford Mennonite Church. "Wetlands." Accessed August 23, 2024. https://waterfordchurch.org/wetlands/.
Weaver, Miriam L. "The Status of Widows in the Church." *Report* 4 (February 1974): 6.
Weber, Max. *The Protestant Ethic and the Spirit of Capitalism*. Translated by Talcott Parsons. New York: Routledge, 1992 [1920–1].
Weingroff, Richard F. "Federal-Aid Highway Act of 1956: Creating the Interstate System." *Public Roads* 60, no. 1 (Summer 1996), https://www.fhwa.dot.gov/publications/publicroads/96summer/p96su10.cfm.

Whapham, Theodore James. "Spirit as Field of Force." *Scottish Journal of Theology* 67, no. 1 (2014): 15–32.

White, Derrick E. *The Challenge of Blackness: The Institute of the Black World and Political Activism in the 1970s.* Gainesville, FL: University Press of Florida, 2011.

Williams, Delores S. *Sisters in the Wilderness: The Challenge of Womanist God-talk.* Maryknoll, NY: Orbis, 1993.

Williams, Rowan. "The Judgment of the World." In *On Christian Theology*, 29–43. Oxford: Blackwell, 2000.

Wittgenstein, Ludwig. *Philosophical Investigations*, revised fourth edition, Translated by G. E. M. Anscombe, P. M. S. Hacker, and Joachim Shulte. Oxford: Blackwell, 2009.

Wittgenstein, Ludwig. *Tractatus Logico-Philosophicus*, 2d edition, Translated by David Pears and Brian McGuiness. New York: Routledge, 2001.

Woodley, Randy. "Early Dialogue in the Community of Creation." In *Buffalo Shout, Salmon Cry: Conversations on Creation, Land Justice, and Life Together*, edited by Steve Heinrichs, 92–103. Harrisonburg, VA: Herald Press, 2013.

Wylie-Kellerman, Lydia. "God's Gonna Trouble the Water: A Call to Discipleship in the Detroit Watershed." In *Watershed Discipleship: Reinhabiting Bioregional Faith and Practice*, edited by Ched Myers, 75–87. Eugene, OR: Cascade, 2016.

Wynward, Todd. *Rewilding the Way: Break Free to Follow an Untamed God!* Harrisonburg, VA: Herald Press, 2015.

Yoder, Anita Hooley. *Circles of Sisterhood: A History of Mission, Service, and Fellowship in Mennonite Women's Organizations.* Harrisonburg, VA: Herald, 2017.

Yong, Amos. *The Spirit Poured out on All Flesh: Pentecostalism and the Possibility of a Global Theology.* Grand Rapids, MI: Baker Academic, 2005.

Yong, Amos. *Theology and Down Syndrome: Reimagining Disability in Late Modernity.* Waco: Baylor University Press, 2007.

Zubovich, Gene. *Before the Religious Right: Liberal Protestants, Human Rights, and the Polarization of the United States.* Philadelphia, PA: University of Pennsylvania Press, 2022.

INDEX

Althaus-Reid, Marcella 8–10, 11, 13, 101 n.102, 143
Anabaptism (*see also* Mennonites)
   environmental ethics 39–46, 56–7
   historical theology 95–8, 124 n.46, 127 n.65, 146 n.121, 171 n.23, 177–8
autonomy 148–51

Baker-Fletcher, Karen 7, 11, 13–14, 48
Bedford, Nancy 8, 9, 11, 13–14, 100, 172 n.24
Bourdieu, Pierre 28–31, 35–6, 105–6, 164 n.3, 169 n.13, 174 n.31

Church
   as community 4–7, 75, 132
   identity of members 136–46
   institutions 80–3, 99–100, 172, 178
   relation to world 131–6
   and social reproduction 101–8
Coakley, Sarah 2 n.2, 20–1, 79–84, 101, 153
Comblin, José 6–7, 11, 13, 24 n.60
communities 4–10, 11–15, 75
Crawley, Ashon T. 9–10
creation 23–8, 46–56, 145–6, 162

discernment 38, 69–70, 105–9, 133–5, 150–1, 160–1
divine economy 23–8, 52–6, 75, 132–6, 153–61

election 23, 50–6, 155–6
Elkhart River Watershed 56–70
evangelical theology 10–11

feminist theology 8, 90, 94–9
field theory 28–31, 67–70, 99–100, 105–7, 131–2, 138, 144–5 (*see also* Bourdieu, Pierre)

global imagination 172–8
glocalization 1–2, 21–2
Gutiérrez, Gustavo 7, 11, 13, 148

Harding, Vincent 115–29, 135–6, 144, 147–51
Hauerwas, Stanley 148
Holy Spirit
   and democracy 175–8
   doctrine of (*see* pneumatology)
   doubling 129–36, 139–42, 145–6
   hovering over creation 46–56, 67–70
   and sanctification 74–84, 98–100
   and Word (Jesus Christ) 46–9, 55, 67, 127–30, 155

INDEX

identity 13–14, 136–46, 167, 171
Institute of the Black World 117–19, 144
institutions 14–19, 56, 69–70, 83–4, 99–100, 104–8, 120–2, 129–46

justice
  environmental 39–70
  gender and sexuality 72–109
  racial 111–51

Kotsko, Adam 162–4

liberation theology 6–10, 13, 42, 132, 139
life 49–55, 69, 74, 98, 128, 132–5

Mennonites (*see also* Anabaptism)
  in Elkhart River Watershed 57, 60–3
  North American women's movements 84–100
  and sexual abuse 71–2
  theology 34–5, 38, 95–8, 123–9
  and Vincent Harding 116, 135–6
Moltmann, Jürgen 13 n.43, 20 n.52
movements 6–10, 13–15, 43–6, 84–6, 98, 131–2, 148–51

neoliberalism 40, 164–78
networks 10–1

participation 36–8, 54–6, 99–100, 105–8, 130–6, 145–6
Pentecostal theology 11 n.40
picture theory 31–3 (*see also* Wittgenstein, Ludwig)

pneumatology 4–19, 95, 104, 161–2
political theology 162–73
postliberal theology 4–6, 13, 42, 132, 148
"principalities and powers" 24, 38, 53, 133 n.82

Radner, Ephraim 5–6, 11, 13–14, 103–8
relational ontology 21–31, 52–6, 163–4 (*see also* Fields)
Rogers, Eugene F. 4–5, 11, 13, 52, 75–9, 83–4

Scott, Peter 49 n.40, 163 n.2, 175–6, 178
sin 23–7, 38, 53–4, 67, 69, 100, 139
social theory
  modern 17–19
  postmodern 28–31
solidarity 51–2, 69, 74, 100, 146

Taylor, Keeanga-Yamahtta 65 n.97, 143–4, 147 n.124, 165 n.5
Tonstad, Linn Marie 9–10, 11, 13–14, 101–8, 143
Turman, Eboni Marshall 139, 142–3

Ward, Pete 10–11, 13–15, 24 n.60
watershed discipleship 40, 42, 43–5, 56–7, 68
Wittgenstein, Ludwig 31–2, 107–8

Yoder, John Howard 26 n.65, 71–2
Yong, Amos 11 n.40, 141–3